GROUP PSYCHOTHERAPY

Published in Columbia, South Carolina, during the one hundred and seventy-fifth anniversary of the establishment of the University of South Carolina and the two hundredth anniversary of the establishment of the United States of America.

Behavioral Science Series

Editor:

Robert V. Heckel
Social Problems Research Institute
University of South Carolina

Consulting Editors:

James A. Morris
Former Commissioner
South Carolina Commission on Higher Education

J. Wilbert Edgerton
University of North Carolina

Robert L. Stewart
University of South Carolina

Number 1:
The Discharged Mental Patient:
A 5-year Statistical Survey

By Robert V. Heckel, Charles Perry,
and P. G. Reeves, Jr.

Number 2:
Group Psychotherapy:
A Behavioral Approach

By Robert V. Heckel and H. C. Salzberg
Contributing Authors:
Mervyn Wagner and Morton Feigenbaum

Group Psychotherapy

A Behavioral Approach

Robert V. Heckel
and H. C. Salzberg

Contributing Authors,
Mervyn Wagner and Morton Feigenbaum

UNIVERSITY OF SOUTH CAROLINA PRESS·COLUMBIA·S.C.

FIRST EDITION

Published in Columbia, S.C., by the
University of South Carolina Press, 1976

Manufactured in the United States of America

Library of Congress Cataloging in Publication Data

Heckel, Robert V
Group psychotherapy, a behavioral approach.

(Behavioral science series; no. 2)
Bibliography: p.
Includes index.
1. Group psychotherapy. I. Salzberg, H. C.,
1931–   joint author. II. Title. III. Series:
Behavioral science series (Columbia, S. C.); no. 2.
RC488.H4   616.8'915   76–5445
ISBN 0–87249–340–7

Contents

Tables

Figure

Acknowledgments

In a work that spans fifteen years of effort, it is difficult to provide due credit to those who have assisted in the research. Through the years, Donald Bidus, Ernest Land, David Strahley, Russell Brokaw, George Holmes, Will Drennen, and most of all Stewart Wiggins, who coauthored many of our early works, have given valuable cooperation. There have also been numerous comments, criticisms, and suggestions from other colleagues, all of which have helped shape our approach.

In preparation of the manuscript, the incisive comments and observations of Stephen N. Haynes have helped supply tightness and rigor where the authors' own involvement reduced objectivity. In the typing of the manuscript, both Renée McKeown and Louise Lowman have worked hard and have been supportive and smiling through the several revisions of the manuscript.

GROUP PSYCHOTHERAPY

Introduction

In writing a book on group psychotherapy, we had to make a decision whether we would present a broad coverage of the history of group psychotherapy, with a discussion of its various approaches and techniques, or would present our own position in depth and detail, concentrating on our views and our biases while relying, not on a broad spectrum of persons or references, but on our own research and those works by other authors which have influenced us or are closely related to our own approach.

We chose to do the latter. In taking such an approach, we recognized that we risk appearing to some as unscholarly, or, even more serious, being accused of unfamiliarity with the extensive literature of group psychotherapy. However, we feel that both extensive coverage of this literature and an explication of both the history and theories have been done well by other authors. Merely to repeat their work appears redundant. Our work is, in essence, a position paper. Most, but not all, of our techniques have been worked through a series of systematic researches involving a variety of therapeutic groups—adolescent, adult, in-patient, out-patient, and special-problem subgroupings such as drug and alcohol. We have studied the effects of different verbal behaviors by therapists on the verbal behavior of patients in many settings. We have observed and studied the effects of patient responses on therapist behaviors as well (see Bibliography, under Heckel and Salzberg). When our joint efforts started in 1961, it seemed probable that our efforts would result in a book at least by 1965. Now, in 1975, we feel that sufficient data have been accumulated to report on our findings. As with most researchers, we find that each question has raised new questions; only rarely are there answers. In this work, little mention is made of nonverbal behaviors. This does not represent an oversight, merely a recognition of the difficulty of obtaining quantifiable data which take into account the three aspects of nonverbal communication—the encoding process, the transmission, and the decoding process. Our work has moved much more slowly in this area and additional research must be completed before we would attempt a statement of our views on nonverbal behavior.

R.V.H.   H.C.S.

1

THEORETICAL FOUNDATIONS

In our approach to psychotherapy there are two major considerations, both of which have relevance to individual psychotherapy.

Our first premise is that the *disordered behaviors for which people seek treatment and for which treatment is most effective are learned behaviors.* These disordered behaviors are responsive to treatment methodologies that involve the application of learning principles to modify present response sequences or to provide the individual with new, more effective, or previously undeveloped responses. In addition, cognitive processes play an important role in problem-solving behavior; frequently they help to mediate change and are responsible for the relative permanence of some changes. The capacity for understanding or insight is uniquely found in man and enables him to effect change more efficiently.

Our second premise is that *disordered behaviors are culturally determined.* As such, they are not subject to the absolutes of definition once adhered to by medically oriented researchers using a disease model. It has been suggested that even the term "disordered behaviors" may be inappropriate, in that these behaviors represent social definitions; they do not necessarily relate to specific behavioral sequences or even to situation-specific responses. In fact, most individuals who seek treatment today cannot be considered "disordered" in the traditional sense. Presenting problems are difficult to classify as "symptoms" and most people do not fall into clear psychiatric classifications of mental disorders.

Individuals present themselves for therapy today with problems in communicating with their spouses and with their peers, vague feelings of uneasiness about their goals or purpose in life, self-consciousness and lack of assertiveness. The typical out-patient is indistinguishable from the average individual except for the fact that he is seeking a vehicle for change, whereas the nonclient has decided to deal with life's problems on his own. In our complex society, everyone must learn many skills essential to psychological adaptation and to growth.

Yalom (1970), in his excellent work on group psychotherapy, believes that the definition of disorder—leaving aside presenting complaints—emerges through consensual validation and self-observation of interpersonal behavior. As an individual becomes aware of his strengths, limitations, parataxic distortions, and maladaptive behaviors, he learns of their impact and consequences, the responses they elicit from others. Though often couched in dynamic terms, Yalom's views rely heavily on a learning model (imitation, interpersonal learning) as he develops his approach to the acquisition and the changing of undesired behaviors.

Some years ago, Ford and Urban (1963) presented a learning model of the development of disordered behavior. Little has occurred in the theoretical sphere to modify or supersede their very cogent observations. They presented three components of disordered behavior which, in their opinion, cover the spectrum of what would clinically be described as disordered behavior:

1. Disordered persons develop patterns and sequences of responses just as do normal individuals, but their acquired patterns are in some way inappropriate to the situations in which they occur.
2. Patterns are developed which are poorly or inadequately linked; something might be amiss in the way in which they are constructed, or one set of responses is inappropriate to another.
3. Perhaps a disordered person fails to develop patterns that others do, and thus his behavior might be characterized as essentially unpatterned or disorganized.

In the first instance, it may be that an individual makes a "right" response, but in the wrong situation. Somewhere in the learning process there has been an inappropriate linking of sets of behaviors. As an example, consider the voyeur given to peeking in windows.

Looking in or out of windows is, in most instances, normal and acceptable behavior. We would expect a person to feel no hesitancy in looking out of a window to determine if it is raining; we would expect him to be able to look into store windows to examine merchandise, to look out and enjoy trees, flowers, or his children playing; and we would also expect the person to look through automobile windows while driving. We would hope to help the individual, through psychotherapy, to restrict his viewing to normal channels of observation and away from situations in which he attempts to violate the privacy of others in their homes or in their rooms. We would not want to remove the response of looking through windows; rather, we would wish to retain the appropriate behaviors while establishing more appropriate linkages in the instances where he was voyeuristic. Thus, it is not the response that is defective. It is only when responses occur inappropriately or in wrong situations that in this instance they are labeled disordered behaviors.

It should be stressed that this voyeuristic behavior is, in large part, socially determined. The same behavior, when in the context of an X-rated movie, has become socially adaptive behavior in recent years. The determination of what is appropriate or inappropriate in any social context is determined by the culture in which the behavior occurs, and standards for appropriateness may change in an individual's lifetime.

Conformity to the standards, rules, and processes present in a culture is necessary for acceptance and status in the culture. When an individual presents a series of inappropriate responses in social situations, his membership in the culture is threatened. A major focus of the family and of the social institutions of a culture is in shaping children to conform to the social-behavior requirements of the culture or subculture. This is achieved through instruction, reinforcement, modeling, and punishment; each of these is also a basic tool of the therapist in modifying behaviors. In addition, because man has the capacity for rational thought, the therapist can present alternative behaviors to the individual and can forecast short-term and long-term consequences of specific behaviors, enabling the individual to make rational choices.

It is important to note that not all inappropriate social behaviors are of clinical significance. A number of inappropriate or inadequate responses may merely reflect a lack of maturity or of understanding, inadequate social training, or ignorance of the requirements of a particular situation. Grammatical errors, poor table manners, poor social judgment, loud or boisterous behavior, or other socially inept responses may be seen, not as a basis for clinical referral, but merely as a lack of instruction or training. In some instances these behaviors are class-related, and someone from a lower class is not expected to make the appropriate response. Children are permitted many of these errors early in life but are expected to show increasing conformity as they mature. When an adult, however, continues to engage in behavior typical of a child or adolescent, he often experiences social disapproval and has difficulty in obtaining adequate reinforcement.

The second category of disorders upon which Ford and Urban placed particular emphasis may be described as inappropriate response—response interrelationships. The authors see these occurring as a result of defective hook-ups in which normal patterns of behavior are established, but they are poorly arranged. They would also include in this category instances of conflict where two simultaneous responses occur but are incompatible with one another. In most theories of personality, conflict is seen as a major component of anxiety or behavioral disorder. One example of inappropriate hook-ups would be the linking of a positive affective response, such as sex, with fear or anxiety about expressing love. Ford and Urban speak of the possibility that paralleled response sequences, which are not affectively related to one another, may operate; these responses may be incongruous even though they may not be incompatible. In many instances the stress or disturbance occurs because of conflicts between verbal-symbolic events and other response sequences. Most often this is seen when physiological responses, motoric behaviors, or affective patterns occur without any conceptual representation of or insight into these events on the part of the person making the response. An individual may show physiological signs of extreme stress, tension, or anger, while reporting verbally that none of these feelings is present. In our culture there is some degree of tolerance for incongruence between the way an individual appears and the verbal responses he makes. As the distance between these behavioral components increases, however, the judged level of deviance or incongruity is also seen to increase, and tolerance for this ambiguity typically decreases, causing others to avoid the person or judge him to be insensitive, unaware, or disturbed. Conflict is the core of most theories of psychological disorder. For Freud, the focus is on the conflict between the id and the ego or between the superego and the ego. The conflict persists because the individual is unaware of its source, and therapy is aimed toward helping him become aware of all its components so that a decision for action may be made on the basis of reality. These comments represent only a few of the possibilities of disorder falling in the category of inappropriate relationships.

In their third category, Ford and Urban described behavioral disorder as unpatterned behavior. The two previous categories were alike in that fully developed responses, albeit inappropriate ones, were occurring, but the concept of disorder in unpatterned behavior encompasses two views: either the individual has been unable to develop an adequate response pattern for the events in question or previously effective patterns of behavior have "become disjointed and fragmented." In the third category one might fit psychotic behavior, which our society does not tolerate very well and which often leads to institutionalization of individuals displaying such behavior.

As indicated, it is suggested that virtually all of the behavior which is treated clinically with psychological techniques would fit one of the three patterns, either singly or in combination. Investigation of the writings of a number of psychotherapeutic theorists seems to indicate that these patterns fit their conceptions of disordered behavior. Even the more cerebral and abstruse complaints that clients present in psychotherapy—malaise, existential crises, identity crises, and concern about the meaning of events—may be reduced to one or to combinations of these patterns, and even more certainly can be related to the learning process by which they were acquired.

Mischel (1968), like Ford and Urban, rejects the disease view of behavior disorders because it suggests a physical disease model, as with cancer or pneumonia, and because concern with behavior patterns is bypassed in favor of inferential references to an underlying mental disease. In the disease model, behaviors are seen as symptoms. Traditional diagnostic procedures suggest that some concrete thing like an invading germ is the source of the behavior disorder. Diagnosis is a process of identifying the pathology, thus leading to differential treatment. In addition, the disease model implies that the individual is not responsible for his behavior; it is incumbent on society or his therapist to prescribe and effect a cure. Szasz (1961) feels that it is an infringement on human rights to label people "mentally ill"; this is to apply a disease-related label to a socially determined phenomenon.

Mischel, in rejecting the disease model, presents a social-learning view of behavior disorders which follows closely the model of Ford and Urban. He views disordered behavior as the disadvantageous consequences that result from inappropriate reactions to diverse stimuli. He groups these problem-producing stimuli into two major behavioral categories.

His first category is those stimuli that are problematic primarily because they evoke disadvantageous emotional reactions in the person. These stimuli can produce aversive emotional responses or avoidance. They also may be responses unique to the individual, since they may have little value, negative or positive, to other persons. Mischel sees the resultant emotional reactions occurring in the form of somatic disorders, tension, fatigue, or intense anxiety. In these emotional responses, the fear and anxiety may be attached to otherwise neutral objects, such as animals and knives, or to simple interpersonal acts, such as introducing someone or speaking. It is also possible for these same kinds of situations to evoke positive emotional arousal and approach responses, even though they may have neutral value to other persons. Examples Mischel cites are those of sexual attraction to one's own sex or fetishistic behavior.

In Mischel's second category, the response of the individual to the evoking stimuli is incorrect, inappropriate, or otherwise deficient. Such situations may or may not evoke intense or disturbed conditioned emotional responses in him. Most often in this category are the behavioral deficits which bring about disadvantageous consequences because individuals have not acquired the necessary skills and competencies to reach an effective level of functioning. Mischel states that "individuals with deficient educational, vocational, social, and interpersonal skills abundantly illustrate the paralyzing social and personal disadvantages resulting from severe behavioral deficits."

Mischel indicates that these inappropriate emotional reactions and behavior patterns can be acquired in a number of ways—observational learning, direct reinforcement, classical conditioning, or a combination of processes at work over an extended period of time.

He feels that, a posteriori, it is impossible to reconstruct accurately the origins of most persons' behavior. As a result, his therapeutic interventions would be to identify present emotional reactions, performance deficits, and inappropriate behavior by isolating the stimuli under which these problems occur. His assessment of the situation facing the person would focus on understanding the current conditions that maintain problems and the interventions or manipulations that would modify them.

The theories of both Ford and Urban and Mischel regarding what is to be labeled as disordered behavior are consistent with one position of the authors, particularly the view that learning plays a major role in its development. It would be redundant, therefore, to restate in slightly altered form a similar view of disorder. Rather, we will present our view of the *process of acquiring* disordered behaviors.

We have already indicated our bias: that it is in the learning process, through instruction, modeling, reinforcement, or punishment, that disordered behavior is acquired and maintained. This process interacts with the organically determined limitations of the individual to produce the behaviors we observe. Though Ford and Urban state that "it seems quite likely that the kind of disorder that develops depends on the kinds of behaviors and situations that become interrelated," our current level of knowledge and research sophistication permits little beyond speculation as to behavioral determinants. Just as there are many ways to acquire knowledge, there may also be many ways to acquire any new behavior. One might hope that certain learning experiences may result in very specific behavioral acquisitions, yet this seems to be of low probability, considering the complexity of most human responses. Franks (1969) offers a potential solution to this complexity—the development of a technology of behavioral assessment. Of necessity, assessment for behavioral approaches would extend far beyond those customarily utilized in dynamic psychology.

The Acquisition of Disordered Behavior

We have already indicated our bias that most disordered behavior is learned. We recognize that obviously there are physiological factors which may predispose one to certain types of disorder, and that certain chemical disorders either internally or externally produced will also result in behavioral change, though in the latter case, unless damage occurs, this is typically a temporary change. We also feel that there is an overwhelming body of information which indicates that even organically based or genetically predisposing conditions can be in part compensated for, or dealt with, through psychological techniques of behavior modification. It does not seem pertinent to cite an extensive body of research to support this, but it does seem relevant to indicate that group psychotherapy, as practiced by the authors, operates on this assumption.

There appears to be widespread agreement among personality theorists, as well as group and individual therapists, that the kinds of disordered behavior observed appear to be based on learning experiences that were inappropriate, inadequate, or ill timed, or are due to the absence of crucial learning experiences. There is also the assumption that someone or some group, usually the family, was instrumental in shaping the behavior of the individual—using instruction, reinforcement, modeling, or punishment; and that that person or group provided the training environment to produce the undesired responses and the necessary conditions (chiefly, some form of direct or vicarious reinforcement) to maintain them.

There is virtually universal acceptance that the major shapers of behavior are the family during the early years, with the peer group and the institutions of the culture providing later shaping and modification of established patterns. It has also been accepted that in some instances parental or environmental training, which may appear adequate for a particular cultural setting, does not provide the mechanisms for generalization or for coping with situations which are to be met outside the home or early learning environment. Training adequate to meet the demands of a subculture may be inadequate to meet the demands of the major culture. Failure to produce adequate responses in a novel setting places the person at a severe disadvantage. If his response is sufficiently inept or inappropriate, he may be labeled as having a behavior disorder because of his inability to respond effectively to new social stimuli. The resultant problem might be viewed as a sociocultural disorder rather than an emotional disorder. A surprisingly high proportion of people seeking help for problems in living fall into this category. Mores and cultural expectancies change so rapidly today that, by the time most of us become adults, we are ill equipped to deal with our society. A good example of this is our changing views about sexuality and marriage. In the last few years, we have seen a tremendous increase in the number of couples seeking marital therapy for problems with sexual dysfunction. The right of the individual to enjoy sex has now become socially acceptable, and couples once embarrassed or afraid to seek help are now reexamining their sexual relationships. With the recent acceptance of open and candid discussion of sexual matters popularized by several best-selling books on sexual behavior,[1] young and old adults now seek help in establishing their right to sexual satisfaction. This has led to many disrupted relationships in instances where, were it not for the changes in cultural standards, individuals would have continued their lack of fulfillment or adjustment in sexual areas.

The appropriate time for adequate learning or training in the development of behavior patterns is a question of importance. If certain learning occurs later in the individual's experience, the information may be acquired too late to cope with situations which have already been occurring or which were met, lacking information, with a failure to respond or an inadequate response.

There is much to suggest that training carried out under conditions of low motivation does not result in the efficient acquisition of desired behaviors. Often it is a rote process with no cognitive understanding. Hence these responses are poorly generalized to other situations as a function of the inadequate training process. In other words, the absence of sufficient reinforcement or, on another level, the failure to deal with the cognitive aspects of response acquisition leads to inadequate learning.

Ford and Urban suggest another dimension, which, though un-

---

1. The serious efforts of researchers such as Masters and Johnson sell almost as well as the overpopularized efforts of several writers attempting to capitalize on a good market. It really amounts to a second wave of openness, the first created by Kinsey and his coworkers almost a generation ago.

familiar in Western culture to most psychotherapy patients, may, in fact, have great relevance to the process of acquiring disordered behaviors. Externally imposed physiological states such as hunger, economic deprivation, cultural impoverishment, and other environmental conditions have an impact on behavior. Those who would work with the culturally disadvantaged should know the implications for psychotherapy. It is not our intent to discuss or describe the unique therapies or approaches suited to the disadvantaged or to those whose cultural experiences are so unique as to render them inaccessible through verbal therapeutic processes.[2]

Much theorizing by researchers has dealt with behaviors which are the result of inadequate training and learning. The target behaviors for change are chiefly the emotions of guilt, fear, anger, and similar less adaptive response patterns.

However, the kinds of developmental hazards we have described would not, in and of themselves, constitute the only ingredients in the acquisition of disordered behavior. Most individuals will experience all the negative emotions we have mentioned and will engage in behavior that would meet, at least on a temporary basis, the previous qualifications mentioned: inadequate, undesirable, inappropriate, ill-timed, etc.

The development of the disorder, in what we would label clinically as behavior disorder, occurs when the individual undergoes recurring stress and arrives at inadequate solutions when attempting to terminate responses that he experiences as uncomfortable, painful, or anxiety-producing, or experiences any other unpleasant reaction described by the labels that have commonly been applied. We are less concerned with labels than with the fact that there is occurring, either externally or within the individual, a distressing or noxious stimulus which his prior learning has not equipped him to terminate effectively. For the child, "Mommie" can often terminate such stimuli; for the adult, continued recurrence of the conditions without adequate solution may place him in the position of seeking professional help to learn more adequate responses to these stressors.

Lest there be some confusion regarding disordered behaviors, it

2. Those who would wish further information on this subject might start by reading A. P. Goldstein, *Structured Learning Therapy: Toward a Psychotherapy for the Poor.* New York: Academic Press, 1973.

should be noted that some distress and some anxiety are normal, useful, and adaptive. When responses are made by the individual in such a way that he effectively and directly copes with his environment or when he heeds the warnings produced by distress and acts, he is reinforced for making these responses by a reduction in anxiety. It is only when the response sequence is inadequate in meeting the demands of the situation that the potential for disorder is present. Furthermore, it is only when these anxiety responses occur with some regularity and intensity, or become generalized to a variety of situations, that the individual fails to cope effectively with his environment and develops defenses against anxiety, such as denial and projection.

Ford and Urban indicate that disordered behavior is made up of various kinds of response/response interrelationships acquired for the purpose of holding off, lessening, and ending negative affects of various kinds. There is a further suggestion that certain behaviors judged ultimately to be inappropriate are acquired not so much to terminate the distress as to produce some positive response instead. Early theorists like Freud saw man as seeking only tension reduction; the best one could hope for was a state of homeostasis. The humanistic movement, as exemplified by A. H. Maslow and C. R. Rogers, implies that man behaves to achieve positive growth and that only a small segment of behavior is directed toward relieving anxiety or distress. There are, apparently, at least these two methods of acquiring behavior. Ford and Urban also speculate that, where an undesired response has been acquired, some combination of events may be used to produce two sets or results: the termination of the anxiety, and, in addition, partially satisfying emotions, such as a feeling of superiority.

Bandura (1969) described disordered behavior or psychopathology as involving social judgments, which are influenced by factors such as the normative standards of persons making the judgments, the social context in which the behavior is exhibited, certain attributes of the behavior, and the characteristics of the deviator himself. Bandura feels that pathology is inferred from the degree to which the individual's behavior deviates from the social norms that define how a person is supposed to behave in social situations occurring in a series of settings over time. He states that "the appropriateness of symbolic, affective, or social responses to given situations constitutes one major criterion in labeling 'symptomatic' behavior." Deviant behavior that creates aversive consequences for others is most often labeled abnormal and typically is met by attempts to modify, control, or eliminate it.

Bandura also cites other behaviors frequently identified as emotional disorders, such as responses of high magnitude, behavioral deficits, and the intention attributed to an individual's behavior by others. He adds two personal components to his definition:

1. Personal attributes may deviate from role demands. An individual's age, sex, social role, occupation, race, and religious or ethnic origin all involve certain expectations of the individual. When he fails to fulfill these expectations, others judge his behavior as deviant.

2. Bandura describes a self-definition of disordered behavior in which the individual views himself as deviant or disordered. This is a component not mentioned in most other definitions of disorder. However, Bandura feels that it is significant because of the evaluative discrepancies caused by such factors as an individual imposing excessive demands on himself, then suffering extreme distress when he fails to fulfill these demands.

Evaluative discrepancies are factors which must be taken into account when describing deviance. Rogers and other therapy theorists place great emphasis on negative self-evaluation as the cornerstone of disordered behavior.

Bandura's approach is important because it does not become enmeshed in judgments about internal processes occurring in the individual. Rather, he is concerned with the consequences which result from judgments made by others about observed behaviors in an individual, and their responses to the perceived deviations. Whatever the label given to the internal processes occurring in a person, it only becomes consequential through the responses of others to the label. Bandura develops his causal process with a behavioral model that provides a complete system for explaining deviant or pathological behavior.

Krasner and Ullmann (1973) used a social determination of be-havior disorder. They suggest that those behaviors that are to be modified are acts that may be described as unexpected, disturbing, or disadvantageous and that are likely to be described as deviant.

Whatever the conditions for responding are, the underlying prin-ciples appear the same. Disordered behaviors are acquired through faulty learning, although the major learning techniques of training, reinforcement, modeling, or punishment are still utilized. When these techniques are applied ineffectively, inadequately, or inappro-priately, or with improper timing, behavioral disorders may occur.[3] When such disorders occur it is incumbent upon the therapist to apply techniques which are solidly based on learning principles. The therapist's efforts must lead to new, more adequate levels of re-sponding that result in more appropriate and effective counter-measures to the disordered behaviors.

Principles of Group Behavior

We have already emphasized the fundamental concepts necessary to the acquisition of new knowledge (instruction, reinforcement, modeling, and punishment). We have also indicated that these same principles are used by the therapist in the modification of behavior. As we more fully develop our approach to therapy, these principles are expanded and simplified throughout the remainder of this book. However, there are shaping and modifying influences from the social environment which have been acquired by the individual seeking treatment and which operate in a lawful manner based on these earlier learning experiences. While they are not fundamental con-cepts, they are important in explaining why group psychotherapy works and what constitutes significant interpersonal interrelation-ships for each person. The materials included in this section are drawn from research in group behavior and group dynamics by social psychologists. Our conclusions have been heavily influenced by the

3. We would agree with C. M. Franks (1969) that it is not possible to view abnormal behavior as solely based on faulty learning. Genetic and biochemical factors determine the base for learning and the parameters of response capa-bility.

work of French (1956), Cartwright and Zander (1968), Collins and Guetzkow (1964), Roby and Lanzetta (1958), Shaw (1971), and Heckel (1972).

Much of the research on small groups has been concerned with problem-solving behavior, demonstrating the value of the group over individual efforts. The therapy group differs from other problem-solving groups only in the nature of its task (solving personal problems as opposed to unraveling the experimenter's anagram), the length of time available for work (months in the case of patients, typically minutes or hours for experimental problem-solving groups), and the possibility that prior deficits of learning may interfere with new learning. In the latter instance, experimental studies can be constructed in which prior learning interferes with solutions to the experimental problems presented, thus creating an analog of situations faced by many patients.

It is apparent that the psychotherapy group is only a variation on many groups in which learning occurs; as such, the same advantages exist for it as for other group settings. For example, when individuals work as a group, not only is there a division of labor or shared effort, but the end product or solution often extends well beyond the possibility of any one individual working separately (a model which would most closely approximate that of individual psychotherapy).

The results of small-group research with few exceptions support what group psychotherapists understand on an intuitive or observational basis. Let us consider the debated issue that group therapy may save time because it treats a number of persons simultaneously. Many experienced group therapists state that the technique is an important learning experience, but it should not be considered as a technique for saving time. Typically, the only support for this attitude is a "feeling," but inspection of problem-solving research has in fact demonstrated that, in many instances, when individuals work as a group they tend to use more total man-hours than individuals working separately. However, the important consideration in group research is that the end product is generally superior to what any individual can achieve working independently. Kelley and Thibaut (1969) and Shaw (1971), demonstrate various aspects to group versus individual performance in their summary articles.

While this would seem strongly to support the value of group psychotherapy, there are deterrents as well. For example, when other persons are present, participants are much more aware of, and concerned about, social motives. Many of these motives are defensive or protective in character, even though the effect may be temporary. This seems to be of special importance when the social concerns of the individual center on how he appears or how he relates to other individuals. Individuals in groups have learned to relate to one another in a superficial manner, as at a cocktail party or tea. Even with structuring, it usually takes considerable time to reduce these established psychological barriers and to reach direct and open communication in group psychotherapy. Initial structuring or warm-up exercises are sometimes helpful, but the members still need time to relinquish acquired habits of group responses. The skill and openness of the therapist are very important during the early stages of group therapy in helping the group get past this first stage of uneasiness and defensiveness. In most social-psychological research on groups, the social content of what individuals report is not highly emotion-laden. Even under these rather mild and unemotional circumstances, defensiveness appears as a block or deterrent to optimal levels of interaction. Consider how much greater would be the barriers when the content of a group member's response might be negated or rejected by other group members.

Another major deterrent to group therapy is the level of motivation of individual members for solving their problems within the framework of a group. In our society we have been taught that when we face difficult problems in living we should seek out an empathetic individual and share our distress with him. We are taught, at the same time, to keep up a facade of satisfaction when involved in groups of people. Group problem solving often appears alien to the prospective group therapy member, and he sees only the group therapist as a potential source of help. Of course, if the group functions well, these expectations change and members see the value of group problem solving, but in the crucial formative period of a group, the therapist must pay attention to the motivation of each member for attending sessions on a regular basis and for taking responsibility for the functioning of the group. This is especially important outside an institutional setting where environmental controls are nonexistent.

Many forces studied by social psychologists play an important role in group behavior. Conformity and social influence are often the basis of rapid behavioral change in group members.[4] For example, a group member who presents his problems and discusses alternatives, in a constructive manner with congruent data, may be reinforced by other group members with suggestions for change or support for some of his ideas. Majority opinion from group members may very greatly influence the decision-making process of individuals in a group. This frequently results in their choosing better alternatives or more effective solutions than they might have determined through their own efforts. While the therapist will almost always be most influential and his opinions more heavily weighted than those of other group members, the cumulative effect of several members supporting a particular solution or response can be very powerful.

Another advantage of group therapy is that behavior learned in a group situation, particularly in a group of peers, can be generalized to the individual's environment. In individual therapy, even though the client is able to build trust in the therapist, he is frequently disappointed when the people he comes in contact with outside therapy are not as understanding or responsive to his needs as the therapist. A group therapy situation, therefore, provides a reality base where the individual can try out new behaviors in relative safety, but not in the completely insulated cocoon of the therapist-client relationship.

A further advantage of group therapy is the very heavy emphasis on training in interpersonal skills, an emphasis that is not always present in individual psychotherapy. Most problems in living are

---

4. "Conformity" as used here is defined as an individual's behaving and valuing in a manner congruent with the behaviors of a particular reference group from whom he receives or would hope to receive reinforcement. A major origin of conforming behavior appears to be through social learning.

"Social influence" refers to the efforts on the part of group members to shape or change behavior in others so that it is more like their own behavior or so that it conforms to the role ascription they have given a particular person. Again, the promise of reinforcement or its withdrawal and the threat of punishment are preeminent in the process of social influence.

reflected in interpersonal conflicts of one sort or another. In individual therapy, the client must describe his interpersonal difficulties to the therapist. In the group situation, he reveals his style as he interacts with others. He is given feedback from the group, composed of persons who may have very different styles of relating. He is able to reply and to give feedback, which rarely occurs in the client-therapist relationship.

Later, in chapter 2, we spend considerable time developing the rationale for a therapist's behavior. At this point it seems desirable to explore the reasons that the therapist must maintain an effective learning climate and the operant social forces that insure his doing so. We do so because research studies indicate that the task environment (the group psychotherapy session) can provide interpersonal obstacles that can greatly affect the productivity of the persons present. In chapter 5 we consider the physical environment of the group and the strategies available to the therapist to minimize obstacles that it might generate. The therapist must seek to provide the most facilitative learning climate possible.

Power and the Therapist

The importance of power in the group session is recognized by only a few group psychotherapists, yet it is a vital dimension in therapists' behaviors. It is also one key to understanding the effectiveness of group psychotherapy. The therapist has many sources of power. These come from the attribution of power by group members, who, on entering a contract for psychotherapy, do so with the understanding that the therapist has the skill to help them. Because the therapist can give reward and punishment to group members, his level of power is further increased. Some social psychologists distinguish these as reward power and coercive power.

There are other sources of power, some of which are available both to the therapist and to other group members. For example, both the therapist and an individual group member may be rated as high in personal attraction to others—which is also a major source of power. The greater the interpersonal attraction, the greater is the power to influence and shape the behavior of group members. This interpersonal attraction is important in shaping the behavior that takes place in encounter groups and in dynamic therapies where transference is utilized as an essential component in the treatment process.

On a much lower level of influence, yet still significant, are the friendly interactions with either the therapist or other group members. Such simple behaviors as nodding, smiling, or other nonverbal reinforcing behaviors, which imply friendship, support, and concern, contain a potential for power.

The experiences shared by group members will further develop interpersonal attraction as contact continues within the group. The degree to which individuals have a commonality of experience or share problems will further increase the attraction and the potential degree of influence or power that they will have over one another. Group members with a history of success and/or status (especially the therapist), who are successful in facilitating group growth and social interactions, will gain increased power over the group. The demonstration of success and competence by the therapist or some group members will lead to power. Other behaviors which are noncongruent with successful interactions will undermine this and lead to a reduction in the power attributed to either an individual group member or the therapist. These findings from studies on leadership relate directly to the ability of the therapist to effect behavioral change.

Once power is established within the group, a series of measurable and observable behaviors occurs. Those persons who are seen as more powerful or competent will influence others more, communicate more often, and initiate more influential communications than persons with less power. Unfortunately for psychotherapy, powerful group members tend to change less readily in their behaviors, for an obvious reason. If an individual is reasonably successful in his attempts at influence or power, he has less need to change his behavior, even though his level of effectiveness may be far from optimum. Many disordered behaviors are rewarded by others (who might, for example, give in to prevent a temper tantrum), and, as a result, they are extremely difficult to modify. Fortunately, in group psychotherapy, most of the more powerful interactions will be those produced by the therapist, especially early in therapy. One important aspect of the development of the therapeutic group, whether recognized or not by therapists, is an attempt to reduce the influence of the more powerful individuals and to increase that of those who are less powerful. Once power has been equalized or balanced within the social context and members feel relatively free to speak, the group is more effective in understanding the work of group therapy—the solving of individual problems. Rarely, if ever, does the psychotherapist give up his position of power, though he may relinquish much of his power potential to the group as it develops the response sequences that he approves.

One of the problems that therapists work diligently to overcome is the well-established tendency that powerful individuals have great numbers of communications directed to them. As we will see in chapter 2, the therapist engages in techniques which redirect responses from himself to other individuals. This, in effect, is a surrender of power to other group members. The system by which he chooses the one to whom he redirects comment is often a deliberate effort by the therapist to raise the power of some individuals in his group. In other instances, he may redirect to those whose views are most congruent with his own, further increasing their power in the group.

Once a therapist has been successful in manipulating the group to the point where there is greater equality of power among members, levels of communication will be more nearly equal in the group. As in all groups, there is considerable variability in these levels based on other, more enduring response patterns of members. Those who retain their high degree of deviance from group norms in the psychotherapy group will receive less response from other members, even if they themselves tend to maintain a high response rate in the group. Typically, those who are granted little power and low status will reduce their levels of communication over time.

Other results from small-group research indicate that the group's effort in solving individual problems leads to group satisfaction or reinforcement for group members. In effect, the problems of each individual in the group become the problems of every member, and there is a level of satisfaction achieved as each member solves a problem or makes some gain in more effectively coping with his environment.

Models that focus on other aspects of the group are available. For example, Whitaker and Lieberman (1964) advocate a focal conflict approach based largely on systems developed by W. R. Bion and K. Lewin. Some theorists concerned with power and social influence approach these subjects from a dynamic standpoint, concerned with the inner processes of the individuals, while still others propose nontheoretical models.

To be sure, these comments reflect only a limited insight into the impact of small-group research on group psychotherapy, yet the evidence on which these comments are based is what psychological researchers would label as "hard" evidence.

Goals of Group Psychotherapy

Our emphasis to this point has been on the nature of disordered behavior, its foundations, and, briefly, on some of the social dynamics derived from small-group research as they apply to the group psychotherapeutic setting. A more fundamental consideration in developing our position is to describe the goals of psychotherapy and their relationship to the psychotherapeutic process.

While examining various psychotherapeutic orientations, Ford and Urban (1963) describe three positions taken by major theorists. One view is that the therapist is an expert in behavior disorders whose insights permit him to determine what is wrong with the individual and to decide what techniques are necessary to produce change in his behavior. From this therapeutic view, goals must be established by the therapist because the patient's difficulties prevent him from achieving the necessary insights to make sound judgments about what is wrong with him and what his therapeutic objectives or goals should be. The patient may have a role in determining alternative response patterns to be substituted for the deviant responses although some therapists would retain control of this decision as well.

A second position is that found in client-centered approaches where the patient is active in choosing his own goals. Theorists using this approach feel that "man's innate nature involves choosing his own goals (organismically valuing); any learnings that interfere with this are undesirable" (Ford and Urban, 1963, p. 664). In spite of theoretical adherence to the complete freedom of the patients in selecting goals, careful study of therapist behaviors reveals that the therapist does make some determination of what conditions are amiss and what behaviors will become targets for change.

Ford and Urban indicate that H. S. Sullivan exemplifies the third position, which they feel is the most defensible in understanding therapeutic goals. In this approach, both the therapist and client agree on goals on which they both can work. Agreement on goals is seen as a precondition to effective psychotherapy. Negotiation (sometimes extensive, sometimes as a contract) is necessary because some of the client's goals may be unacceptable to the therapist; conversely, some of the therapist's goals may be unacceptable to the client. This negotiation is a continuous process and agreed-upon goals may change during the course of therapy. Such negotiation becomes especially important to therapists who work with individuals or groups whose value systems are at variance with those of the therapist. Since most therapists have middle class, or unusually mobile lower middle class, values, they may encounter difficulty in relating to those groups least accessible to psychotherapy—the black, a member of another minority group, the deviant, the elderly, or others with whom there is a marked divergence between the values of the therapist and those of his clients.

Mahrer (1967) writes at great length on desirable outcomes in psychotherapy, but he does not explicitly state who sets goals. Separating his comments from those of the therapists and the therapeutic system he reviews in his book, it appears that he supports the position that the client's goals are given high priority, though the therapist must make judgments about a patient's capacity for goal setting. He seems to adopt an interaction model somewhat like Ford and Urban's third category.

Mischel (1968) presents a strong behavioral model of psychotherapy in which he contrasts the role of the experimenter with that of the therapist. He views the experimenter as one who considers what he wants to study, determines and defines his independent variables and the dependent measures to be used in measuring the effects of his treatment and manipulations. The experimenter determines what measurements and manipulations he will engage in and those with which he will be most concerned. By contrast, in the clinical situation, he indicates that "it is the 'subject' or client who must define the problematic behaviors and the objectives he seeks." In that sense he assumes something of the role of the scientist who must delineate his problems. The dual role of the therapist-scientist has been emphasized by C. R. Rogers and the client as scientist has been most explicitly expounded by G. A. Kelley.

It would seem that the existential view of goals would be most unlike Mischel's behavioral model, yet those holding this view agree with him that the individual must set the goals and develop the terms on which psychotherapy will be carried out.

Bandura (1969) expresses the belief that the therapist plays a major role in determining therapeutic goals. He feels that when a therapist, regardless of his theoretical orientation, claims to be successful in modifying his client's behavior, "he has either deliberately or unwittingly manipulated the facts that control it" (p. 81). Much of his research has supported the view that psychotherapists are models and selective reinforcers for the behaviors of their patients. While recognizing the considerable impact of the therapist on the process, Bandura suggests that, in most behaviorally oriented psychotherapy, the efforts of the therapist in modifying behaviors are designed to deal with those problems presented by clients. He views the therapist as exercising responsible controls over conditions which affect the relevant segment of a client's behavior in carrying out his psychotherapy. Under these constraints Bandura feels that the therapist is far less likely to shape behavior in accordance with his own belief system.

We believe that target behaviors selected for change in psychotherapy are determined by the client. These behaviors form the basis for negotiation between therapist and clients, which results in a contract for psychotherapy. Most often the contract is informal and not made explicit. The initial contract is subject to modification during later phases of the therapeutic process. New goals may be learned or discovered as interactions take place in therapy. Some goals of the client may be unacceptable to the therapist, and views may change regarding the reasonableness or desirability of some goals. Such altered conditions become the basis for further negotiation between therapist and client. Like Ford and Urban, the authors feel that there must be agreement between therapist and client on goals. The initial agreement is a precondition for effective psychotherapy. Part of the contract, implicit or explicit, must recognize both the limitations of the therapist-client relationship as an exclusive vehicle for effecting change and also those imposed by the realities of the environmental situation in which the client finds himself. Too frequently, clients seek therapy as a panacea for all their troubles and see the therapist as a wonder-working magician. The client quickly becomes disenchanted with the behavior process of change, if he does not recognize the limitations built into the therapy relationship, and if he does not recognize that the major responsibility for change will rest on his own shoulders.

The Goals

In determining the specific goals of psychotherapy, theorists typically have indicated a range of attitudes, values, and behaviors which they see as deviant and needing to be modified or eliminated. In some instances the definition of the goals of psychotherapy is very simple, as with Ford and Urban; in others, highly elaborate and descriptive (Mahrer, 1967).

Ford and Urban (1963) see the goals of psychotherapy as (1) modifying disordered responses, and (2) developing alternative responses. While many goals and categories are subsumed in each of these major categories, this definition cuts through the complexities and confusion found in the definitions of goals of other psychotherapy theorists.

A much more elaborate descriptive system is provided by Mahrer (1967), who includes in his goals of psychotherapy the following: (1) reduction of psychopathology, (2) reduction of psychological pain and suffering, (3) increase in pleasure, (4) increase in experiencing, (5) any self-relationship, (6) enhanced external relationships, (7) the achievement of mediating goals that serve as pathways toward the ultimate goals of psychotherapy. While Mahrer's categories do not conflict with those of Ford and Urban, they lack the behavioral rigor of the latters' definition and deal primarily with internal processes or constructs.

Krasner and Ullmann (1973) indicate that the goal of treatment is to change the behavior of the individual, a process which may involve an increase or decrease of certain behaviors or a change in their timing. They further indicate that the decision to alter a specific behavior or to choose what new behaviors to reinforce depends on concepts of what is "good, right, useful, proper, and so on." They further feel that an ethical question always exists in behavior change in regard to the legitimacy of the change and the direction it should take.

Bandura (1969) would not disagree with the objectives of psychotherapy described by Ford and Urban. He does add an important consideration that is only implicit in some of their statements. "Behavioral problems of vast proportions can never be adequately eliminated on an individual basis but require treatment and prevention at the social systems level . . . and the decision processes by which cultural priorities are established must, therefore, be made more explicit to ensure that 'social engineering' is utilized to produce living conditions that enrich life and behavioral freedom rather than aversive human effects" (p. 112).

Yalom's (1970) approach combines both goals and the process for change. He describes the goals of group psychotherapy and the curative process as possessing ten elements which interact in the change process:

1. Imparting of information
2. Installation of hope
3. Universality—developing the knowledge that problems are universal, not unique
4. Altruism—recognition of the help one patient may give another
5. The corrective recapitulation of the primary family group— the group serves as a medium for working out unfinished family business from the past
6. Development of socializing techniques
7. Imitative behavior
8. Interpersonal learning
9. Group cohesiveness
10. Catharsis

These factors, both behavioral and dynamic in nature, parallel at many points the position of the authors.

Our position is congruent with that of most other therapy theorists. Once the preconditions for psychotherapy have been met, that is, some agreement on the type of behaviors to be modified and the willingness of parties involved to engage in processes aimed at bringing about such change, the work of therapy can proceed. The goal of the therapeutic process is (1) to attempt to extinguish behaviors that are nonadaptive, inappropriate, ill timed, and/or disorganized, and (2) to aid individuals in developing or acquiring responses to meet their needs more adequately and in achieving their goals. Achievement of these goals would in turn produce changes in the constructs descriptive of internal processes, such as those in Mahrer's system or in the systems of dynamic theorists.

Therapeutic Change

In our initial comments, we described our position with regard to disordered behavior, the role of the culture in determination of disordered behavior, who determines the goals for psychotherapy, and the objectives of psychotherapeutic change. In subsequent chapters of the book, we shall develop and describe psychotherapeutic techniques and the way these techniques interact with conditions within the individual to produce changes.

2

THERAPISTS' BEHAVIORS
IN GROUP PSYCHOTHERAPY

Most previous descriptions of therapist behaviors have approached this subject on three levels. The first is an abstract approach in which the traits of the successful therapist—a series of ideal internal characteristics—are described. An excellent example of this approach is Grotjahn (1971). He delineates important qualities of the therapist, such as spontaneity, trust, firmness, humor, performance (fulfillment of duty, openness, self-disclosure), the ability to deal with countertransference, a recognition of the therapist's fallibility, and the ability to encompass the many transferences which occur in groups. Grotjahn goes on to explain the necessary personal therapeutic experiences for the therapist and comments on desirable qualities in a therapist's *wife* and *her* necessary understanding.[1] While approaches such as Grotjahn's are interesting and challenging, the qualities described as desirable in a therapist are difficult to specify operationally and appropriate training to achieve these qualities cannot be specified either.

The second level of approach to the therapist's traits is research-oriented, emphasizing the unique characteristics of the therapist or the patient. These studies have been provided by a series of psychological researchers, among them C. R. Rogers, W. U. Snyder, L. M. Brammer, E. L. Shostrom, R. R. Carkhuff, C. B. Truax, A. E. Bergin, and Barbara J. Betz—to mention some of the better-known persons

1. There seems to be little doubt that the social and interpersonal environment in which the therapist lives has considerable impact on his work and professional attitudes, yet the literature is devoid of any research on this important topic. Anecdotal and highly speculative accounts are found, but even these are limited in number.

who have developed these systems. It is not our intent to review these systems in depth. Inspection of one contemporary system may be informative.

One prominent system concerned with the interpersonal skills of therapists is found in the work of Truax and Carkhuff, summarized in Truax and Mitchell (1971), Carkhuff (1969) and Truax and Carkhuff (1967). They have been primarily concerned with measuring such qualities as the therapist's genuineness, nonpossessive warmth, and the accuracy of his empathic response.[2] Truax and Mitchell state (1971) that "the evidence is convincing that the depth and accuracy of therapist empathic responses, his warm non-possessive responses, and his non-defensive or 'non-phony' responses, do indeed play an important role in the process and outcome of psychotherapy." Measurement of these qualities typically involves the use of trained raters or judges who sample segments of therapeutic interaction either from video or audio tapings. Measurements generally are made in the middle and third portions of psychotherapy, because Truax and Mitchell, like the authors, have found that initial moments of psychotherapy tend to be its least relevant portions.

Truax also indicates that these qualities and other interpersonal skills have:

indirect effects upon patient change in four modalities: (1) they serve to reinforce positive aspects of the patient self concept, modifying the existing self concepts and thereby leading to changes in the patient's own self-reinforcement system; (2) they serve to reinforce self-exploratory behavior and thereby elicit self-concepts and anxiety laden material that can be then modified by selective reinforcement; (3) they serve to extinguish anxiety fear responses associated with specific use, both those elicited by the relationship with the therapist and those elicited by patient self-exploration; and (4) they serve to reinforce human relating, encountering, or interacting, and

2. The principles and techniques of data gathering, whether this is in the form of observation, history taking or psychological testing, or various combinations of these techniques, are fully developed by many authors and researchers and will not be discussed in this chapter. Virtually every text describing clinical techniques presents a methodology for data gathering. Emphases range from strict behavioral techniques to dynamic-analytic procedures. It is possible to select from this array an approach to data gathering which approximates the reader's orientation.

serve to extinguish fear or avoidance responses associated with human relating.

Truax and Mitchell's system, while interesting and challenging, lacks sufficient specificity to be a truly behavioral system. Relying strongly on ratings and heavily weighted in judgment and interpretation, it requires more clearly specified behavioral measures in order to progress beyond the present level of development.

The third approach, which we will develop, is less concerned with traits than with methods for effecting change. Many researchers have developed behaviorally oriented systems, most prominently Bandura (1969), Mischel (1968), Krumboltz (1966), Ullmann and Krasner (1969), and Mahoney and Thoreson (1974).

We would not summarily reject the useful approaches of the humanist or trait-oriented therapist. Rather, we would hope to understand the behavioral system which underlies a particular approach and utilize those successful principles in our system.

In the present system, five therapist behaviors are of major importance: (1) instruction, (2) modeling, (3) reinforcement, (4) aversive control, and (5) data gathering. Though this may not constitute the range of therapist behaviors, each can be fully specified, and each is learning-based. Each area will be described in detail with development of the specific therapist behaviors related to each class of response.

Instruction

Much of the therapist's behavior in psychotherapy lies in specifying to the patient those behaviors that are desired, those discriminative stimuli that ensure that if certain behaviors are emitted, they will be reinforced. The term "structuring" has been used to describe this pattern and is an appropriate term to be subsumed under the instructional label. The instructional process details for the patient the behaviors that are expected of him inside and outside the group. It is critical to the whole psychotherapeutic process because it provides the arena, the game plan, the behaviors expected of the patient which will then be reinforced by the therapist when they occur, or appropriately shaped to more efficient and effective levels.

Structure

Regardless of the orientation of the therapist, structure plays a major role in all therapeutic systems. It is through structuring that the therapist sets the contract or specifies the behavior desired. Even were the therapist to provide no structure (requiring patients to engage in a process of trial and error with a series of responses, then reinforcing certain types of responses), he has in effect provided the structure—one of trial and error. Techniques involving a trial-and-error approach to structure are frequently used in group dynamics, but only rarely in psychotherapy groups. The rationale is that in training groups the level of awareness and sophistication and the expectations and behavioral interactions of the members are higher than in most patient groups. The dangers of providing an unstructured situation for these more efficiently responding individuals is far less than for those having disordered behaviors.

In the approach used by the authors, instructions tend to be quite specific:

1. *Patients are informed that participation in therapy groups is on a voluntary basis.* Such information is presented before the patient enters the group and often is restated early in the group. Patients who are ambivalent are reinforced for the adient response toward the group. Involved in such interactions are some reassurance about the nature of the groups, how they work, and what the therapist and other group members expect of the patient. Once this information has been supplied most ambivalent individuals agree to "try."

2. *Punctuality in arriving for group therapy sessions is stressed.* If this factor is not clearly elaborated upon, the ability to use it as a criterion of resistance or other avoidance responses is diminished. Instruction on this point is typically provided several times early in the therapeutic process if it appears necessary.

3. *Regular attendance is stressed as a requisite for effective group psychotherapy.* Here again, the ability to interpret resistance or other avoidance responses is diminished if regular attendance is not stated as one of the ground rules for group therapy. The need for establishing this point extends beyond the group itself. If the group is held in an in-patient setting, agreement on the part of all staff that

group therapy has highest priority must be established. Otherwise patients will set their own priorities, and the resistant patient typically will find that occupational therapy, recreational activities, or ward duties have priority over the therapy session. With full agreement gained from staff on the priority of therapy, the meaning of absence can be more adequately assessed.

4. *The therapist stresses the confidential nature of interactions taking place in the group and of the data revealed by members.* This is often done before the patient enters and almost invariably becomes an early topic of discussion in the group. This confidentiality should be observed as well by the therapist, and material revealed to him by a patient in an individual session should not be introduced without permission. Where such material is deemed important by the therapist, he may encourage the patient to present such material to the group but should not break the patient's confidence or engage in revealing materials supplied by others.

5. *All patients have the same access to the therapist for individual psychotherapy.* Access to the therapist is an especially difficult problem where some patients are seen individually by the group therapist and others are not. Where possible it is desirable to see individuals only in the group, referring those who need individual treatment to another therapist. Where several persons are working together, they may exchange patients who need individual therapeutic attention. Where this is not possible, the group's understanding of the basis on which individual attention is given should be made quite clear. Problems may arise from greater contact time with some patients than with others (the greater number of reinforcements given to those seen individually) and often become the basis of status within the group or an implied special relationship between the individually seen patient and the therapist. While it is possible to solve all such problems in the group setting, it is best to avoid them if possible.

6. *Structure to patients includes those topics and areas of discussion which are not encouraged.* For example, all topics which are not problem-relevant—discussion of the weather, sports, or mere generalities—should be discouraged in structuring the therapy session. Usually reserved for other kinds of groups (patient government, ward management groups, etc.) is the discussion of an in-patient's disposi-

tion in the hospital or the arrangements for a weekend pass. These are best handled before or after the group session, if this is a responsibility of the group therapist. At times, such topics will be problem-related and group members may be able to make valuable comments and evaluate the patient's readiness for certain in-hospital actions. Of course, in such cases, discussion with the therapy group is appropriate. However, most patients use such topics in a manipulative manner and, as typically utilized, they have little to do with therapy in the group.

7. *Patients are instructed on the appropriate focus of their relevant responses.* If the group concentrates primarily on current behavior, feelings, and attitudes, this concentration should be made very plain to the patients. If childhood experiences, dreams and fantasies are considered important by the therapist, they should appear in the description of the structure of group psychotherapy. There is ample evidence that when instructions require the development of certain kinds of responses, as with the reporting of dreams in the group, patients not only report more dreams, but dream more frequently. Short-term group psychotherapy primarily focuses on the present. Responses to current situations are reinforced. Focus on past events, except when the past history specifically fits into present problems, receives no reinforcement.

An example of research into therapist-provided structure is reported by Gross (1969) in a dissertation conducted under the direction of Salzberg:

Forty hospitalized patients in a VA hospital were assigned to one of four therapy groups in which a therapist variable and structure variable were manipulated. In two of these groups a therapist was present (TP) while in the other two groups the therapist was absent (TA). Structuring materials were administered to patients in two of the groups (S) and not to the other two (US). Structuring materials were designed to clarify patients' perception of group therapy and provide information to facilitate learning. Frequencies of relevant, spontaneous and group verbal responses were used as measures of the effects of the two independent variables. The Barron Ego-Strength Scale and the Finney Group Therapy Scale were used as pre-post measures. Group sessions were run every day, five days per week, until a total of twenty sessions were completed. Those groups receiving structuring materials (TA-S & TP-S) were found to have a significantly greater number of relevant, spontaneous, and group responses although the structuring factor appeared to have enhanced spontaneity in the absence of a therapist and it also seemed to diminish the frequency of group responses over time in the TA-S group. The presence of a therapist (TP-US & TP-S groups) resulted in greater numbers of relevant and group responses while therapist absence increased spontaneous responses. This result confirmed other studies which report similar results using much the same measures as well as different measures of change. Overall, the relative strength of both the variables was consistent and indicated that therapy groups would most likely be most productive if a therapist was present and structure was administered. No significant results occurred on the pre-post measures, a result that was interpreted as meaning that: (1) these scales were not sensitive to the structuring materials or the presence of a leader; (2) therapist presence or absence and structure may have "overdirectionalized" the content of therapy; (3) possibly not enough of a time lapse occurred between pre-post administrations of the scales to allow for significant differences to occur.

8. *The therapist structures for spontaneity.* Spontaneity is defined as a response that is made by a group member that does not occur as the result of a question or other method of eliciting a response. In structuring for spontaneous inputs, patients are instructed not to wait for the therapist's questions, but to bring forth their feelings, ideas, and problems. There is evidence that the therapist's silence is a strong motivator for spontaneous responses. Middle class patients, particularly, have a reasonably high operant speech level in social situations; protracted silence appears to activate such persons. Unfortunately, this is not an effective means of working with persons who interact on a very limited level verbally. In such instances, spontaneity may only be achieved by extended training and use of techniques such as modeling. The work of Goldstein (1973) is particularly important in this regard. His technique, structured learning therapy, is geared to overcome deficiencies in skill so that group members may respond effectively and therapeutically. Modeling and role playing are important features of his approach.

Little formal research exists on structuring and its impact on the group psychotherapeutic process. Many informal studies have been carried out by therapists who try certain structural techniques, or eliminate them in order to measure their impact. Some group therapists provide patients with an explicit contract which fully details the structure of group psychotherapy as they practice it. Having read the contract patients sign it, signifying their willingness to follow the rules of the group. Brammer and Shostrom (1960) utilized what they described as a "Preparation Sheet for New Group Members." This form, based on one devised earlier by G. R. Bach, delineates many of the specifications of the therapy group and reduces group time spent in discussing these matters.

Preparation Sheet for New Group Members

1. *Size of group:* The group's size is limited to a minimum number of six and a maximum number of ten clients.
2. *Admission of new members:* When an old member leaves the group his or her place in the group will be filled by a new member. The selection is made on two bases: (a) which group is best for the prospective member, and (b) which prospective member is best for the group.
3. *Extra-office meetings:* The regular office meetings of the group with the therapist, while of central therapeutic importance, are only part of the total program. Experiences during the post session between members of the group, provide important material for self-observation and analysis. No extra-office meetings other than post-session meetings are allowed.
4. *Sharing of mutual experiences:* Group members usually adhere to the principle that everything anybody says, thinks or does, which involves another member of the group, is subject to open discussion in the group. In other words, the emotionally important experiences of any member are shared by all members. There are no secrets *inside* the group.
5. *Ethical confidence:* In contrast to principle No. 4, everything that goes on within the group—everything!—must remain an absolute secret as far as any outsider (non-member) is concerned. Anyone participating in group therapy automatically assumes the same professional ethics of absolute discretion which bind professional therapists.
6. *The group's goal:* The group goal is free communication on a non-defensive, personal and emotional level. This goal can be reached only by the group effort. Experience shows that the

official therapists cannot "push" the group; the group has to progress by its own efforts. Each member will get out of the group what he puts into it. As every member communicates to the group his feelings and perceptions and associations of the moment as openly as he can and as often as he can, the group will become a therapeutically effective medium. The goal of free communication is freedom to be oneself most fully and comfortably.

I have read the above and agree to cooperate fully.

Signed   *

Structure aids such as the contract used by Brammer and Shostrom are valuable, especially when utilized by verbal, middle class patients. For others, the ability fully to comprehend the various parameters may be limited by marginal reading skills or by failure to understand the implications of what they have read. For groups from other than middle class background, credibility of group rules is increased when presented by peers or other group members who have been in attendance in the group, or when the therapist shares with the new members the basis for the structure proposed.

While most structuring occurs early in therapy, it is also included during all stages of therapy. For example, some aspects of feedback, evaluation of progress, and summarizing behaviors by the therapist provide additional structure to the patient. These are complex behaviors and each may also utilize reinforcement, punishment, and modeling.

Modeling

The most important recent advance in group psychotherapy is related to the use of modeling and what Bandura (1969) refers to as other "vicarious processes." Modeling has been long recognized as an important factor in the acquisition of behavior, but only in recent times has it been fully used as a major therapeutic technique. Even following the important work of J. B. Watson and Mary C. Jones early in this century, modeling remained largely a curiosity, used

*Reprinted by permission from *Therapeutic psychology,* pp. 301–2. Copyright © 1960 by Prentice-Hall, Inc.

occasionally, and then only in the modifying of certain highly specified behaviors. It was not really developed until Bandura and his students tested and implemented modeling procedures and techniques for purposes which were only hinted at in the earlier work of Miller and Dollard (1941).

Bandura (1969) distinguishes three different kinds of behavioral modifications which result from exposure to modeling stimuli:

First, an observer may acquire new response patterns that did not previously exist in his behavioral repertoire. Second, observation of modeled actions and their consequences to the performer may strengthen or weaken inhibitory responses in observers . . . third, the behavior of others often serves merely as discriminative stimuli for the observer in facilitating occurrence of previously learned responses in the same general class.

Basically, he is describing observational learning, an inhibitory or disinhibitory effect, and a response facilitation effect, each of which can be utilized in successfully modifying behavior under the conditions of group psychotherapy.

Acquiring New Response Patterns

Bandura (1969) has indicated the importance of modeling in acquiring new social learnings and, thus, new social behaviors. He further indicates that were individuals forced to acquire complex behaviors by a trial-and-error approach or successive approximations, many of the hazards of living would not be avoided, with either dangerous, or possibly lethal, consequences. Modeling permits the acquisition of large segments of behavior rather than fragmented or fractional behavioral bits that must then be organized into a more complex form—the only explanation one could arrive at on the basis of earlier learning theory.

The importance of modeling for group psychotherapy is inescapable. New patients who observe the therapist reinforce patient verbal-behavioral sequences can, and frequently do, rapidly acquire those complex verbal behaviors that we describe in chapter 3, especially those classed as functional group roles. The therapist may also model many of the desired verbal behaviors himself, though acquisition of such behaviors in the absence of reinforcement is somewhat more complex. However, it is possible to speculate that there are inherent reinforcing properties in having or taking the role of therapist, and, thus, the emitted behaviors of the therapist follow the reinforcement paradigm of identification—which Kohlberg (1963) indicates is maintained by the intrinsic reinforcement of perceived similarity. While our position is not quite that of Mowrer (1964) in having the therapist actively model a majority of verbal response sequences which the clients are supposed to learn, we want the therapist to develop in his approach sufficient openness to present the patient with a response style or response set that would facilitate communicative acts, thus permitting the therapist selectively to reinforce those behaviors and responses desired in his patients.

Inhibitory and Disinhibitory Effects in Modeling

Observing a model may act to inhibit or disinhibit previously learned response patterns. This particular aspect of modeling has special consequences in group psychotherapy where the group sets about to alter response styles of participants. Bandura states (1969): "The occurrence of inhibitory effects is indicated when, as a function of observing negative response consequences to a model, observers show either decrements in the same class of behavior, or a general reduction of responsiveness." He also indicates:

Behavioral restraints, established through previous modeling or direct aversive conditioning, can be reduced on the basis of observational experiences. Such disinhibitory effects are evident when observers display increases in socially disapproved behavior as a function of viewing models either rewarded or experiencing no adverse consequences for performing prohibited responses.

Procedures for modeling vary somewhat depending upon the orientation of the therapist, the level of sophistication of the group members, their ability effectively to monitor their behaviors and report them, and their ability to specify their goals. Gutride, Goldstein, and Hunter (1973), following procedures developed by Goldstein, provide an excellent example of modeling techniques for use with psychiatric in-patients. They used four modeling videotapes as stimulus materials. Each tape depicted an increasingly complex social interaction.

The first tape contained enactments indicating how one individual (the model) can interact with another individual who approaches him. The second tape indicated how an individual (the model) can initiate interaction with a second person. The third tape indicated how an individual (the model) can initiate interaction with a group of people. Finally, continuing this progression reflecting increasing complexity of social interaction, the fourth tape depicted how an individual (the model) can resume relationships with relatives, friends, and business associates from outside the hospital. In several respects, in both the development and experimental usage of these modeling displays, we sought to be responsive to laboratory research findings that have identified characteristics of the observer, the model, and the modeling display that function to enhance the level of vicarious learning that occurs. This included our portrayal of several heterogeneous models; the introduction and summarization of each tape by a high-status narrator (hospital superintendent and clinical director) who sought by his introduction to maximize observer attention and by his summary to reemphasize the nature of the specific concrete social interaction behaviors; portrayal of the model's characteristics as similar to that of most participating study patients (age, sex); and frequent and readily observable reward provided to the model contingent on his social interaction behavior. . . .

Each session began with the modeling tape display, during which the group leaders actively drew attention to those model behaviors representative of effective social interaction. At frequent intervals the sound was turned off and the importance of nonverbal aspects of social interaction was highlighted, for example, forward leaning, eye contact, smiling, etc. Each tape was immediately followed by an "idiosyncratizing" group discussion in which the behaviors and circumstances depicted were related to each patient's personal experiences and environmental demands. The remainder of each session was devoted to role playing both the depicted and personalized social interaction sequences. The role-playing enactments were themselves videotaped and played back to the group for comment and corrective feedback. Both the group leaders and, frequently, other group members provided the role-play enactor with frequent social reinforcement as his depiction more and more approximated that of the videotaped model's. [p. 410]

In group psychotherapy, patients in most cases enter with high-level verbal skills, particularly if they come from a middle class background. However, even highly verbal, middle class individuals have situational inhibitions about certain kinds of verbally expressive behaviors. Prior learning has taught them that highly personal statements are not emitted in groups of strangers, and in some family configurations, these verbalizations may never occur. For most individuals, verbal interactions tend to fall in what we class as the environmental or non-problem-relevant levels of responding. That is, they may talk about baseball, the weather, or current news events, never highly personal problems. The use of modeling to inhibit irrelevant verbal responding, and disinhibit the responses that are problem-relevant, personal, and high in emotional content follows a two-stage sequence.

In the first stage, the therapist may model or give examples, or may role-play the modeling sequence directed toward inhibiting or disinhibiting the verbal behavior. Patients may observe the therapist and cotherapist (if one is used) modeling the verbal behavior, with verbal reinforcement being given for appropriate responses. For example, the therapist playing the role of patient might model a personal, problem-relevant response: "It's hard for me to talk to anyone. I get this feeling of tension, anxiety, and I walk off rather than say anything." The reinforcement is also modeled: "I'm glad you could tell us that. It took a lot of determination, feeling as you do."

In the second stage, the whole group becomes an observer as the therapist reinforces a patient for appropriate verbal responses. Modeling is not limited to verbal behavior. Appropriate nonverbal behaviors relating to attending, observing, and avoidance of withdrawal (e.g., by moving one's chair out of the group), and other negative nonverbal behaviors may also be modeled.

Unlike individual therapy, the group setting offers an almost infinite number of modeling opportunities to the patient-observer. He will see hundreds of therapist-patient interactions which will shape his response patterns, particularly if the therapist reinforces them nonverbally or verbally, by nodding positively or "mhmming" during the interaction, or in words following its termination.

Response-Facilitating Effects of Modeling

In Bandura's third category, dealing with response-facilitating effects of modeling, the model's behavior provides discriminative cues for the patient-observer that facilitate the expression of "previously learned responses that ordinarily are not subject to negative sanction." There is not always a one-to-one relationship between the modeling sequence and the actions of patient-observers, because persons serving as models may have a differential impact on the observer's actions. For example, a patient-observer may model quite readily a behavioral sequence by the therapist, but fail to respond to the behaviors of the cotherapist. Bandura indicates that factors affecting the patient-observer's susceptibility to social facilitation is governed by the characteristics of the observer, the reinforcement contingencies associated with matching behavior in the setting, and the model's attributes. Thus the emitted behaviors of the therapist or cotherapist may quickly facilitate a response, while the same behaviors occurring in other patients observed by the patient-observer may have far less influence, or possibly none at all. Power and status are of great importance in determining degrees of influence. There exists a wealth of social-psychological research into the effects of both on communication patterns in groups. Those interested in further study in this area are directed to Shaw (1971), Collins and Guetzkow (1964), and Cartwright and Zander (1971). Whitaker and Lieberman (1966) describe a conflict model of group psychotherapy in which power and status are important considerations.

Finally, we recognize that many things subsumed under our category of instruction may also blend with what Bandura and others describe as a part of the modeling process. Indeed, all categories proposed for classifying therapist behaviors blend into one another, rather than being totally discrete entities. They appear either singly or in concert with other categories. It is not uncommon for a therapist to instruct or structure, then model the behavior and immediately reinforce patients who are able to comprehend what he offers.

Reinforcement

Reinforcement is a cornerstone of the therapeutic modification of behavior. It plays a major role in the two preceding sections, Instruction and Modeling, and is used (Bandura, 1969) individually as well as in combination with other methods to maintain existing patterns of response, to modify behavioral deficits and to change deviant behaviors which are supported by their rewarding effects. Bandura further develops his position on reinforcement by describing three sets of variables which are involved in the successful use of the principles of reinforcement. The first is related to the development of an incentive system capable of producing a high level of responsiveness over extended periods of time. The incentives available to the group therapist are quite limited. Unless the patient is able to respond effectively to verbal stimuli, and hence be responsive to social reinforcers, as in verbal conditioning, the therapist's options are quite limited. Two researchers in our group, Drennen and Wiggins (1964), utilized food, candy, and cigarettes as rewards for verbal responding but were successful only with patients who had at least a limited baseline of verbal responses. They were not effective with patients who could not or would not initially respond verbally.

Second, reinforcement occurs only upon the emitting of the desired behavior. Because of the complexities of the group, with the simultaneous occurrence of many verbal and nonverbal behaviors, the therapist must be alert to reinforce appropriate responses and not inadvertently reinforce inappropriate responses—a behavior sometimes particularly difficult to avoid in a group situation. Fortunately the number of emitted responses by group therapy patients in any given session is sufficiently high that the occasional "miss" proves insignificant.[3] Also, partial reinforcement, although less effective than continuous reinforcement in building effective responses, leads to behaviors that are more resistant to extinction.

Third, reinforcement must involve rewards of sufficient strength, and the responses to be reinforced must potentially occur often enough for them to be strongly established through positive reinforcement. In most instances, the therapist will be required to

3. Studies by the authors reveal that numbers of patient statements range from about 140 to 200 in their typical group session.

engage in an extended shaping process in which the various classes of verbal responses from his patients are refined and developed through successive stages (successive approximations) to a precise and appropriate level. Irrelevant, impersonal verbal responses by a patient, through shaping, become problem-relevant, self-disclosing verbal responses.

As indicated, reinforcement in its various forms and special conditions is fundamental to the therapist's behavior when interacting with patients in the group, regardless of his orientation or theoretical base.

While often reinforcement is combined with other therapist behaviors to shape the responses of patients, there are many instances in which the therapist directly reinforces a patient's verbal response. Some examples are as follows:

1. *The therapist should reinforce patient interaction about specific personal problems.* When patients make statements that are problem-oriented or problem-relevant, the therapist should encourage this behavior by using verbal reinforcement. This is especially true early in therapy, when the goal for the individual is to uncover his areas of adjustive difficulty. As therapy progresses, group responses are more desirable, and the patient who fixates on personal responses to the exclusion of interaction responses (awareness of and a willingness to discuss the problems of other persons) will no longer be reinforced for giving only personal responses. Personal responses are no longer reinforced when the patient repeats earlier personal statements, especially when these have been dealt with effectively by the group or by the therapist.

2. *When patients are verbally interacting in the group the therapist offers nonintrusive verbal reinforcements—such as, "That's good, mmm; I think that's important, etc."—or utilizes nonverbal reinforcers such as nodding approval, encouraging, smiling, etc.*

3. *The therapist should reinforce patients when they show signs of emotional involvement and when they express emotion-laden material.* Typically this takes the form of either verbal or nonverbal approval for the behavior as it is occurring (immediate reinforcement), or making approving comments at the end of the interaction, or, in other instances, at the end of the group session.

4. *The therapist should reinforce the presentation of emotional*

material by insuring that the patient catharting is protected from potentially punishing or nonreinforcing comments from other members. The reinforcing behaviors used by the therapist at this point tend to be more subtle and are often displayed by a gesture or a quieting motion to other group members. When more vigorous attempts are made to interrupt the introduction of emotional material by irrelevant intellectualizations or other intrusive comments, the therapist may use verbal forms of punishment with the intruder, while strongly supporting the verbalizations of the patient experiencing emotion.

5. *The therapist should talk to the group as a whole frequently, particularly to let them know how they are behaving in group therapy.* By reinforcing appropriate responses on the part of all group members, the therapist is able effectively to shape all their behaviors through feedback. These behaviors promote the development of group-delivered contingencies, an important part of shaping as controlled by group members. This is sometimes necessary as a part of restructuring or reminding the group about previously agreed-upon structural guidelines.

6. *The therapist should reinforce verbal behaviors in patients who appear visibly upset or disturbed.* When the degree of disturbance in a patient is acute, usual procedures and techniques are set aside in favor of developing a one-to-one relationship with the disturbed individual, and his organized and appropriate verbal responses are highly reinforced until the level of stress is reduced. Responses from other group members are then encouraged and incorporated. In a mature group of long standing, it is possible that the highly individual attention will not be necessary and that group members themselves can help manage the emotional distress of the disturbed group member.

7. *The therapist should focus on acutely disturbed patients whose symptoms are active rather than on those whose symptoms have subsided after having been in the group for an extended period of time.* This is done to allow the new patient to catch up, to become thoroughly integrated into the group process and to receive sufficient behavioral shaping to work effectively as a group member. The therapist makes ample use of older group members for supplying data, modeling, reinforcing the new patient and instruction

regarding group structure and function. The motivation of patients experiencing distress is quite high. Their willingness to accept new response sequences which may reduce this distress permits rapid behavioral change if the therapist actively involves them in therapy.

8. *The therapist should reinforce patients discussing or reacting to the behavior of other patients within the group.* This behavior does not often occur spontaneously in group psychotherapy. It must be carefully shaped from less complex interactions. This is the essence of the group response, a major factor in group psychotherapy in our view. Thus, when a group member spontaneously offers a group response, the therapist makes efforts to reinforce the behavior to insure its recurrence. He must be careful to reinforce only those interactions that he feels are problem-relevant or are useful in problem solving.

Aversive Control

While the majority of the therapist's behaviors are concerned with shaping and reinforcing the verbal responses and behaviors of patients, there are also available to the therapist two major kinds of aversive stimuli: punishment—the most frequently utilized—and negative reinforcement. Briefly, punishment is utilized by the therapist to reduce or inhibit certain classes of responding. In negative reinforcement, desired behaviors are maintained or increased by removal of the aversive stimulus, following models of avoidance or escape.

Punishment

When a particular behavior or set of behaviors meets with aversive consequences (punishment), the behaviors involved typically are reduced or terminated. Learning theorists have long concerned themselves with the fact that behaviors, once extinguished, may reappear and have argued that punishment serves a repressive function and does not actually remove the punished behavior. If reinforceable alternative responses are available, however, punishment may be used quite effectively.

We will not attempt to elaborate upon this in any depth, but the prior reinforcement history of the behavior is crucial in determining the effectiveness of punishment in its reduction or removal. For example, it is much more difficult to extinguish verbal aggression in a person during psychotherapy if he is reinforced for this behavior in his interactions outside treatment. A parent may buy a child a toy or desired object in order to end his verbal aggression, thus actually increasing the probability of its recurrence when needs are to be filled.

Bandura (1969), like the authors, feels that punishment is more effective in life situations than might be concluded from laboratory research. He states:

The relative ineffectiveness of punishment in producing durable reductive effects in laboratory situations has probably resulted from the fact that, with few exceptions, the punished response constitutes the sole means of securing rewards. Hence, it comes as no surprise that, in single-response situations, punished behavior is performed for some time even though it incurs aversive consequences, and it often reappears when punishment is discontinued. In contrast, people generally have numerous options available in everyday life. Even though punishment may only temporarily inhibit dominant responses, during the period of suppression alternative modes of behavior may be strengthened sufficiently to supplant the original response tendencies. Moreover, brief cessation of behavior that is highly disturbing to others eventually draws positive reactions from appreciative associates. The new conditions of reinforcement created by cessation of deviant responses may foster and maintain their relinquishment. By the same token, rodents or pigeons that were suddenly showered with food pellets and increased positive attention from relieved comrades, after inhibiting a socially distressing bar-press response, would undoubtedly abandon the cherished bar more rapidly than they would if no alternative activities were available and response inhibition produced no outcomes other than the removal of aversive stimulation and loss of food rewards. [p. 347]

Bandura further suggests that:

Punishment based upon the removal of positive reinforcers often reduces undesired behavior without producing fear learning or avoidant behavior. This procedure also tends to maintain strong approach tendencies toward change agents, and, when reinstatement of approval, possessions, or privileges is made conditional upon more appropriate behavior, it provides more positive support and guidance than mere administration of negative outcomes.

Lasting elimination of detrimental behavior can be most effectively facilitated by punishment if competing response patterns are simultaneously rewarded. Negative sanctions may therefore be successfully employed to hold undesired responses in check while alternative modes of behavior are being established and strengthened. [p. 348]

The results of two studies by the authors, using one negative reinforcer, produced sufficient behavioral change to encourage more use of this technique in therapy and therapy research. Wiggins and Salzberg (1966) have speculated that it might be possible to:

select two comparable groups, have an experienced therapist agree with E on the behavior to be manipulated, and make it a contest to see if E is more successful in manipulating behavior in a therapistless group than the group psychotherapist, using all of his vast experience and knowledge about behavior in group psychotherapy? Is it possible selectively and consecutively to reinforce or extinguish a number of behaviors in the group psychotherapeutic situation with simple conditioning techniques so that only one or two desirable behaviors would eventually remain? [p. 598] *

It is apparent that behavior in group psychotherapy follows predictable principles and that conditioning techniques established in the laboratory can be applied effectively in the clinical setting. If we keep our measures simple, yet meaningful, there is much to be gained by working directly with the complex behavior of human interactions.

Punishment and the Therapist

In general, the therapist should not be identified as an aversive stimulus to group members. Thus, when punishment can be applied by external forces, as in the case of a noxious auditory stimulus (see Heckel, Wiggins and Salzberg [1962]), it is not necessary to deal with the complication of the therapist becoming the "bad guy." In groups where cotherapists are utilized, it may be that one can play the role of the aggressive confronter (aversive) when undesirable responses appear, while the other therapist maintains a reinforcing role, responding only to appropriate verbal responses. If they were to alternate in these roles patients in groups might not come to expect any exclusive response sets in either therapist.

When the therapist uses punishment in the group it should be mild and well specified, that is, directed toward specific actions or responses of the patient or the group. In many instances the non-verbal communication of disapproval is sufficiently aversive to produce behavioral change. Often punishment is used after structuring has failed or when insufficient numbers of reinforceable behaviors have occurred.

Aversive verbal comments may be used with patients who frequently interpret comments of other patients or with patients who monopolize groups for long periods of time, respond only to the therapist, or otherwise emit negative, blocking, or impeding responses. We would stress that aversive techniques initiated by the therapist rank low on the hierarchy of responses and other methods should be tried before they are employed. However, it is possible to use aversive control after the group has met for a series of sessions and group members have a history of reinforcement from the therapist. Early in therapy aversive control may be less effective.

Negative Reinforcement

A special condition, closely related to punishment, is that of negative reinforcement. In negative reinforcement the therapist's withdrawal of an aversive stimulus results in a maintenance or increase in the patient's response rate. The stimulus producing this effect is called a negative reinforcer.

As a technique to be utilized by the therapist, negative reinforcement is quite limited. Often the presentation of a negative reinforcer in an effort to produce an avoidance or escape response in patients may go beyond the goal of eliciting and increasing desired responses and instead result in the patient's flight from treatment. For example, a therapist may decide to berate his group for certain responses, only stopping this negative reinforcer when the group or some member emits a correct response following an escape paradigm. This might work, but it might also be sufficiently confusing or disrupting that patients' responses were extinguished before the correct response pattern was discovered and increased.

Somewhat less dangerous to group functioning is the avoidance paradigm, in which the therapist produces a signal or cue which requires the emitting of an appropriate response to avoid the beginning of an aversive stimulus. For example, the therapist might require the group to complete certain tasks or behave in a particular fashion. If they fail to fulfill these, then he initiates a negative reinforcer.

Because of the complexities of negative reinforcement, and the greater difficulty of predicting an individual's, let alone a group's, response to a negative reinforcer, it would seem to be of limited utility in most therapeutic situations.

Data Gathering

Many of the therapist's early efforts in group psychotherapy are directed toward the gathering of data relevant to the problems of patients in the group. This is achieved through a process of searching and probing, questioning and at times pushing patients to emit appropriate classes of verbal behavior. It is also gained through use of the techniques of role playing and self-observation, including enumerating or counting occurrences of specific behaviors in order to establish baselines, establishing goals and methods for measuring them, setting reinforcement contingencies, and determining types of reinforcement (see Williams and Long [1975] for techniques of self-management).

The process is, however, quite complex. Data must be elicited in such a manner as not to become a simple question-and-answer sequence—a dialogue between patient and therapist. Heckel, Froelich, and Salzberg (1962), in one of their earliest research efforts, demonstrated that if the therapist frequently responded directly to patients' verbalizations levels of communication were lower, and there were fewer total responses and more silences, and the material that developed was far less therapeutically significant than when the therapist sought to develop data through redirection (described later in this chapter) or other shaping techniques. In effect the probing and development *must* be a shared inquiry involving the therapist and other group members. The reinforcing properties of the interest demonstrated by the therapist and other members in a patient's relevant verbal responses produce the behavioral patterns of inter-action which dynamicists have labeled a "climate of trust," a "shar-ing atmosphere" or "permissive group environment." Whatever the disciplinary label, reinforcement from multiple sources appears to be a necessary condition for the development of relevant and deep verbal responses. Once the member has observed the rewards that ensue from interaction between one group member and the therapist and other group members, similar interactions are much easier to elicit.

Most probing and data-gathering statements by therapists are simple and straightforward, as "I wonder if you could tell the group more about that." This statement is preferable to "Tell *me* more about it" because it involves the whole group and frequently other group members will verbally or nonverbally support the therapist's request. It probably makes little difference whether the response of other group members is based on a genuine desire to learn more about a particular member's problems or on a response set to agree with whatever the therapist suggests. The net effect is that the responding patient is able to observe verbal and/or nonverbal rein-forcement when others in the group (and the therapist) support additional relevant verbal responses. As we have already indicated, dialogues between patient and therapist do not provide a desirable model for group responding and do not foster group interaction.

Complex Therapist Behaviors

As indicated, many therapist behaviors are complex, combining several of the five classes (instruction, modeling, reinforcement, punishment, data gathering). One such behavior, which occupies a cornerstone of the authors' approach, is *redirection,* in which group interaction is shaped through redirecting those responses directed to the therapist or cotherapist to other members of the group.

1. *Redirection.* Redirection can only occur effectively when pa-tients are at least minimally communicative on a personal level and the group itself has evolved sufficiently—or the therapist is sure enough of the response potential of the group member to whom he

redirects the response—that there will be an adequate, and thus nonpunishing or nonextinguishing, interaction.

The components of this interaction are reasonably straight-forward once the previously mentioned conditions are met. The patient emits a personal response which is directed toward the therapist. The therapist, after reinforcing through some form of positive acknowledgment (at least in early stages of the group), redirects the response to another group member for a response. The process of involving the other member may be reinforcing to the person selected to respond and fits closely as a behavioral paradigm of the dynamic concept of countertransference. It may, of course, also be seen as aversive to the individual who actively opposes verbal inputs, who may be relating to the therapist in a counterdependent way, or who may dislike the other patient to whom he is to respond. These aversive conditions are relatively rare, and behavioral observa-tions suggest that almost invariably the person to whom the response is redirected perceives the act as reinforcing, i.e., "The therapist likes or trusts me."

The nature of the response offers multiple options: it may be reinforcing, punishing, may involve the giving of information, or may involve the responding individual in presenting data about himself. These contingencies are largely under the control of the therapist, as the following examples illustrate:

Patient 1: What should I do? My family really needs me at home. I need to get out of the hospital!

Therapist (nodding, accepting): Mhm. (Turning to Patient 2) Bill, last time you were in the hospital you had feelings like these, didn't you? Maybe you could share some of them with Jim.

Patient 2: Well, I went out early, before I was ready, because I thought my family had to have me back. But it didn't work. I messed it up, had to come back. I decided that this time I'd stay till I got well.

or

Patient 1: I'm really not sure what kinds of things I'm supposed to say in the group.

Therapist (accepting gesture): Betty, could you help Cal? Tell him something about how our group works.

Patient 2: It's not too difficult, really. We try to be open and say what we are feeling—talk about what's happening to us. Most of the time we try to understand what the rest are feeling and try to respond to them.

In the first example, the response to the redirection was mildly aversive, suggesting to the original respondent that his action might fail. In the second instance, support for verbalization was augmented by structuring.

The failure of a patient to respond appropriately to a request from the therapist occurs on occasion. Only rarely are the comments antitherapeutic. More often, there is an unwillingness to respond— "Gee, I don't know"—or a failure to see the point of the initial comment. Under these conditions the therapist may redirect to another member, or correct the response which missed the essence of the original response. In cases where the response was disruptive or antitherapeutic it may be necessary temporarily to set aside the original comment and deal with the pathological value of the re- sponse, as "You really seemed to overreact to _____'s com- ment. I wonder why it bothered you so much?" In this way it would be possible to neutralize the negative experience for the original respondent, and to permit some better understanding of the basis for the negative response in the second patient.

2. *The therapist should use interpretation when patients are covering up their problems by using typical and obvious defenses. This trains the group to pick up obvious defense maneuvers and eventually, through modeling, the patients can engage in interpretive behavior.* Involved in this complex set of behaviors are questioning and challenging responses which may be perceived by the patient as aversive, or at the very least nonreinforcing. In effect the patient is saying, "This is how I perceive my behavior"; the therapist does not concur and rejects the patient's response. Challenges and interpre- tations by the therapist are typically based on the lack of con- gruence between the verbal comments and the observable behaviors of the patient. The models that the therapist provides to other group members are those of recognizing and challenging when such incon- gruities appear. In many respects the paradigm involved is close to one of negative reinforcement, in which the therapist punishes all verbal responses that are not desired until the patient makes a

"correct" response, for instance, in switching from an irrelevant, impersonal response to one which is problem-relevant. If the approbation of the therapist is important, and his criticism is experienced as painful, the cessation of his negative responses should reinforce the response emitted just before the response shift by the therapist. In addition, the therapist will positively reinforce the appearance of a "correct" response. A potential problem in using negative reinforcement in treatment is the danger that what will be suppressed is not just the irrelevant or "incorrect" response, but all verbal responding. This can be minimized if alternative behaviors are reinforced by the therapist.

3. *The therapist should control for extremes of behavior in group members through actively moderating. When a patient in the group is hostile toward another group member, the therapist can reduce his hostility and prevent drastic behavior or acting out on the part of either patient.* The complexities involved in this behavioral sequence are those related to maintaining an adequate level of verbal expression in the patient, while controlling or limiting his need to take more direct physical action. This may involve the use of structuring, extinction, and selective reinforcement of controlled or responsible responses emitted by the patient.

4. *The therapist should not feel obligated to rationalize or justify his behavior in the group. When he is attacked by a patient in the group he should carefully consider the motivations of the patient. If he is able to understand that motivation, his defensiveness will be reduced.* Frequently patients seek to manipulate therapist's behaviors through attacking the therapist. Often this is done by the patient's questioning the therapist's qualifications and credentials, or finding fault with his personal characteristics—his age, sex, appearance, etc. Young or beginning therapists are particularly vulnerable to patients' verbal attacks and often become involved in defending or presenting their credentials or justifying their behavior as it occurs in the group. The more desirable response is one in which initially the therapist does not respond directly to the attack, but allows it to dissipate through extinction. Occasionally, other patients will speak in defense of the therapist. In such instances group pressures are brought to bear on the attacking patient to shape his behavior in more appropriate ways. A direct response to a patient's verbal attack

often reinforces him and may increase the occurrence of negative or undesirable behaviors. In the psychodynamically oriented group such attacks are seen as part of a transference response in which the patient desires attention or affection from the therapist. Many of the questions and inquiries which may later be aggressively sought after have been interpreted as part of the patient's desire to see the therapist as a "real" person, to receive his attention, or as anger at his failure to give a more personal response. It is not necessary to interpret these aggressive, inquiring behaviors in a dynamic manner to work effectively with them. The behavioral model would suggest that a patient's high need for reinforcement from the therapist coupled with the therapist's unwillingness to reinforce one group member minimally reinforcing other group members could result in the expression of aggressive behavior. The aggressive response is most often modified by withdrawal of reward or mild punishment.

5. *The therapist should enable every group member to participate in each group session and should not allow any member to absent himself psychologically for any extended period of time.* Though it constitutes an apparently simple behavioral sequence, the complexity of involving all members in a group session may require the therapist to use structuring, modeling, reinforcement, redirection, and punishment in order to shape each member's participation effectively. In psychoanalytically oriented group psychotherapy groups, sessions are often started by "going around," with each member speaking. This forces interaction on the part of each group member, but requires a higher degree of therapist control than we typically use. Because of the emphasis on spontaneity, ample time should be given for group members to comment on their own, or in response to questions from other group members. Failing this, the therapist may use appropriate techniques to involve each person in the group session.

6. *The therapist should seek problem areas where several members of the group have difficulties and should turn the group to mutual conflict areas.* This requires careful monitoring by the therapist or cotherapist in continuously seeking commonalities of problems or difficulties which can be presented to the group for further investigation and development. Involved in this is again a series of

strategies in eliciting data from group members and reinforcing the sharing of information relating to common problems. The therapist's ability to recall accurately earlier information discussed in the group is necessary. Notes, tapes, and videotapes can greatly facilitate this use of past verbal interactions.

3

PATIENT RESPONSES
IN GROUP PSYCHOTHERAPY

In the previous chapter we specified and defined five classes of therapist behaviors: instruction, modeling, reinforcement, punishment, and data gathering. These behaviors can, however, only be effective in the therapeutic situation when the classes of patient response are well defined. In this chapter we will present our approach to classifying patients' verbal responses and information on how the therapist shapes various classes of response. Methods of classifying the verbal behavior of patients must be broad and inclusive. They must also go well beyond the highly specific verbal conditioning studies which deal with such entities as plural nouns, tense of verbs, etc. (Greenspoon, 1955; Krasner, 1958; Dinoff et al. 1960; Drennen, 1963; and other similar efforts).

Patient response categories must be readily identifiable, so that even the beginning therapist can reinforce, punish, or otherwise deal with the response in a direct, appropriate, and immediate fashion. Categories must include something of the content of the verbal response and be relevant to the social context in which the response occurs. In our search for some method which would allow full use of the therapist's skills as a shaper of behavior, many systems were investigated. Various systems of classifying patient and therapist response that had been utilized in the past were generally rejected because they were too specific, too static, or failed to deal effectively with both content and process. Snyder (1961) provides an inclusive system of classifying both patient and therapist responses, but it does not lend itself to easy recognition and thus is not effective in identifying a full range of responses to be shaped by the therapist. Bales's (1950) system, which is described in this chapter, is more functional, but deals only with process variables.

It was only through the use of the efforts of small-group researchers that a viable system was finally developed. It was necessary to find systems that would permit analysis of verbal behavior occurring under conditions that might be described as free, with no explicit limits on the frequency of member inputs, on the person to whom the verbal behavior was directed, or any qualitative control on what the patient was allowed to say. Controls typically used in small-group research, such as group size, time, frequency of meetings, and the physical settings, are controls appropriate to group psychotherapy research. The authors used such controls and attempted where possible to manipulate a limited number of variables in each study.

The interest in process analysis as used in small-group research appeared to offer promise for solving the problem of classifying patients' verbal behavior. Heckel (1972a) states:

In process analysis studies, goals have been to understand something of the emergent qualities of group behavior, individual behaviors and their relative frequency at various stages in the process of problem solving, and the refining of techniques for assessing this ongoing process. Through these methods we may learn the behaviors which are related to emerging leadership, what kinds of responses are most typical of "follower" behavior, an understanding of a whole range of blocking negative responses, and an appreciation of the complex interactions which constitute a group's "working well" together. While most groups of the type studied by Bales were short-lived small membership groups, others have extended his methodology in studying emergent behavior in groups given the task of setting their own goals and determining their own problems. In other instances through manipulation of group composition, types of problems, and situations which the group must confront, experimenters have gained extended knowledge of problem solving and the decision making process. They also have been able to chart those factors which work against decision making or closure in a group.

The basic difference was that our efforts were directed to identifying classes of patient response, shaping those behaviors, and suitable criteria for measuring behavioral change or improvement.

Bales's Process Analysis

Our initial efforts attempted to utilize Bales's process analysis system (Bales, 1950) as a possible way of classifying patient behaviors.

In the typical experiment with Bales's system of analysis, multiple observers are utilized for reliability. These observers systematically record the behaviors occurring in the group, using a coding system developed by Bales. Group members are rated on every statement, question, gesture, and any other communication method they might use. According to Bales, these behaviors occur at a rate of about fifteen or twenty per minute in the average group, requiring a prodigious effort from the observers to rate all that occur. In addition, it is necessary to keep track of the person speaking, the person spoken to, and, of course, to assign the behaviors observed to one of Bales's twelve process categories (see figure 1). Time sampling is often used to reduce this effort.

The twelve categories cover a wide range of behaviors. Most verbal behaviors (and some nonverbal) occurring in groups fit into them. The division into task and social-emotional roles fits well with virtually all theories on group therapy. That is, it is necessary to have both areas dealt with in a successful therapy group. That some of the attempts at interaction and dealing with group problems may have negative valences is covered in the section on negative or blocking responses.

It should be noted that negative interactions do not greatly reduce verbal rate in the group, though it may reduce verbal behavior between specific individuals. The person who is uncomfortable or disagrees with a hasty or ill-formed decision may be scored as giving a negative response, yet for the effectiveness of the group may actually be engaging in extremely valuable and necessary behavior. If you listen to a group of persons interacting with the list of categories before you, it is possible for you to learn quickly to rate their responses. It becomes apparent at once that Bales's system, whatever its shortcomings, has high reliability and great flexibility in dealing with what is taking place in the group at any moment.[1]

---

1. It is unlikely, however, that twelve classes of verbal behavior are sufficient for providing data necessary for shaping.

In examining the frequency of occurrence of the twelve response categories, Bales has found that when a group is given a task or problem to solve, about one-half of the responses during a session are devoted to problem-solving attempts. Interactions in therapy follow this same general pattern. The remaining responses are distributed with less predictable focus in the remaining categories. Some other researchers (Lieberman, Yalom, and Miles, 1973) have shown that when the group must set its own goals and priorities a quite different pattern emerges, with the task often becoming that of solving the group's social-emotional difficulties before it can move toward a work task. Therapy has well-defined goals, and with shaping by the therapist, groups are not required to establish their own goals.

As groups extend their contact with one another over time, the behaviors they use as classified in Bales's categories undergo change. In his study of group process, Bales arrived at seven stages which occur in the decision-making process. These stages involve perception, memory, association, inductive insights, as well as internal and external pressures which may operate to block or facilitate process and markedly affect group decisions.

Bales further amplified four factors in the process by which a small group arrives at a decision. These processes are: (1) observation of an event, (2) the classification of the event or a comparison of it with previous events and experiences, (3) attempts at considering all relevant facts related to the event, and finally (4) the initiating of some appropriate form of action with regard to the event.

On the basis of verbal content, Bales observed three broad stages of behavior in decision-making groups. In the first stage, verbal behavior consisted of a great deal of information-seeking. Questions typically involved: "What should we do?," "How do we get started?," "What are our plans?," all aimed at developing a structure which lessens anxiety and provides a basis for action. In the middle phase the need for structure lessens, and interaction greatly increases, particularly in relation to the task. It is something of a collecting and organizing phase which prepares the group for stage three, wherein the group must somehow come to a decision. In the last phase, opinion, a frequently used category earlier, is no longer effective. If new ideas or decisions are offered by group members at

Figure 1

Bales's System of Process Analysis

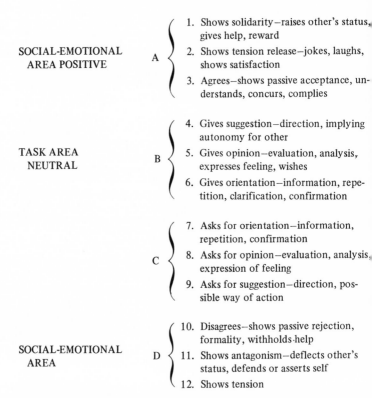

A Positive reactions; B Attempted answers; C Questions: D Negative reactions

Source: System of categories used in observations and their major relations based on data from R. F. Bales, *Interaction process analysis: A method for the study of small groups* (Reading, Mass.: Addison-Wesley Publishing Co. 1950). Reprinted by permission. Copyright © 1975 by R. F. Bales.

this late stage, they must be supported by something other than personal opinion.

In the third phase, verbal rate increases as does the level of both negative and positive responding. It is also a time for evaluating and discarding possible solutions and ideas that do not seem to meet the group's needs. This in itself is sufficient to arouse conflict. This is especially true if one of the ideas discarded is one's own. The inability to deal with or resolve the emotions aroused in this third stage can reduce verbal interaction in the group and prevent its reaching a decision. Other groups may indicate that only if all the members agree completely on any phase of problem solution can they go on to the next phase. If the group is finally able to break through these hazards and reach some level of agreement and make a decision, it will then attempt to regain some of the harmony by reducing negative responses and reinforcing interaction between opposing members. Also increased are positive responses, explanations, and rationalizations, as, "Well, that wasn't so bad!" This tendency is prevalent in many groups, but especially in problem-solving groups. We would describe therapy groups as a special class of problem-solving groups.

Bales's system was promising, but failed to meet the requirements of a viable system for group psychotherapy because it did not contain a measure of relevance or of direction, and the scoring system he developed was more molecular than desired for our purposes. It appeared that it would be quite difficult for a therapist to shape verbal behaviors as defined by Bales, since several of them might occur simultaneously. What was needed was a more identifiable unit of verbal behavior in which responses were specified in a behaviorally testable manner. This should not be taken to suggest that Bales's work does not have major implications for group psychotherapy. He has carefully researched group behaviors in such a way that the components he has uncovered apply equally well to all kinds of groups. Indeed, the psychotherapy group is a problem-solving group, and the processes it utilizes are clearly described in Bales's work. In an effort to develop a more effective process model, we made extended use of a process model concerning itself with functional roles, developed by Benne and Sheats (1948). Their work concentrates on the functional roles which each group might play.

These roles cover a wide range of responses which form even greater numbers of complex behaviors. It has been suggested that the more flexible and versatile an individual is in playing a wide range of roles within the group, the greater the possibility that he functions as a leader or high power figure in the group (Heckel, 1972b). Concomitantly, these behaviors should correlate highly with recognition from others. We may find that certain other behaviors—blocking, aggressive, and negative responses—are very infrequently found in leaders, at least as expressed to members of one's own group.

Even though twenty-five years have passed since their original formulations, there have been few improvements over the categories set up by Benne and Sheats. They described three major role classifications, those connected with the task of the group, those connected with both group tasks and group maintenance roles (those which help the group to continue to develop and interact), and those concerned with group building and maintenance roles. These categories and their descriptive content follow:[2]

Task roles
1. Initiating activity. Proposing solutions; suggesting new definitions of the problem, new attacks on the problem, or new organization of material.
2. Seeking information. Asking for clarification of suggestions; requesting additional information or facts.
3. Seeking opinion. Looking for an expression of feeling about something from the members; seeking clarification of values, of suggestions, or of ideas.
4. Giving opinion. Stating an opinion or belief concerning a suggestion or one of several suggestions, particularly concerning its values rather than its factual basis.
5. Giving information. Offering facts or generalizations; relating one's own experience to the group problems to illustrate point.

2. Adapted from K. D. Benne and P. H. Sheats (1948), Functional roles of group members. *Journal of Social Issues* 4:41, and report of the First National Training Laboratory in Group Development sponsored by the National Education Association and the Research Center for Group Dynamics, MIT, Bethel, Maine, 1947.

6. Elaborating. Clarifying, giving examples, or developing meanings. Trying to envision how a proposal might work out, if adopted.
7. Coordinating. Showing relationship among various ideas or suggestions; trying to pull ideas and suggestions together; trying to draw together activities of various subgroups or members.
8. Summarizing. Pulling together related ideas or suggestions; restating suggestions after the group has discussed them.
9. Testing feasibility. Making applications of suggestions to real situations; examining practicality and workability of ideas; preevaluating decisions.
10. Testing consensus. Tentatively asking for group opinions in order to find out if the group is nearing consensus on a decision; sending up trial balloons to test group opinions.

Both group tasks and group maintenance roles

1. Evaluating. Submitting group decisions or accomplishments to comparison with group standards; measuring accomplishments against goals.
2. Diagnosing. Determining sources of difficulties, appropriate steps to take next, and the main blocks to progress.

Group building and maintenance roles

1. Encouraging. Being friendly, warm, responsive to others, praising others and their ideas; agreeing with and accepting contributions of others.
2. Gate keeping. Trying to make it possible for another member to make a contribution to the group by saying, "We haven't heard anything from Jim yet," or suggesting limited talking time for everyone so that all will have a chance to be heard.
3. Standard setting. Expressing standards for group use in choosing its content or procedures or in evaluating its decisions; reminding group to avoid decisions that conflict with group standards.
4. Following. Coming along with decisions of the group; somewhat passively accepting ideas of others; serving as audience during group discussion and decision making.
5. Expressing group feelings. Summarizing what group feeling is sensed to be; describing reactions of the group to ideas or solutions.

6. Mediating. Harmonizing; conciliating differences in points of view; making compromise solutions.
7. Relieving tension. Draining off negative feelings by jesting or pouring oil on troubled waters; putting a tense situation in wider context.

While the system of Benne and Sheats was not meant to be a complete system of behavioral analysis for the small group, its value in understanding what behaviors make a group function, and what roles each individual plays in the process, has been proven great.

In a series of studies over a period of years the authors have developed a process analysis model based on Bales, Benne and Sheats, with several modifications (Salzberg, 1962) which allow for additional insights into group responses without complicating either the collecting of data or their analysis. All responses occurring in the group are scored on the following categories:

Each response of a group member is classed as either:

(a) *Environmental*—defined as statements in which members talk about topics not relevant to the group's task or goal, as in talking about baseball, the weather, current news events, etc.

(b)*Personal*—statements through which a member conveys his feelings, attitudes or problems to others in the group.

(c)*Group*—a member expresses an interest in another member's values, feelings, attitudes or problems or is concerned with matters relevant to the whole group.

Where a designated leader is present, all responses directed to him are enumerated in the "therapist-directed response" category. Finally, all responses are scored in one or more of the following categories:

1. *Negative interaction responses* which act to block topics of conversation, interfere with the participation of others, or decrease the depth of focus with the group session.
2. *Initiating activity* a measure of spontaneous behavior in the group wherein members start topics, put forth ideas, comments, or suggestions not predicated on previous remarks made by other group members or the designated leader (an

exception would be when in a subsequent session a member might reintroduce a previous topic or view for rediscussion or examination).

3. *Seeking information, opinion* in which group members seek information or opinions from others in the group.

4. *Giving information, opinions* in which members offer either information or opinions to other members.

5. *Elaborating* in which opinions, information, suggestions, etc., of either the original respondent or another member are followed by a related statement.

6. *Summarizing, testing feasibility, and testing consensus* the process whereby plans and solutions developed by the group are subjected to the scrutiny of the group or are "tried on for size."

7. *Evaluating and diagnosing* a group role in which functioning and purpose are explored by members of the group, with evaluation and diagnosis of possible problem areas in group functioning.

8. *Group building roles* in which group members perform a variety of group building roles such as supporting, gate keeping, standard setting, mediating, and relieving tension.

Our original work utilized a full range of categories as in both Bales and Benne and Sheats. Studies of rater reliability suggested that while adequate judgments could be made on many categories, reliability was quite low on many instances of information vs. opinion.[3] Although we thought that combining the two categories might entail some losses, the low reliability suggested that the distinction was not clear in the rater's mind, possibly because the construct itself was not well defined as it occurs in therapy groups, thus combining represented less of a loss than was originally believed. In the case of group building roles, when multiple categories were used, they appeared with very low frequency and suffered because of low rater reliability in individual instances. As a class, however, these responses were highly reliable. Thus, by combining

3. These studies were conducted by the authors during the development of the scales and reported as part of many of their early researches.

them we lost a little in interpretation but gained in reliability of measurement.

As simple as the final process analysis system appears, it provides classes of verbal responding to which the therapist may respond with ease and little confusion. Patients may be instructed in the appropriate classes of responding, these response classes may be modeled, and, when base rates of responding are established, patients may be reinforced or punished to increase or decrease certain responses, as will be described in connection with several researches by the authors.

At this point we will look more carefully and in depth at the classes of patients' verbal responses.

Classes of Patient Responses

Environmental Responses

Nearly every social group that comes together initially engages in a series of environmental responses which are characterized by personal opinions or attitudes.[4] Most topics chosen are neutral and of little consequence to all persons concerned. Most inputs might best be described as conversation openers. (Typical topics are: the weather, baseball scores, price of groceries, offerings at the local theater; or in institutional settings, complaints of food quality in the dining hall, etc.) Few of the verbal responses by patients have anything to do with the personal problems of the individuals who are participating in the group. They represent initially a lack of adequate response set, uncertainties about the patient's required role, or, to use dynamic terminology, are an attempt to defend against anxiety. In many instances initial superficiality can be reduced by instruction—structuring of the group goals by the psychotherapist. When environmental responses occur in later sessions of group therapy they represent a defensive maneuver on the part of group members against more deeply exploring their personal problems or feelings. They may also be a defense against the patient's

4. One exception in psychotherapy is family therapy, where members come ready to work and give very low percentages of environmental responses, even in initial sessions.

special feelings toward the group as a whole or the group therapeutic process itself. The appearance of superficial topics is not unknown in the training groups described in our comments on group process. In training groups it is necessary for the group to agree upon a task suitable for the group. In the case of the psychotherapy group, goals and ends are established in the structuring offered by the psychotherapist. There is no need for the group to find itself a goal. When superficial interactions occur, the therapist may handle the "resistance" by use of the shaping procedures available to him. Whether he instructs, models, reinforces desired responses or punishes undesired ones, he should not permit the continuance of these superficial, environmental, verbal responses, for once they are permitted and reinforced they are extinguished only with difficulty. Focusing on one's personal problems in a group setting is not only difficult but extremely anxiety-producing. Unless the therapist is successful in rewarding and shaping behaviors in such a manner that the rewards for relevant responding appear greater than the immediate rewards of talking about noncritical topics, the individuals will tend to respond on a superficial and impersonal level.

The presence of the therapist seems to be crucial in minimizing the frequency of environmental responses in therapy groups. Salzberg (1967) attempted to ascertain how a group would function if the therapist was present on some occasions and absent on others. Results indicated that there were significantly more environmental responses when the therapist was absent than when he was present. In fact, there were times during group sessions with no therapist present where conversation broke down completely and group members talked simultaneously in pairs about environmental events. This is the lowest level of group functioning, where the group no longer functions as a unit. The phenomenon occurred even though this group was given a considerable amount of training in proper group responding through modeling and reinforcement while the therapist was present. Gross (1969) confirmed this finding in his study of leaderless groups.

Interaction on an environmental level is, in the early stages of a group, a desirable response, at least as compared with silence or other noncommunicative acts. The therapist must, as therapy develops, extinguish most environmental responses, but not reduce the verbal communication which takes place. Thus, he must at times "go along" with the extraneous material while shaping the environmental responses into personal or group responses which are problem-oriented and problem-relevant. This is effectively done by procedures such as accepting the environmental response while suggesting alternate responses or seeking relevant data. For example, the therapist might say, "That's interesting (positive reinforcement), but I wonder if you could tell us why you are coming to the group." When verbal responding is well established in the group, environmental responses may be ignored in the hope of extinguishing the response, or the therapist may verbally punish environmental responding.

Personal Responses

Much of the shaping process engaged in by the therapist has as its goal the verbal presentation of personal problems. He does this several ways: the first is through structuring or modeling to encourage the production of personal responses. Rarely, in a group of from six to ten patients, will all patients refuse to model or fail to express personal problems. Once the therapist elicits a personal response from a group member, reinforcement of the response increases the frequency of that response class in the member and provides a model for the observing group members. Probing and data gathering can draw in group members, whose relevant responses can be reinforced.

Other options exist for the therapist in shaping behavior in the therapy group. Principal among the therapist's techniques is redirection, in which he fosters group interaction by involving other group members in discussion of a relevant topic. Following a personal statement by a patient, the therapist may redirect for further exploration of one individual's problems or draw others in on the basis of "Isn't _____'s problem similar to some problem you've had?" or "I wonder, _____, if you have had any experiences similar to _____'s?" Such techniques have the value of producing interaction and drawing all individuals into the discussion undertaken in the group. The therapist's behavior in this situation also may serve all members of the group as a model for group interaction. Thus, it is not uncommon to see other group members picking up these cues and utilizing them in their future interactions with other members of the group.

Group Responses

Much of the therapist's shaping of responses is directed to developing the group response. A group response contains, as defined, interaction with others in the group on a problem-relevant basis. Subjectively described, the deepest and most effective interaction responses possible in group members are those in which they respond in a spontaneous manner to the problems, feelings, and attitudes of other members within the group. Over a period of sessions in which the therapist has been effective in shaping behaviors, there is a gradual increase in the number of group responses emitted by members. Concurrent with the increase in group responses are a decline in environmental responding, and a decrease in the number of personal responses. Equally concomitant is a decrease in the number of statements by the therapist in the functioning group. When members are interacting with one another, the therapist responds infrequently, except to shape group responses further or to help the members focus more adequately on their tasks.

It should be stressed that the group response is one that evolves over time in group members. That is, following initial structuring by the therapist, there are tentative inputs which may be highly loaded in environmental content. Gradually, as responses are shaped, more personal responses appear, and finally the more interactive, sharing group response appears. In group psychotherapy as conducted by the authors, group responses reach a plateau during the seventh to tenth group session. This progression in responding is emphasized because occasionally patients enter group psychotherapy and immediately model the therapist, emitting group responses without sharing any material on an environmental or personal level. They in effect immediately become a patient "cotherapist." In this role they operate effectively in terms of eliciting responses from other group members, but fail to make personal statements about themselves. In such instances it is necessary for the therapist to draw attention to this behavior in the patient and to instruct, orient, or shape his production of personal responses. Restructuring of the patient's behavior under these circumstances is somewhat difficult, in that the group response is so highly desirable and so strongly reinforced. However, if the patient is too obvious in using the group response as a means of avoiding personal involvement, he may be punished by other group members for playing of the "therapist" role. Fortunately, this is not a frequently occurring response in most groups. It is seen most frequently in groups made up of highly intellectual or sophisticated individuals. The sophistication of other group members serves to offset this behavior.

Therapist-directed responses

Initially, and in decrements through the first three to five sessions, patients address their comments primarily to the therapist. This is almost without exception. Regardless of the amount of structuring, modeling, or other preparatory activities, patients focus on the therapist. Often the therapist is called on to provide structure for the group, repeat guidelines, and reassure as to confidentiality. The apparent reluctance fully to accept instruction for appropriate responding in groups and the need to seek restatement of its goals relates to the therapy group's sharply different expectancies for verbal behaviors as compared with those of other social groups. When these concerns of patients are met, and with appropriate shaping, responses directed to the therapist decline, but do not extinguish. His ultimate control over the group, his level of knowledge, and his role as reinforcer prevent this.[5]

Though the number of statements directed to the therapist decreases over time and he speaks infrequently in a highly interacting group, patients are almost invariably aware of his role as reinforcer (or punisher). Films of groups reveal that patients frequently monitor the therapist even when actively interacting with one another. Despite the diminution in verbal responses, nonverbal responses by therapists continue virtually unchanged through all sessions.[6] What does occur, largely through modeling and recognition of those behaviors that the therapist reinforces or punishes, is an additional component, wherein other patients, paralleling the therapist, emit

5. The exception to this occurs in what Bion (1961) describes as the "counter-dependent phase" of the groups. In this phase the group punishes the therapist by excluding him and attempting to assume group control for themselves. A fuller discussion of this is provided in the section on "The Patient as Reinforcer."

6. Unpublished data of the senior author. Further, as groups continue, there is an increase in synchronous nonverbal behaviors between the therapist and group members.

nonverbal responses supporting, questioning, or punishing the verbal behavior of the patient who is speaking. For example, when a formerly silent member of a well-established group begins talking, not only the therapist, but other group members as well may be observed nodding in approval or otherwise reinforcing the verbal behavior.

Initiating

This patient response is one of the most difficult for the beginning therapist to deal with. However, it is an easy behavior to identify. The first spontaneous comment by a patient is an initiating response. Similarly, new topics, different ideas, and "changing the subject" represent initiating responses.

Difficulties arise in determining whether to reinforce an initiating response. For example, when a patient is experiencing catharsis or beginning to explore a personal problem in depth and another patient attempts to change the topic or to deal instead with his problems, the therapist must be able to maintain the original discussion, while not punishing or extinguishing the verbal responding of the second patient. The therapist can intervene with comments such as "I wonder if we can come back to you in a moment. _____ was into some very important material." This reinforces verbalizing, but also retains the original discussion. In other instances the intervention may be an attempt to avoid uncomfortable topics or material. If this has happened before the therapist may note, "It seems that when the discussion in the group gets serious, you change the subject to something light or superficial." In this latter example, the therapist by confronting the patient signals a willingness to focus on the disrupting behavior in the hope of extinguishing it in future groups, before returning to the patient who had been interrupted. The important judgment that the therapist must make in this instance is whether or not to deal with the interruption or to stay with the original topics.

A further problem occurs early in groups and occasionally in later sessions to group members who are difficult to understand or who are unpopular with other group members. This is the situation in which a patient initiates a response and no one reacts or responds to his comment. In group dynamics, this is called a "plop." In those groups several persons may initiate responses and receive no response. This lack of reinforcement for the verbalization may prove discouraging. The therapist must not let verbalizing go unrewarded or at the very least unrecognized. The exception would be when the therapist wishes to reduce the verbalization of a highly verbal but irrelevant group member.

Giving Information/Opinion

It will be recalled that these categories were combined for scoring because of the difficulty sometimes encountered in distinguishing between them. While in many instances distinctions are clear—statements of "I think ____," "feel ____," "in my opinion ____," and other similar beginning statements precede the rendering of an opinion. Conversely, information is frequently given in more absolute form, as in recounting experiences or recalling factual data much as is required in obtaining a case history. Unfortunately, the distinctions are very often not so clear and judgments are required of raters and of the therapist. This becomes critical if it is important to respond differentially to the giving of information and the giving of an opinion. To exemplify the confusion, consider the following interaction:

Patient A. The one difficulty I have in marriage is my husband's getting angry with me.
Patient B. My husband never gets angry with me.

This appears to be a simple and straightforward presentation of information. But is it? Supporting data from the husband may be lacking. In other instances the statement may contradict information gained in an interview with the husband. Frequently statements such as that by Patient B are overturned in the ensuing discussion, as:

Patient A. I find that hard to believe. You can't live with another person on a day to day basis without both of you getting angry at each other sometime.
Patient B. Well, if he does the only way he shows it is to walk out of the house.
Patient C. Does that ever happen?
Patient B. Well, yes—it does.

In retrospect, was the original statement opinion or information? It was a decision of the authors that the distinction, for research or therapeutic purposes, was not critical, in that "information" or "opinion" would only rarely be differentially reinforced. Thus the amount of error introduced in being unable to distinguish between these categories would minimally reduce the validity of any conclusions drawn.

This is not to suggest that some differentiation is not important. In early group sessions, when patients are giving extended amounts of both information and opinion, the therapist attempts to shape their responses to provide a rich and full picture of the patient and his problems. If only opinions are obtained, the picture is incomplete and shadowy. If only factual, demographic inputs are made by the patient, the data may lack affect and feeling. Ideally, information should be accompanied by the feelings associated, and opinions should be enriched by some factual support. For example:

Patient A. I didn't quit wetting the bed until I was nearly ten years old.
Therapist. How did that affect you?
Patient A. Well, I didn't accept many invitations to spend the night out (laughs), and it cut me out from kids I wanted to be friends with. I was afraid they might find out, or if they came to my house my family would say something.

Our research in group psychotherapy indicates that early sessions are matched by a preponderance of giving responses. As the group matures, responses change and there is an externalizing or movement away from personal responses and a growing concern for the problems, reactions, and feelings of others in the group. As a result, patients seek information and opinions from one another and there is a drop in total numbers of giving responses.

Seeking Information/Opinion

As was true in the giving of information/opinion, rater reliability was low in distinguishing between these categories. Since again the distinction did not require differential responding, the seeking categories were combined.

Unlike the "giving" category, "seeking" responses occur with great frequency in early sessions, undergo a decline, then as the group matures, undergo an increase which remains high throughout the course of therapy.

These phases are quite distinct. Initially the seeking response is directed at the therapist, the cotherapist, or anyone from whom the patient feels he can obtain structure or information on his role, the expectations or goals of the group. Once these structural questions have been dealt with, seeking responses drop, patients spend weeks pouring out (giving) information and opinion. Once sufficient ventilation or catharsis has occurred, response patterns shift, with interest in and concern for other patients in the group occurring. In this second seeking phase there is a healthy externalizing of feelings and a sharing of mutual problems. More explicitly, patients have been reinforced for their interaction with other members and seek actively to demonstrate this. For some this does not occur, and those who remain on a dominantly personal level, giving information and opinion about themselves, are labeled as unsuccessful. Success is determined in part as the ability to shift roles and behaviors in concert with the demands of the therapeutic situation—what Heckel (1972b) has described as role flexibility.

Elaborating

The elaborating or further development of a topic initiated by a patient is necessary to obtain the depth and understanding required for effective group psychotherapy. Once a patient has presented a problem-relevant personal or group response, it is necessary for the therapist or other group members to reinforce a thorough development and exploration of the material presented. Such reinforcement is relatively easily achieved, since the patient who has just spoken can be immediately reinforced. The real danger is that the patient's statement may go unreinforced. Since one of the goals of therapy is to foster group interaction and communication, the therapist should not always rush to provide the reinforcement which would lead to the less desirable form of therapy where all comments are directed to the therapist. However, if the patient's response might be lost because of the failure of other patients to respond, the therapist should provide the reinforcement. This can be done, though somewhat awkwardly, through redirecting, with the therapist eliciting reinforcing comments from others in the group.

The therapist must also judge when elaboration has been sufficient and other group members should be brought into the discussion more actively, or when some change of focus is desirable. Both verbal and nonverbal cues may reflect exhaustion of a topic: discomfort, boredom, the arrival at a solution to a problem, or conclusion of a certain sequence of ideas.

Evaluating and Diagnosing

Initially, very few patient responses fall in this category. The therapist may use it as part of his shaping and reinforcing, but it only appears with any frequency in patients when the group has become cohesive and its members show mutual concern rather than primarily focusing on themselves. Typical subjects in which evaluating and diagnosing play a major role are decisions—termination from the group, leaving the hospital, changing employment, divorce, marriage, etc.—in which other group members are sufficiently aware of the needs, characteristics, problems, and potential of the responding group member to provide useful feedback to him, or they have had parallel personal experiences, the results of which may be useful in helping the respondent form an adequate solution.

In short-term therapy as occurs in brief, 30-to-90-day hospitalization, the urgency for decision-making requires the therapist to shape this response, rather than to wait for its more spontaneous appearance. He may model these behaviors or structure for them, but all group members should have had the opportunity to evaluate and diagnose their difficulties before leaving the group, even if their departure from the group occurs prematurely. Sometimes early termination takes place through the patient absenting himself without notice or explanation. In such instances the therapist should attempt to determine the reasons for termination, discuss them with the patient, and, with permission, inform remaining group members of the reasons for termination. Unless such information is known to the group, the termination may be interpreted as hostility toward the group or the therapist, or as evidence that the group had offended the patient, or as a series of other fantasy explanations, the exploration of which could be disruptive since actual data from the patient would be missing.

Group Building Responses

One of the most valuable responses patients can make in a therapeutic group is that which is reinforcing to other group members or enhances their interaction and participation. This response class is so labeled because occurrence of such responses results in positive behavioral change in the group: verbalizing by previously silent members, increases in verbal rate, a movement to more relevant discussion, and a removal of blocks to communication, the reduction of negative responses, and the resolution of conflicts. Research on group process both in therapy and sensitivity groups has supported these observations.

When group building responses occur, they should be strongly reinforced, both because of their desirability and their relatively low frequency. They occur on the average of three or four times per session and may not occur at all in early meetings.

Originally, group building responses were broken down into a series of subcategories, including encouraging, gate keeping, standard setting, following, mediating, relieving tension, and expressing group feelings.

Most frequently occurring in group psychotherapy are gate keeping and the relieving of tension. Gate keeping, the bringing in of persons who are not responding or who have been excluded in some way from the group activity, is an important activity, one frequently engaged in by the therapist, who thus models the response for group members. This is not the entire story, however, as not all group members use this response and those who do may make their major contribution to the group through this behavior.[7]

Relieving group tension most frequently occurs through a humorous response. The responder may be able to find humor in the responses to the encounter that produced the tension or he may

---

7. Unless a patient is able to make a fuller range of responses his opportunities for reinforcement are diminished. However, a gate-keeping response is often strongly reinforced by the person who is so brought in to the group by this action, as "I really appreciate your asking my opinion."

break in with a comment such as, "Everyone is taking this too seriously, maybe we should wear guns to our next group." The combatants become aware of their intensity, the tension is reduced. It is then possible to moderate the situation, change the subject, or to explore the reasons behind the tension.

Negative Responses

Negative responses are those verbal interactions which block, challenge, attack, confront, assault and otherwise serve to impede communication in a group. As compared with task groups as studied by Bales or sensitivity/encounter groups, psychotherapy groups use far fewer negative responses or negative interactions. The exception to this is family group psychotherapy (Heckel and Levenberg, 1975), where negative response patterns may be well established and, during role playing, this is part of the therapeutic approach utilized.

The reasons for the differences in the frequency of negative interactions between the various groups are related to the different goals in each. Task groups aim to solve a problem or to reach a decision group members can agree on. Because each member may have different ideas or solutions, there is a resultant struggle, often unpleasant, during which ideas and solutions are tested and abandoned. In sensitivity/encounter groups the struggle occurs over developing agendas and priorities. In therapy, group goals and agendas are not the subject of negotiation or struggle. The acceptance of therapy, and the instructions (structuring) regarding the role of the patient and response modeling, reduce conflict and establish an appropriate behavioral role for the patient. This high degree of role definition as compared with other kinds of groups keeps the negative response to a minimum.

Negative responses do occur, often directed toward the therapist. This may be because the therapist has: failed to reinforce the patient in a way the patient desired; used punishment, causing a negative reaction; or ignored (perhaps in an attempt to extinguish) some response classes emitted by the patient. Negative responses also occur as part of a pattern of resisting the therapist's perceived goals (counterdependence). In the section on the "Patient as Reinforcer" we will again examine many of these negative responses.

In patient-to-patient interactions negative responses occasionally occur, but only infrequently. Patients who are highly aggressive and attacking toward others can elicit negative responses, but even in these instances, active moderation by the therapist serves as a protective shield for the potential victim in the therapy group.

Negative responses are only rarely destructive to the group process or to the patient emitting the response or those who are verbally attacked. When they are irrational, extremely overstated, or unusually prolonged there is some increased possibility of a negative result, though the therapist can exercise controls which would prevent this. Cathartic experience in which negative responses occur, free from the restrictions or punishments received in interactions outside the therapy group can be highly beneficial to virtually any patient.

The Patient as Reinforcer and Aversive Controller

Many psychotherapists doing either group or individual therapy naïvely assume that they are in control of the therapeutic process with their patients, except when patients cancel appointments, arrive late for sessions, leave treatment prematurely, or somehow fail to make the appropriate responses during the psychotherapeutic process. These behaviors are seen as part of the illness, and not under the control of the patient himself. For example, it is not unusual to hear a therapist say that "his pathology is so overwhelming that he is unable to respond to treatment." This suggests that the process producing the unresponsiveness to the therapist's efforts is not under the control of the patient. In other instances, failure to respond is seen as "resistance," again related to the illness and again not directly under the control of the patient. While it is possible that the "illness" may impede responsivity, virtually all of the responses in therapy are potentially under the control of the patient (or the therapist).

Even more clearly in group psychotherapy than in individual therapy, it becomes apparent that the role of the patient is far beyond that of a passive recipient of the reinforcements, aversive controls, and special techniques of the therapist. Not only do patients in group settings exercise considerable control over the group, they attempt to exercise counter-control measures over the therapist, using virtually all of the five classes of responding that he himself uses (instruction, reinforcement, aversive control, modeling, and data gathering).

This does not provide a complete picture. Other dimensions of patient behavior directly under the control of the patient himself are related first to the goals of the therapist, and may be part of the instructional process that the therapist gives to the patient. These are the processes and parameters related to self-control. Unlike older concepts of self-control, which related to "will power," the behavioral concept of self-control skills, is, according to Thoresen and Mahoney (1974) "tightly bound up with the person's ability to discriminate patterns and causes in the behaviors to be regulated," and, "to exercise self-control, the individual must understand what factors influence his actions and how he can alter those factors to bring about the changes he desires." This is not unlike the therapeutic approach suggested much earlier by Kelly (1955), in which he advocated that the patient should become a "personal scientist" in which he would play an active role in observing, recording, and analyzing personal data and utilizing certain techniques to modify these behaviors.

Basic to the self-control model is emphasis on the individual's full awareness of the relationship between his behaviors and his environment. Thoresen and Mahoney provide an excellent description and model for understanding the process of self-controlling responses, including understanding of how the individual might use environmental planning (stimulus control) and behavioral programming (self-presented consequences). The implications for the use of self-controlled responses in group psychotherapy are intriguing, but largely unstudied. There have been extensive studies, using specific problem areas such as obesity, smoking, etc., of work toward self-regulation using stimulus control techniques. Similarly in behavioral programming the use of factors such as self-observation, positive self-reward, negative self-reward, positive self-punishment, and negative self-punishment offers a range of strategies some of which may appear to be immediately unpleasant but which ultimately lead to the production of desired consequences. In many instances it is necessary to institute these self-control strategies where competing responses involve immediately pleasant but ultimately aversive results, as in weight control or where acting out is used in place of constructive problem solving. It is recommended that Thoresen and Mahoney (1974) and the works of A. R. Marston and F. H. Kanfer be read by those wishing to understand more fully the implications of behavioral self-control as it applies to the psychotherapeutic process.

A second and more basic problem for the therapist relates to the behavior directly under the control of the patient. For example, Krasner, after describing the therapist as a "reinforcement machine," broadened his concepts to the view that "behavior control is a two-way affair and counter-controls are being asserted by the patient. Yet, part of the training of the therapist is to be able to counter the counter-controls and, to the extent that he can do so, he will be a successful therapist (Krasner, 1963)."

This seems to be a most important and compelling idea. The difficulty arises because in many instances the therapist is unaware of the nature and extent of counter-controls in the patient. Often, it is only the overwhelming response, as in counterdependency and overt aggression, that he recognizes, overlooking the more subtle shaping that the patient uses. Over the past ten years a series of studies has moved from the concept of the therapist as a reinforcement machine and studies of the behavior influencing his characteristics, to a view in which the therapeutic equation is something far beyond the concept that patient or client behaviors are merely dependent variables. Only a few have studied the control process available to the patient, which looks at the obverse of the usual therapeutic equation to one in which the therapist's responses are viewed as the dependent variable. No studies, to our knowledge, have concerned themselves with a third stage in which the results of the dependent therapist's responses are then viewed in terms of their impact in shaping patient behaviors, or a second stage of dependent variables. Though extremely complex, the groundwork found in studies of therapist behaviors as dependent variables provides important directions and suggestions for this further study.

As early as 1958, Cutler, using a dynamic base, studied countertransference reactions in therapists on the basis of his perceptions of his own and his patients' behavior in psychotherapy and his effectiveness in dealing with patients' material that was closely related to his own personal areas of conflict. Conflicts in the therapist were identified by a rating scale in which disparities between the therapists' ratings of themselves and judges' ratings of them were seen to indicate the presence of conflict. Other factors relating to task orientation or ego orientation in the therapist were included in this study. The results suggested strong support for the concept that patients' statements containing material that impinged on the conflict areas of the therapist resulted in an inadequate immediate following response from the therapist. In a later study, Bandura, Lepsher, and Miller (1960) found that when a patient's hostility was directed toward the therapist, he displayed a significant tendency to show avoidance responses. When this hostility was directed to objects other than the therapist, therapists who rated high in direct expression of hostility, and low in their need for approval emitted more approach responses to those patients than therapists who were rated as being in need of approval and low in their direct expression of hostility. Somewhat later, Winder et al. (1962) studied two hypotheses: (1) Whether, if the therapist approaches more often than he avoids a patient's expressions of dependency need, during the initial phase of treatment, the patient will remain in treatment; conversely, if there is infrequent approach as compared with avoidance of expressions of dependency, the patient will avoid the treatment relationship; (2) whether the frequency of expressions of dependency will be sustained or will increase if they are approached by the psychotherapist, but decrease if they are avoided. Both hypotheses were supported. The second hypothesis was also confirmed for expressions of hostility.

In an even more striking study, Moos and Clemes (1967), using a well-designed method of content analysis, found that therapists showed more variation in their behavior with different patients than patients showed in their behavior with different therapists, suggesting that therapists may be more modifiable than patients during psychotherapy!

Conger (1971), in research using social reinforcement, hypothesized that clients could alter the response classes of past or present verb forms emitted by interviewers. In this study, two graduate students who acted roles of "real clients" attempted this experimental manipulation in the brief interview session. Each "client" was interviewed by two groups of interviewers. The target response for one group was past verb forms and for the other present verb forms. Analysis indicated differences between clients and interviewers on such measures as total time spent talking and number of interactions. Palisi and Ruzicka (1974), in a study of patient interaction with trainees, produced data which suggest the shaping of counselor trainee behaviors by the nature of patient responses, though this theme was not fully developed in their article.

Other studies on this theme are worth noting: Russell and Snyder (1963) found hostile client behavior led to greater therapist anxiety on several measures; Heller, Myers, and Klein (1963) found that interviewers who received friendly responses from clients responded with agreeable behavior, while those confronted with hostility countered with hostility.

The results of these and other studies suggest what has been informally noted by therapists over an extended period of time: that certain kinds of patients are successful with certain kinds of therapists. What has been lacking to this point has been a careful analysis of the kinds of behaviors emitted by patients that may lead to the kinds of interactions that produce therapeutic success. It is quite conceivable that a thorough understanding of the role of the patient as reinforcer and aversive controller can lead to a further development of the instructional process so that more of the appropriate kinds of responses can be designated for patients. Through this process the therapist could enhance the therapeutic relationship by instructing the patient to engage in a series of self-controlled behaviors which would facilitate the psychotherapeutic process. Too often, therapists fail to specify patient behaviors, allowing instead a somewhat random exploration to occur with reinforcement taking place when desired responses occur.

4

SELECTION FOR GROUP PSYCHOTHERAPY

Effective group psychotherapy requires the recognition of a number of personal characteristics in the individuals chosen. Though it might be said that it is possible to deal with all patients in groups regardless of diagnostic classification, age, degree of contact with reality, etc., this is only true in the most limited sense. Lightly structured, interactive forms of group psychotherapy may effectively meet the needs of a highly verbal and sophisticated group of out-patients, but be totally inadequate in working with groups composed of regressed psychotics. Similarly, highly verbal forms of therapy are typically beyond the understanding of the very young, the acutely disturbed, and the socially and educationally disadvantaged. Each of these might respond more adequately to a more concrete, action-centered approach which includes directed role-playing, tokens, behavioral modeling, and other instructional forms. This chapter will focus on some of the research and opinions of therapists on selection factors as they affect several models of group psychotherapy.

Size of the Group

Three parameters are of particular importance when considering the proper size for a psychotherapeutic group: the length of time the group is to meet per session; the frequency per week; and the depth the therapist would hope to attain with his group. When the number of patients is small (less than ten) it is possible and reasonable to conduct therapy sessions for periods of fifty or sixty minutes. Observations of group process over a period of years reflect that when groups of larger numbers are held within this time period, both numbers of statements decrease and qualitative depth attained is lessened. Further, measures of member satisfaction show a decrement as the number of members increases above ten persons. Groups of 7–10 members show consistently higher satisfaction per session than do groups with 16–18 members.[1] Larger groups tend to dissolve more rapidly, to appear more dependent upon the therapist, and to create less interaction. When forming an out-patient group, however, it is frequently necessary to select several more than the optimum number of members until a core of regularly attending individuals develops. If this is not done, the therapist runs the risk of having the group die as individual members drop out early or do not show up for early sessions.

Verbal Rate

These observations may in effect be an artifact. Since patients can only give a relatively limited number of statements within the period of an hour, the more persons in a group, the fewer response opportunities for any given person. Thus, unless the person in a large group (10–12 members) is highly vocal, forceful, or well focused on his problems, he could not possibly attain the depth in a given period of time that would be possible in the smaller group. We have noted that in a series of groups studied the numbers of patients' statements in the sixty-minute hour typically ranged from 145–75, with an average of 158 for our model of group psychotherapy. Statements were defined as patient verbalizations which terminated when the subject stopped speaking and either was silent for ten seconds before resuming speech, or another individual began to speak. One-word statements were not included in our count. Statements might contain only a few words or might consist of a lengthy discourse, though typically they were not brief, tending to be several sentences in length.

Different types of group psychotherapy can and do produce

1. A review on this subject is found in A. P. Hare, *Handbook of small group research* (New York: Free Press, 1962). The authors have found in measurements of growth groups a sharp drop in satisfaction with the group process as the group size rose above ten with a high level of dissatisfaction and decline in productivity with twenty members.

markedly different operant speech levels. An early study by Heckel (1966a) revealed that northern therapists' groups tended to operate at a higher speech rate than those conducted by southern therapists. The differential was small but consistent over time. The difference averaged five statements less per session for groups conducted by southern therapists. This occurred in spite of the fact that numbers of statements by the therapist (not included in the above rates) showed no qualitative difference. One might well account for the fewer statements by the length of time involved in having a northerner versus a southerner speak the same word sequences, though this was not measured. In another study, Heckel (1966b) combined group procedures described in this text with a directive, challenging, and confronting approach and found a speech rate three times as great as this 158 average, with shorter sentences, and more statements by the therapist.

In the sixty-minute hour, the differential between therapy with a group of six compared with one of twelve persons, each with opportunity to participate, is apparent. In the first case each subject on the average would be able to give twenty-six statements. In the larger groups the opportunities would afford each person only thirteen statements. (If we assume that qualitative change follows predictable patterns, as reflected in the article by Heckel, Holmes, and Salzberg [1967], in which there appears to be a definite form to the development of certain response patterns, differentiated only by the subject's rated responsivity to group psychotherapy, it is possible to conclude that it should take twice as long to attain specific response goals in the larger group.)

This is, of course, not the case. With the larger group there is a greater tendency for one or two persons to dominate the group; the therapist is required to assume a more active role, and the depth achieved for a few in the larger group may be equal to that found in smaller groups. But for most persons, opportunities to participate are decreased. As a result, experiments involving larger groups have been generally less successful than those with smaller groups unless they followed a more directed, therapist-controlled pattern of socialization or therapists were content to seek less depth with participants in larger groups.

Many of the negative effects described remain constant even with

longer periods of time (e.g., 90 or 120 minutes) given to the larger
therapy groups (ten members). Total numbers of statements do not
reflect half again as many statements for ninety minutes as are found
in the sixty-minute hour. Indeed, statement counts for both types of
sessions reveal considerable overlap, perhaps due to the lack of
urgency in groups with longer time limits, particularly when they
meet for the same number of sessions per week as do sixty-minute
groups. How is this lack of urgency reflected? Most often it is seen in
slight delays of arrival, longer extraneous conversation at the beginning of each session, more and longer periods of silence within the
group. The difference in pacing should not be regarded as a basis for
avoiding longer group sessions, though those that extend beyond
two hours may lose efficiency due to the physical discomfort of
participants.

The last fifteen minutes of both groups (after initial orienting
sessions) are the most active and verbally productive. Over time
more statements occur in this segment than any other. Silence is
most frequent during the first fifteen minutes of each session and
can be minimized by using simple operant procedures, as in the
research utilizing aversive tones.

Although no optimum group size has been firmly established
through research with psychotherapy groups, therapists report a high
degree of agreement on group size at an ideal of seven with a range
from four to ten. Above this level therapists have felt groups were
superficial and unwieldy. Below this number the character of a true
psychotherapeutic group setting becomes difficult to maintain. Research on this problem reveals that the smaller group is more
desirable because of greater opportunity for each group member to
participate, greater depth and pertinence attained in a shorter period
of time, and fewer demands placed on the therapist to shape, direct
and maintain the group.

The most extensive research data available on group size are
summarized in Hare (1962) and Shaw (1971). Optimum size for a
variety of group experiences—learning tasks, problem-solving exercises, leadership, etc.—appears to be a group of five persons, a figure
smaller than that suggested by group therapists. Goals and motiva-
tional levels for persons in the above groups tend to be less than for
patient groups. At least anecdotally, it would appear that these

factors would permit a somewhat larger number of persons than five to operate effectively.

There are other parameters which affect the above observations and are suggested by the study by Heckel, Froelich, and Salzberg (1962). Therapists who maintain a greater degree of control over persons in their group and who tend to respond with methods derived from individual psychotherapy, such as reflecting the feelings, ideas, and attitudes and in other ways responding directly and consistently to therapist-directed statements, generate less interaction and have fewer total patient statements. Group therapy under this approach appears much like a series of individual psychotherapies conducted in the group setting. Persons who intentionally follow such courses of action would then expect that the operant speech patterns they obtained were much different from those described thus far. They might well, under such circumstances, find that other time limits were more efficacious than those suggested.

Group Attendance

Considerations regarding group attendance are presented in two aspects: "How often should the group meet?" and "Should attendance be voluntary or compulsory?"

Voluntary Versus Compulsory Attendance

Those who attend group psychotherapy sessions voluntarily have demonstrated more active participation and greater motivation to work on their problems; they stay in treatment longer than persons who are coerced into attending. Coercion typically takes the form of court-ordered treatment, at the insistence of persons controlling the patient's behavior: parent, employer, school principal, etc. This is not to suggest that only persons who actively seek treatment respond well in psychotherapy. Many individuals enter with mixed or neutral feelings and are able to function effectively. Even individuals with strong resistances, can, if they are willing to try, benefit from psychotherapy. Typical high-resistance interactions involve the group member expressing grave doubts about treatment, fearing it would not work or be beneficial to him. If the therapist selecting group members is able to obtain some indication of a willingness to give the group therapy sessions a "try," it is sufficient acceptance or acquiescence to provide an opening for the skilled therapist to reach most patients through the medium of group psychotherapy.

It is only when patients are adamantly opposed and forced to participate in group therapy that success rates are lowest. Even in some instances like these, a token economy system accompanying group therapy has been successfully used to break down these great resistances. Researchers have found that tokens or other reinforcers can be utilized in getting even highly resistant individuals to attend groups and to participate actively.

Research by the authors has suggested that individuals poorly motivated for group psychotherapy and those who have been coerced by others to attend groups with little personal conviction of its benefit tend to drop out of groups early, typically during the third to fifth session (though some drop out after one). They interact on a superficial level or not at all, seek a higher degree of interaction with the therapist, and make fewer total statements than other group members who attend on a voluntary basis.

While it is not possible definitively to identify personal characteristics of those who choose not to volunteer for group psychotherapy when it is offered, there are some commonalities which have been drawn from the works of Hollingshead and Redlich (1958) and more recently Goldstein (1973). Disadvantaged individuals, those with limited social assets and social awareness, those who have grave doubts and reservations about professionals and treatment in general, are the most oriented to refuse group treatment or are likely to participate on an involuntary basis. Group therapeutic treatment with disadvantaged individuals is most effective when it does not follow the traditional, verbal group psychotherapy model typically utilized with middle class individuals.

This is not the entire story. In addition to disadvantaged individuals, certain other individuals are quite resistant to group psychotherapy. Those with very high status needs may see treatment as potentially demeaning, especially when they are a part of a heterogeneous group which may contain people whose social status is perceived as below them. Often "VIP's" demand the exclusive attention of the therapist and may resent being placed in a psychotherapy group. Suspicious, oppositional, and paranoid individuals may also actively resist group treatment and may perceive the therapist's efforts as manipulative and controlling. In each of these instances resistances can be effectively overcome through careful explanation and suggestion of potential benefit, and when the group therapist presents group psychotherapy as the *preferred* method of treatment. Group therapists report that severely disturbed paranoids are the most difficult group to reach in the group psychotherapeutic setting. They are reported to develop extreme hostility, tending to incorporate the group or the therapist into their delusional system rather than giving up their more disturbed behaviors for greater orientation to reality. Individuals with a somatic rather than a psychological orientation toward their problems are less likely to be motivated for group psychotherapy.

Consensus indicates that voluntary attendance is necessary when dealing with any therapy group. Attempts at working with captive audiences rarely produce positive rewards, at least with adult patients.

Frequency of Sessions

Ideally, group psychotherapy should be geared to a model that would maximize effective learning in terms of time, length of session, and frequency of meetings. Unfortunately, there are no clear indices that suggest appropriate parameters of these dimensions for the acquisition of behavioral changes, as they occur in group psychotherapy. The range of possibilities is great, from a 3-to-5-times-per-week analytic group, to a 1-time-per-week client-centered group, or even a once-in-a-lifetime marathon experience. Modal values for frequency per week may indicate much about the therapist, but often little about most effective learning or patient preferences.

Frequency of group sessions per week is most often determined by criteria such as financial status, times available to the patient, times available to the therapist, or length of stay in an in-patient setting. It may not be geared to the ideal requirements of either therapist or patient.

For those who work in an out-patient setting, in private practice, or with limited opportunity for patient contact, factors may operate to set limits on the number of sessions per week, the time at which they are held, etc. One meeting per week for six patients may fall far short of the goals of the therapist but may represent the extent of available time or financial commitment that members of a group may be able to give. The busy out-patient clinic might also have to decide whether it can afford more than one session per week for six patients when it has a waiting list for treatment containing the names of forty persons. A careful review of the writings of group psychotherapists on this subject suggests that those who work with group psychoanalysis prefer five sessions per week, with a minimum of three sessions lasting from an hour to an hour and a half. Those who follow more eclectic patterns indicate that a minimum of once per week is necessary, with two to three sessions per week as an ideal number.

There are no comparative studies over extended periods suggesting that less effective results are produced by fewer sessions per week than by three or more sessions per week. In part the difficulty of comparison stems from the results reported by various therapists who follow one extreme position or another, utilize differing group therapeutic techniques, and set different treatment goals.

The pace of time is less critical in the out-patient setting than in an intensive treatment unit of the hospital. With in-patients, the therapeutic goals are sought within a minimum time period, usually from thirty to ninety days. When treatment is compressed into this short period of time, groups must, of necessity, attempt maximum interaction in as short a period of time as possible. As a result, many of the research studies described by the authors have been concentrated in three sessions per week. This has been carried on with little difficulty either for therapists or patients involved. Operating within this framework, researchers have demonstrated shaping of verbal responses for those patients who have attended as few as a total of seven or eight group sessions (Heckel, Holmes, and Salzberg, 1967). The objective fact of verbal behavioral change does not in any sense constitute a definitive sign of improvement, but is only one aspect of psychotherapeutic change. The results of the studies by Heckel, Salzberg, and their colleagues suggest the value of a process analysis system in measuring verbal behavioral change and the utility of role flexibility as a potential measure of outcome or success, but we realize full well that our critical factors are not included in this system.

Lacking definitive research studies, group therapists, like small group researchers (Shaw, 1971; Hare, 1962) are left with personal opinion and preference as the major criteria for optimum frequency of sessions. There is some indication that patients' acceptance of the therapists' model for frequency of meetings may be geared to the patients' effort in making the socially desirable response (agreeing with or accepting therapist dictates).

The frequency of sessions per week has not been subjected to extended experimental scrutiny in group psychotherapy. At present, expediency, inclination, and personal preferences (as well as the more mundane factors of cost) set the session frequency of group psychotherapy. This ranges from one to three sessions per week for eclectic forms of psychotherapy to three to five sessions per week for the psychoanalytic forms. There is some suggestion in the work of Heckel (1965) that verbal behavior operates along predictable lines in the group psychotherapeutic session. Shaping is gradual and predictable, provided that some evaluative prerating is available to indicate each patient's accessibility to group techniques. It is possible to infer that, if this shaping takes place at predictable intervals (Heckel, Holmes, and Salzberg, 1967), fewer sessions per week should result in more time being needed to bring about behavioral shaping on a verbal level. There is no information available, at present, on the degree of verbal shaping (or learning) that takes place in the period of time between sessions. There is much to suggest that implicit behavioral change does take place, if we inspect the accounts that both group and individual therapists give of patient behavior occurring between sessions or following periods of psychotherapy. An experimental paradigm exists for investigating the proper spacing of group psychotherapeutic sessions and changes that occur during the periods of latency between sessions. This is found in the learning experiments on massed versus spaced learning and the work on modeling by Bandura (1969). Bandura demonstrated that it is possible for a person (patient) to observe a model's behavior (the therapist, another patient) and, while performing no overt response, acquire the modeled response as it occurs, only in a cognitive or representational form. The patient may observe the correct handling of a behavioral sequence by the therapist or another group member and may incorporate the behaviors through an encoding process on either an imagery or a verbal basis (or on both).

Heterogeneous or
Homogeneous Grouping of Patients

Most group psychotherapists select patients for group psychotherapy in a relatively heterogeneous manner. There is occasionally
an inclination to draw rough guidelines and to place certain limits as
to age, diagnosis, sex, socioeconomic level, and other sociocultural
and psychological variables. In general, these constraints only relate
to extreme ends of the continua. For example, many therapists
would hesitate to put preadolescents in a group with adults or
adolescents. Similarly, they would only occasionally place young
persons with those of old age. Chronic psychotics are only occasionally, and then usually for research purposes, placed in groups
with acutely disturbed patients or those with mild neuroses. There
are reports in the literature of grouping depressives, schizophrenics,
as well as other diagnostic categories in homogeneous groups, though
these reports tend to represent minority positions and results of
therapy with these groups have not shown uniform success. More
characteristic are groupings that are based on length of time in the
hospital, acuteness of illness, and living together on the same ward.

The intended goal of placing a severely disturbed patient in a
group of mildly disturbed persons may be to achieve a salutary
effect upon the disturbed person. This often fails to materialize. In
one such attempt, a severely delusional patient who had been hospitalized for nearly five years was placed with a group of newly
admitted, mildly disturbed patients. Far from acting as a moderating
influence on the disturbed patient, the group nearly dissolved because of the persistent and highly vocal delusional productions of
the disturbed patient. The authors had similar experiences in other
groups with both male and female patients. This generalization
seems to apply regardless of the level of sophistication of the group
members. That is, a highly experienced and well-oriented group and
therapist were no more successful in dealing with severely delusional
patients in their group than were the newly admitted, mildly disturbed patients mentioned earlier. Land (1962) and Drennen and
Wiggins (1964) have demonstrated the modifiability of the severely
regressed and disturbed patient through group psychotherapeutic
techniques when they are homogeneously grouped. Their goals were

only to modify and increase verbal interaction, not produce "cures." That they were able to achieve this suggests that disturbed patients may find some benefit in group psychotherapy, at least in terms of increased verbal interaction, communication, and self-care. Such benefits fall short of goals typically established for most therapy groups.

Group psychotherapists have expressed a reluctance to group in a heterogeneous manner patients whose primary disorder is alcoholism, drug addiction, homosexuality, sociopathic behavior, paranoid schizophrenia, or a primarily psychophysiological disorder. Homogeneous grouping of persons sharing common difficulties in these categories can offer the therapist some opening wedge into problems that may, in mixed groups, remain concealed because of the social implications of the disorder.

The homosexual placed in a group with heterosexuals may experience extreme difficulty in developing a sufficient level of trust in other group members to share this fact with them. Such revelations are not a requisite to successful therapy. The homosexual's problem is often, not the sexual implications of his label, but the implications of seeking an alternate life-style in a society in which heterosexuality is the accepted response, and the attendant anxiety and uncertainty that is a part of being in a deviant or a minority role. Homogeneous grouping appears necessary in cases when the presenting symptom is so overriding that it can only be effectively dealt with in a group where others are empathic and aware of the "power" of the presenting symptoms.

Experimental data on the above problems are available to the therapist who would analyze therapeutic sessions in which these differing conditions might be established. Specific sessions analyzed such as those in which the disturbed individual was seen with those of lesser degrees of disturbance, clearly reflect a domination of the total numbers of responses by the disturbed patient, a lack of problem-relevant responses, and an autistic level of functioning in which the patient makes an extended series of comments on an environmental level. Unfortunately, in the following case, the environment perceived by the disturbed patient was unreal, preventing, at least by conventional techniques, effective communication. The patient imagined that he was on the planet Pluto and that persons in the group were Plutonians. His comments, which were incisive, literate, and most entertaining, nonetheless provided little that might be labeled as therapeutic interaction. Success in reducing or removing delusional material appears to be more readily achieved in groups when there is opportunity for extended communication on a problem-relevant basis. The chances are greatly enhanced when patients appear somewhat more homogeneous in their depth or degree of disturbance.

In general there appears to be benefit in heterogeneous grouping of persons from differing socioeconomic and cultural backgrounds. By including persons of varying backgrounds, reality problems of society and of particular subcultures may be expressed and dealt with. In more personal spheres, an occupationally or maritally unsuccessful patient may benefit from being in group therapy with a patient who has been successful in these areas. In groups where members have experienced sharp contrasts in their success in life, these disparities might lead to resentments, projected feelings, and distortions. However, such feelings might never be expressed were groups more homogeneous. Highly mixed groups may produce extensive concern in both therapist and group members, yet the result may maximize therapeutic benefit for group members. Such instances may take on psychodramatic overtones. The therapist should be willing to alter the structure of group functioning by utilizing techniques of group dynamics such as role playing or behavioral interaction exercises in order to deal effectively with special problems that may arise from such individual differences.

Process analysis offers an excellent medium for analysis of the efficacy of utilizing techniques of grouping along homogeneous or heterogeneous lines. Most plans for grouping at present are dependent upon the judgment and the preferences of the psychotherapist. Quite often the therapist will construct his therapeutic group with definite parameters in mind to foster the exacerbation of specific problem areas. He may also bring together persons who have conflicting, complementary, or dynamically similar problems. He may work toward having groups made up of all one sex or a similar age, or conversely he may try to duplicate in some manner the age ranges and sexes generally found in a family constellation composed of young adults and their grouping. Experimentally, all combinations provide dimensions of understanding not readily accessible under homogeneous grouping patterns. Some few experiments in this area reflect that placing very disturbed patients in a group of only moderately disturbed individuals in the hope that such a combination might have a palliative effect on the disturbed members has not been of noteworthy success, at least in the research of the authors. In such cases, as with certain specific symptomatology or character disorders, homogeneous grouping appears to offer some promise. For the alcoholic and the homosexual, groups composed of persons with similar problems may strip away the reluctance to deal directly with the major symptom or problem. Though in both cases the homosexuality and alcoholism may be merely symptomatic and not the basic adjustive difficulty, therapeutic groups do not always have sufficient emotional resources and insight to be able to deal effectively with such persons in mixed groups. The potential rejection of a disturbed person, already a social outcast, might precipitate a break with treatment or with reality, or foster a suicide attempt.

Ethnic and Racial
Factors in Group Selection

Though this topic would appear to be more germane in the discussion of homogeneity-heterogeneity, it is of sufficient importance to warrant a separate section for discussion. There is no question that groups of differing ethnic and racial backgrounds pose special problems for the group therapist. Therapists of different racial, ethnic, and cultural backgrounds in turn pose special problems for the groups whom they serve. Over the years, observation has provided information that certain patients would be unable to respond, would drop from psychotherapy, or in other ways present sufficiently complex and difficult blocks as to inhibit the process of psychotherapy. These extended beyond the normal levels of resistance to interaction and were felt by the therapists involved to represent deep-seated prejudices against particular groups—i.e., a group conducted by a Jewish therapist containing rigid fundamentalist Protestants who could not work through their resistance to someone from another area of the country, especially one of a differing religious belief. Other examples include: occasional white southern therapists-in-training who had difficulty accepting, on a peer level, black patients or patients with strong ethnic, in-group, or nationalistic beliefs which limited the depth to which they would communicate with other patients or with the therapists involved.

When group psychotherapists have encountered problems stemming from this source, the solutions have typically been radical surgery—removing such patients from groups or placing them in a more homogeneous grouping as a defense against such occurrences.

This solution, while drastic, is not without merit. Attempts to solve these problems within the structure of a group may result in disorganization of the group and the withdrawal of other group participants as well as the "blocked" patient. An example is provided by a group in which Salzberg was the therapist. In a long-term intensive psychotherapy group he had occasion to place a disturbed black patient with a history of a series of traumatic experiences with white southerners. The group, largely composed of white southerners, was felt to be of potential value in that the patient might benefit from a new, more positive learning experience with a more therapeutic, benevolent group of white persons. Unfortunately, previous conditioning was so pervasive that concerted efforts by senior group members, Salzberg and another, less sensitive black were of no avail in reaching this man. His responses in the group became increasingly more hostile and noncommunicative until communication broke down entirely. This occurred despite every effort that was made to form a positive meaningful relationship for him and with him. Though resistance to this degree is not common, group therapists will encounter a steady stream of patients who will for reasons related exclusively to ethnic and racial problems fail to make effective use of group psychotherapy.

Heckel (1966a), in an attempt to study this problem, structured a series of therapeutic groups to involve the following components: racial and cultural heterogeneity of patients (northern white, southern white, and black) and cultural heterogeneity of therapists (white nothern and white southern; black therapists were not available to provide that additional dimension). Patients were assigned to groups so that each group would contain at least two persons of each patient classification—black, northern white, southern white. A total of four groups were involved—two were conducted by a white northern therapist, two were conducted by white southern therapists. In the original design of the study data collection was to have taken place over ten sessions. By the end of three sessions, however, the character and structure of all groups had changed so drastically through drop-outs and refusals to participate that the study had to be discontinued. The analysis of what had taken place up to that point provided many pertinent insights into the breakdown of communication within these groups.

Blacks in groups gave significantly more environmental responses (.028 level of significance) when the group was conducted by a southern therapist than by a northern therapist. White northern patients gave a higher incidence of personal responses to a northern therapist than to a southern therapist (.028 level of significance). White southern patients tended to respond to northern therapists with environmental responses. (Though this does not quite reach a satisfactory level of confidence, the obtained level of .07 is highly suggestive of a predisposition to respond in this manner.) These findings appear to have been generated within the patient group as there was no unique differential response rate or pattern on the part of either northern or southern group therapists. Other important findings were that southern white patients did not relate to other southern white patients in groups conducted by the northern therapist. They did, however, in the presence of the southern therapists. Black patients showed little inclination to interact with one another either in the presence of a white northern or white southern therapist. Their interactions were limited chiefly to nonspecific, irrelevant, or environmental topics.

The conclusions to be drawn from the patterns of interaction found in this research suggest that the blocked avenues of communication based on cultural, ethnic, and racial differences can lead to the dissolution or the impairment of groups. In many instances such barriers can be overcome under the following conditions: (1) when the therapist can exercise more control over attendance in therapy groups, (2) when other forces can be utilized to maintain the group until the communication barriers based on these perceived differences can be lessened, better understood, or worked through. The study was not carried out over a long period of time, and we can draw no conclusions as to what might eventuate under such conditions. Though the study was carried out through the intended ten sessions, the balance of the original design was lost and conclusions can only be regarded as tentative and unsupported by other than the therapists' perceptions. A general hypothesis would be that mixing racial, ethnic, and cultural groups in the South may provide the therapist with problems which could lead to a breakdown of the therapeutic process. It would require extended effort and the resolving of these differences before full therapeutic benefit could be gained. Further, it appears very likely that racial resolutions may be limited only to the therapy group and cannot be generalized to other settings.

Heckel (1975a) in a recent article describes communication problems that occur between a white therapist and black patients. He indicates that there are four characteristic response patterns in black patients who seek psychotherapeutic help: (1) those who are identified closely with the white culture; (2) those who acquiesce to the white culture, feeling that white ideas are correct or right (or at least better than their own); (3) blacks who are ambivalent in their response to the white culture, deserving some of its rewards, but resenting the basis on which they must seek them; (4) the unconcerned black who denies that there are important racial problems or differences. Each presents unique treatment problems. Missing are the militant blacks who are seen with increasing frequency everywhere, who are acting out their personal problems, and who would find treatment aversive, especially with a white therapist. Thus caution and careful study should precede any racially mixed groups. Surprisingly, with alcoholics in a residential treatment center in the southeast United States, racially mixed groups did not present nearly as many difficulties. It may be that the alcoholic is already receiving so much social censure for his behavior that he is more accepting of other persecuted minorities. Another hopeful possibility is that racial barriers have been slowly breaking down in recent years in our society and are resulting in better reactions to racial mixing in group psychotherapy.

Selection Factors Produced by Open and Closed Groups

There is general agreement that therapeutic groups gain maximum benefit when the group membership remains relatively stable and meets over a period of many months. There is also agreement that members can gain *some* benefit after having participated for much shorter periods of time. The critical period of time appears to be the first several sessions, when group therapists consistently aim toward a stable group. In later phases of group development many therapists are willing to take additional persons into ongoing groups.

One of the experimentally determined bases for trying to maintain stability through this period has been suggested in studies by Heckel (1972b), which clearly illustrate that significant changes occur in the verbal behavior of group members both in the content and in the types of interactions (process) they form. In the first instance movement is from extraneous, irrelevant content to problem-oriented, group-centered responses. In the latter instance movement is toward greater versatility in the roles (role flexibility) taken on by each group member; members orient themselves toward the group rather than depending upon the group therapist.

Changes of group membership during this early, formative period could disrupt the developing deep interaction which appears so vital to the group therapeutic process. Such conclusions reach beyond mere conjecture. Salzberg, Brokaw, and Strahley (1964) attempted to study the differential effects upon spontaneity, problem relevance, total responses, and spontaneous relevant responses in two groups, one stable and the other adding new members periodically. The findings in general confirmed the clinical observations that group therapists had suggested. In the changing group, in which a new group member was added at each session, spontaneous responses were maintained at a uniform and low level. Total responses decreased for the changing group while there was a marked upsurge in the stable group. In the area of developing problem-relevant responses, the changing group, after an initial period of many fewer relevant responses, had "caught up" with the stable group by the ninth session. In the area of spontaneous relevant responses the changing group, while not matching the stable group, did show signs of merging by the ninth session. Conclusions suggest that the changing group can form the behaviors seen as occurring with high frequency in the stable group, but that it does so at a much slower pace. The authors conclude:

Spontaneity perhaps takes a longer time to develop in group psychotherapy than does problem relevance. It is possible that problem relevance is more of a situational factor than spontaneity whereas spontaneity is more peculiar to the type of individual rather than to the group setting. Spontaneity is a much more stable response and does not change significantly within a short period of time during group psychotherapy. Relevance on the other hand changed fairly drastically for the new group which indicates that they learned very quickly the type of response that was required of them in the situation. [p. 693] *

The general evidence suggests that verbal behavioral changes occur before changes in the gross behavioral patterns of each patient. Delays in development of these verbal behavioral changes cannot help but delay the total therapeutic process. These results need parallel studies at later periods in the therapeutic process, especially for periods after the critical early sessions that shape verbal behavior. The results of the study by Heckel (1965) suggest that the responses of "good" group-psychotherapeutic risks, as determined by selection screening techniques reported by Salzberg and Heckel (1963), Salzberg and Bidus (1966), Salzberg (1969), and Heckel (1966b, 1972b), stabilize into a group-centered, sharing pattern, sometimes as early as the eighth session of group psychotherapy.

Selection of Patients
for Group Psychotherapy

Psychotherapists, beginning with Sigmund Freud, have long been the target of critics for their selectivity regarding patients suitable for both group and individual psychotherapy. These critics feel that psychotherapists have no controlled data indicating the success of psychotherapy over other methods, but that they make extensive claims for their methods, even though their successes are with those

*Reprinted by permission from *Psychological reports.* Copyright © 1964

patients who are highly motivated, educationally and occupationally successful, and have an emotional illness of low intensity and short duration. In short, critics feel that the tendency has been to treat those most healthy, while abandoning all others to the less certain modes of treatment provided in state mental hospitals or other custodial agencies. To date, psychotherapists have produced little research to refute this criticism. Bergin and Garfield (1971) have done a very thorough job of reviewing the research in the area. There have been extensive observational and anecdotal studies by group psychotherapists on what they feel are the important selective criteria leading to psychotherapeutic success, though few therapists have systematically worked with selection procedures in an experimental framework.

Land (1962), in his study of the accessibility to group psychotherapy of chronic hospitalized patients, sought out groups consisting of continuously hospitalized individuals with a poor prognosis and markedly limited assets as measured by the Finney Scale (which rated the behavioral and social assets of each patient). Even with this regressed, chronic group, there was change in the verbal responses of group members. A study by Drennen and Wiggins (1964) was a sequel to the work of Land. They selected the most resistant and inaccessible patients from Land's study—those who demonstrated minimal verbal change. By concerted effort and the addition of concrete rewards for verbal behavior, they were able to generate verbal activity even in this group, which represented those of poorest prognosis among members of the chronic population in a Veterans Administration Hospital.

Salzberg and Heckel (1963), Salzberg and Bidus (1966), and Heckel (1971) present techniques for the group screening of patients which provides information of a dynamic and demographic nature and which was later found to be predictive of success in group psychotherapy (Salzberg, 1969).[2]

2. A child-screening scale based on Salzberg's work has been developed by Heckel. Preliminary results suggest that similar items plus developmental and family factors are useful in predicting success in psychotherapy with children. A report of research on this scale has been submitted for publication (Frey, Heckel, Salzberg, and Wackwitz, *Journal of Clinical Psychology,* in press), and is illustrated on pp. 102–3. Used by permission of the *Journal of Clinical Psychology.*

Table 1

Child Scale

NAME: _____

	1	2	3	4	5
1. Intelligence	Borderline defective	Below average	Average	Above average	Superior
2. Length of illness (problems)	5 yrs.	4 yrs.	2–3 yrs.	1–2 yrs.	6–12 mos.
3. School work history	Grades repeated	Some failures in grades	Average school performance	Above average performance	Very successful in school
4. Somatic	Very high	Above average	Average or not ratable	Below average	Very low
5. Motivation for psychotherapy	Very low	Below average	Average or not ratable	Above average	Very high
6. Interaction spontaneity and psychic energy	Very low	Below average	Average or not ratable	Above average	Very high
7. Reality	Very low	Below average	Average	Above	Very high

PARENTAL:

9. Marital status	Single	Divorced or separated over 6 mos.	Divorced-remarried	Widowed or separated 6 mos.	Married
10. Socio-economic level	Very low	Upper lower class	Lower middle class	Middle class	Upper middle class
11. Mobility	Frequent moves last 5 yrs.	3 moves last 5 yrs.	2 moves last 5 yrs.	1 move last 5 yrs.	No moves last 5 yrs.
12. Authoritarianism					
a. Mother	Very high	Above average	Average	Below average	Very low
b. Father	Very high	Above average	Average	Below average	Very low

DEVELOPMENTAL FACTORS:

13. Physical maturity (for age)	Very low	Below average	Average	Above average	Very high
14. Emotional Maturity	Very low	Below average	Average	Above average	Very high
15. Dependency on others	Very high	Above average	Average	Below average	Very low

Group Screening for Group Psychotherapy

The group screening scale was developed in an attempt to overcome a serious staff deficiency problem which prevented adequate screening of the twelve to eighteen new admissions a week to an admissions and intensive treatment ward. Prior to the development of the group screening techniques, evaluations were carried out by staff persons on an individual basis utilizing standard interview and testing procedures. These interviews attempted to assess each patient's: (1) suitability as a psychotherapy candidate; (2) ability to adjust to ward and grounds privileges; and (3) need for further psychological study. In many respects the individual screening sessions created as many problems as they answered. It was often necessary to recondition patients to a group orientation, the major mode of treatment on the ward, after having established a "set" for individual sessions through individual screening. This inevitably led to additional loss of staff time.

With group interview screening techniques, each patient's verbal productions are much more easily controlled. When dynamics are obvious or when patients become repetitious, tangential, or disorganized, the therapist can focus his attention on other persons in the group. This is done with much greater ease than the "turning off" of individually interviewed persons. In this model, six patients were seen for a period of one hour. Thus the maximum time spent on evaluating the group psychotherapeutic potential of eighteen persons was three hours, as opposed to the much longer time required when patients are screened individually. In addition, group screening provided a better evaluation of each patient's potential for group psychotherapy by adding a "work sample." Since patients were seen in a group, interpersonal reactions and interactions were presented for the therapists' evaluation and observation.

The work sample was limited by the fact that the goals were: to learn something of the patient's presenting problems, to evaluate him for psychotherapy and ability to utilize privileges, and to determine whether additional study was indicated.

The therapist took an active role in eliciting from all patients being screened behavioral incidents that indicated and defined the extent of their deviant or problem behavior. In this manner the therapist was then able to assess emotional response patterns as well as noting areas of avoidance and denial.

The direct and probing approach of the therapist was designed to circumvent each person's defenses and to keep him off balance. This prevented the formation of stereotyped answers, fixed responses, and extensive rationalization. Each patient was asked to present his ideas about why he was in the hospital (in out-patient groups, why he was being seen). This discussion was limited to several minutes per person. Following this, the therapist utilized techniques such as redirection (see chapter 2) to produce interaction between group members.

Utilizing this basic screening process, a series of additional studies were undertaken. Table 2 presents the rotated factor matrix of screening scale items from Salzberg and Bidus (1966), utilizing 100 new admissions to a psychiatric hospital.

The rotated factor loadings of the scale items are presented in Table 4.1. Factor I can be identified as intellectual achievement, particularly along the lines of verbal skills. Factor II is interpreted as

Table 2

Rotated Factor Matrix of Screening Scale Items

Item	I	II	III	IV	h^2
Marital Status	−.11	.64	.07	−.12	.44
Education Intelligence	.74	−.10	.27	.21	.68
Chronicity	−.07	.76	.03	.05	.58
Work History	.22	.75	−.10	.32	.72
Work Level	.74	.32	.11	.01	.65
Somatization	.06	.07	−.08	.87	.76
Motivation	.16	−.02	.38	.71	.67
Interaction	.73	−.13	−.17	.12	.59
Contact	.30	.54	.43	.02	.57
Extrapunitiveness	.03	.06	.93	.09	.87
Sum squares	2.64	1.71	1.31	1.06	6.54
Percentage total variance	26.4	17.1	11.3	10.6	65.4

Source: Salzberg and Bidus (1966), p. 479. Reprinted by permission. Copyright © 1966 by Clinical Psychology Publishing Company, Inc.

premorbid adjustment or social adaptability. Factor III is associated with the ability to recognize and accept the responsibility for one's problems. Factor IV can be identified as a psychological rather than a somatic attitude toward treatment. Factors I and II are most heavily loaded with demographic items, while factors III and IV are primarily composed of judgmental items.

An analysis of variance for unequal Ns as described by H. Walker and J. Lev (1953) was performed to determine if screening scores differentiated between successes and failures. Patients in psychotherapy had significantly higher screening-scale scores than those not in psychotherapy ($F = 121.23; P < .001$). Successes had significantly higher screening scale scores than failures ($F = 10.27; P < .005$). The interaction was not significant ($F = 0.27$). Screening scores were therefore able to significantly differentiate between those patients who received psychotherapy and those who did not, and between successes and failures.

There was a .21 point biserial correlation between screening-scale scores and whether or not patients were selected for psychotherapy that was significant at less than the .001 level. The fact that psychotherapy patients had higher screening-scale scores confounded any test for the effects of psychotherapy on success or failure. The relationship between psychotherapy and success or failure was tested separately for patients with screening-scale scores above the mean and for those with scores below the mean. The resulting Chi square of .01 for scores above the mean was not significant. A test of the relationship when screening-scale scores were below the mean yielded a Chi square of 2.7 which was significant at the .10 level. These two comparisons essentially indicated that when screening-scale scores were high, psychotherapy did not facilitate success but when low there was a tendency for psychotherapy to result in greater success.

Salzberg (1969) reports an extended study of the screening scale over a three-year period. In his study, all first admissions to one psychiatric unit of the same V.A. hospital were screened and rated on the scale for a period of three years. The ratings were made prior to selection for group psychotherapy. Records of movement in and out of the hospital were kept for these patients throughout the three-year period as well as for one year after the last patient had been screened.

Of the 977 patients who were screened, 407 participated in group psychotherapy and 570 did not. An analysis of variance indicated that patients in psychotherapy had significantly higher screening-scale scores ($F = 329$, $P < .001$). This finding was influenced partly by the fact that the screening-scale score was one criterion used for selection of group psychotherapy candidates. Successes (those who were discharged with maximum hospital benefits and were not readmitted) also had significantly higher screening-scale scores than failures (all other categories), ($F = 13$, $P < .001$). In an attempt to ascertain the separate effects of the screening-scale score and participation in group psychotherapy on success, four subgroups were compared. Of 316 patients who both scored above the mean on the screening scale and had participated in group psychotherapy, 195, or 61.7 percent, were successes. In contrast, of 386 patients who scored below the mean and did not participate in group psychotherapy, 175, or 45.3 percent, were successes. Of 91 patients below the mean but in group psychotherapy, and 184 patients above the mean but who did not participate in group psychotherapy, the corresponding percentages of successes were 50.5 and 56.0. A large proportion of the failures were composed of patients who were discharged from the hospital, were readmitted once, and then were discharged with no further readmission. This could be considered a partial success. Of the group psychotherapy failures, 44 percent fell into this category, in comparison to 30 percent of those failures who did not take part in group psychotherapy. Nineteen percent of the group psychotherapy failures as compared to 30 percent of the failures who did not have group psychotherapy remained in the hospital at the conclusion of the study. This seemed to be an additional indication that psychotherapy had some positive effect on prognosis, although, in this instance, screening-scale scores may also have been a factor. The screening scale also differentiated among the failures. At the conclusion of the study, only 13 percent of all screened patients were still residing in the hospital. Nine percent of these had scored below the mean and only 4 percent above the mean on the screening scale.

Finally, Heckel (1972b) used the screening scale in conjunction with the process analysis system to predict "role flexibility," which he sees as an affirmative set of social behaviors related to socially successful interactions and hence potentially valuable as a criterion of outcome.

The screening scale successfully predicted the degree of role flexibility for the initial sessions (2–3) and for all sessions at the .10 level of significance. In subsequent sessions (7–8, 12–13), the decline in the number of subjects and the increasing similarity between verbal response patterns of Ss lowered the correlations below significance, although the direction of the relationship was retained. The lowered correlation also may suggest increasing similarity among Ss, an observation that was verified through examination of response patterns in later sessions.

Role flexibility as determined by process items required that an S demonstrate a sensitivity toward both himself and other persons. It also required that Ss interact with a full range of responses: supporting at times, listening at others, etc., in adequate percentages of their total responses.

Heckel states that, "In a complex world, role flexibility, defined as the ability to fulfill regularly a variety of roles in the social environment, promises to be a major criterion of emotional health ... it is felt that role flexibility can be utilized as a new dimension in the study of therapeutic outcome."

In all, the results of the studies thus far completed with the screening scale suggest its value as part of a selection and prediction process for group psychotherapy.

The Role of Psychological Tests in Selection

The major limitations of psychological tests in selection for group psychotherapy are related to the nonspecific or abstract characteristics and qualities desired by therapists in their patients. Thus while there is general agreement that intelligence is a requisite for success in psychotherapy, there is no solid evidence that limited goals cannot be attained in groups even by retardates. Further, some models of group therapy appear to require more thought and independence on the part of members, suggesting for that model that intellect may carry a larger weight than in an activity-oriented group which employs modeling, role-playing, and other concrete and specific actions by members under the careful scrutiny and direction of the therapist.

Personality tests have offered much promise but less prediction than most researchers had hoped would be the case. Here again a combination of factors works against prediction: desired characteristics are not specific, tests are not relevant to those specific qualities therapists emphasize, and the tests, both projective and paper and pencil, fail to generate a high degree of confidence in what they purport to measure. Personality tests have been much more successful in providing background data, response predispositions, and current patient status than in selection or prediction of success.

The factors that personality tests isolate allow for some prediction. Yet two overriding elements of the treatment process at the time of selection are not currently well tapped by testing—motivation of the patient, the impact on the patient's behavior of the social systems in which he functions, and the way such systems might respond to behavioral changes the patient might undergo. When effective measures are designed to evaluate these factors, then the true worth of both projective and paper and pencil tests as predictors can be more clearly assessed.

Most current testing procedures are of limited use in selection or prediction for group therapy. Somewhat greater degrees of success have emerged with situational tests, behavioral samples, and other techniques which do not follow the usual dimensions of most psychological tests. The screening scale described in this chapter is one such test.

In summary, research results regarding the use of psychological tests in selecting for group psychotherapy have not been encouraging. Many believe in these techniques both for selecting patients for group psychotherapy and for evaluating their change or improvement. Others hold a more conservative view: they believe most psychological tests are valuable for research into selection and for providing answers to specific questions about patients. Not infrequently, when one is using only case history material or screening scales, questions arise that cannot be answered without the additional use of special tests. For example, it might be impossible from his statements to determine whether a patient's academic difficulties are (1) due to anxiety and frustration because of his limited intellectual assets, combined with his unrealistic choice of occupation, or (2) whether the anxiety he shows is the cause and not the result of his academic difficulties. An individually administered intellectual evaluation would, in this case, be very helpful in answering the question. Many verbal reports by patients cannot be satisfactorily evaluated. In these instances there is much to gain from the behavioral sample provided by such tests as the Rorschach, the Minnesota Multiphasic Personality Inventory, or the Thematic Apperception Test. Other instruments also may provide clarification and answers to specific diagnostic questions and problems. Rarely, if ever, do they provide the major selective impressions that can predict with a high degree of confidence those patients who would or would not modify their behavior through group or individual psychotherapy. Until finer and more precise measures are developed which can predict change along those parameters presently observed to change in group psychotherapy, psychological testing will be of some value, but limited in scope. Perhaps the inarticulate voice of psychological testing in this area is due to the failure of psycho-therapists to establish what behaviors are to be modified or what techniques are necessary to bring about this modification, and to identify those personal characteristics that may or may not respond to the techniques utilized by the therapist to modify behavior.

Other Methods of Patient Selection

There are a series of other methods of patient selection for group psychotherapy. Luchins (1964) indicates that, in some group settings, patients select the group they wish to attend. Utilizing what appears to be a modified sociometric technique, patients select other patients from a ward or more general grouping with whom they would like to meet in group psychotherapeutic meetings. Luchins does not present data on the relative effectiveness of this approach but does reveal that, in some instances, it is necessary for the therapist to veto a choice of a particular group as well as permitting some mobility for group members in their search for an appropriate group setting.

Luchins also discusses groups that have the responsibility of selecting their own new members. This technique is not unknown in many in-patient and out-patient settings. Quite frequently members of ongoing groups will indicate that they have a friend who is in need of group psychotherapy and request permission of the therapist and other group members to admit this friend to the group. In some instances this is permitted without much question. In other cases a preliminary series of interviews screens prospective members prior to assignment. In cases where groups are given some degree of freedom in carrying out selection, the therapist, at least in an in-patient setting, solicits suggestions from group members for new persons from their ward who might be interested in or "fit in" their group. Some degree of control and discretion is necessary on the part of the group therapist to prevent the emergence of an autocratic clique which would set arbitrary standards for the group and attempt to determine all parameters of group action and behavior. While such discretionary powers are permitted in training groups and other group situations in which normal subjects constitute the group's population, this degree of freedom is only extended to psychiatric groups insofar as their personality integration and control will permit.

Though this statement appears highly subjective, it is readily converted into behavioral measures. Groups that reflect a high degree of problem-relevant interaction, consistent use of group building and group maintenance roles, and who have shifted the group focus from narcissistic or highly personalized, noninteractive discussions, can be permitted extensive freedom in forming decisions on group action. Each of the relevant variables mentioned is measurable from an analysis of the process of verbal behavior within the group.

Prospective Research

Though there have been no formalized studies of the selection variables suggested by Luchins, both lend themselves easily to experimental investigation. Utilizing techniques of process analysis, matched ratings on selection criteria, and control groups, the relative merits of each system may be measured. Admittedly the analysis would not provide data beyond the group process level. "Cures," degrees of improvement, better adjustment, alterations of self-perceptions, etc.—the more phenomenological values these terms suggest—could not be assessed except from an introspective or longitudinal observational position. Because ultimate outcome can not be reached in a single study, this should not deter the clinician from undertaking investigative procedures which may fill in some of the existing unknowns in group psychotherapy. The paradigms of small-group research are applicable, necessary, and vital to the body of knowledge about group psychotherapy.

In this chapter we have attempted to provide some of the subjective conclusions of many persons who have written on the subject of patient selection and organization of the group for psychotherapy. Without the clinical experience provided by actually doing group psychotherapy, it would not be possible to take the subjective hunches born as a result of studying the interplay of individuals in a group setting and arrive at a design suitable to measure the interactions and the behavior change which are the core of the group psychotherapeutic process. The demand for research on all structural and interactional aspects of group psychotherapy may seem excessive. Some research projects may appear to be mere exercises in validating what is common knowledge and accepted practice. Yet even in the mechanical process of establishing basic parameters for selection, subtle yet meaningful differences continue to appear which lead to changes in therapists' perceptions, variations in technique appropriate to specific persons, and the abandoning of beliefs, opinions, and practices that no longer may be valuable or efficacious. Each small advance lessens the possibility that extraneous selective factors will operate to impede the flow of the group process. Shaping of behavior will thus become more certain and more smooth, and have far fewer unknowns than presently confront the group psychotherapist.

5

THE PHYSICAL SETTING FOR GROUP THERAPY

Clinical and social psychologists have been aware of the importance of seating arrangements within groups in determining important dynamic features of social interaction. Numerous research studies have demonstrated the most effective communication networks, the limiting and facilitating properties of seating arrangements, and the impact of other physical properties such as heat, light, humidity, auditory stimuli, and length of time per session on social interaction in groups. Studies reflecting a variety of these researches are summarized in a series of clinical and social psychological works by Hare (1962), Cartwright and Zander (1968), Gottschalk and Auerbach (1966), McGrath and Altman (1966), Glanzer and Glaser (1959, 1961), and Shaw (1971). While much of the research reported was laboratory-based and done with volunteers, work in this field is significant and growing.

No group leader or group psychotherapist is for any lengthy period unaware of the effect of seating arrangements on the social interaction patterns within his groups. Pairing, counterdependency, dependency, resistance, and other dynamic behaviors of group interaction may be identified and signaled by the seating choices of group members. In a purely behavioral model, sociometric interaction measures, response rates, and other counting procedures provide significant data for the group researcher. Special consideration should also be given to the physical properties of the group setting. This is especially important in research when it is necessary to exercise a high degree of control over the environment so that the effects of the experimental treatment will not be confounded by uncontrolled environmental stimuli. Examples of the importance of

113

the physical environment on activity within the group can be found in a series of studies by Heckel, Wiggins, and Salzberg (1962, 1963, 1966), in which verbal behaviors were successfully manipulated by auditory stimuli. Both verbal rate and response patterns were modified within the group during psychotherapeutic sessions. While some of the stimuli used in shaping behavior were of a penetrating and intrusive nature, as when an aversive tone was used to eliminate group silences, more subtle applications of fast and slow music played at a minimal auditory level were also effective in manipulating verbal rate. This suggests that less intense stimuli have potential value for behavioral shaping, conceivably without the awareness of the individuals involved.

Of special importance for this chapter are the effects of seating plans, physical properties of the group room, and external auditory stimuli on group behavior, time factors in group therapy, special problems arising from one-way mirrors and recording equipment, as well as suitable arrangements for sound recording, filming, and televising of group sessions.

Seating

The most preferred of seating arrangements for conducting group psychotherapy is an oval or circle. This places people equidistant from one another and from microphones used to record group sessions. Adequate recording is essential in research for training purposes or when it is necessary to keep an audible, recorded account of group sessions for other purposes. This seating arrangement has the added advantage of making each person observable to each other person within the group. It does pose special problems when films are to be made or when the group session is to be televised unless multiple cameras are available, for with limited equipment, some individuals would ordinarily be photographed only from the rear. Open-ended seating in order to accommodate a camera may, however, impede adequate communication or fail to record adequately the observable behaviors of some group members. Heckel, Froelich, and Salzberg (1962) worked out a unique arrangement as a part of their study during which they filmed group therapy sessions. The patient group was seated in a semicircle around

he therapist, whose back was to the concealed camera. Because the
therapist's responses were considered of prime importance, the
therapist was seated opposite a mirror so that his image was reflected
and consequently observable on all filmed sessions. Thus, no one was
excluded from the filming and a complete record was provided for
the analysis of both the verbal and nonverbal interactions taking
place among group members and the therapist.

Studies on Seating

The literature has relatively few research studies of seating choice
by group participants and its relationship to leadership behavior in
the group and in other activities. Several are relevant to seating in
psychotherapy.

It is accepted in our culture that a group leader typically occupies
the head of a table or other focal position in interpersonal
interactions. Such seating typically provides the opportunity to
communicate with the largest number of persons present. There is
the further qualification that, when a person takes this seat, he is
perceived by others as occupying a leadership role. The voluntary
choosing of focal seating positions may indicate a willingness or a
desire to play a leadership role.

Bass and Klubeck (1952) testing a hypothesis of Steinzor (1950)
studied the effects of seating position on the emergence of
leadership in leaderless group discussions. Two seating arrangements
were utilized, a rectangular table with four chairs on either side and
an inverted V-arrangement with six or seven chairs. For two of seven
groups, when balanced for previous leadership status (how often a
person had been a leader in other groups or organizations), one
position proved significant. In a study designed to test the
hypothesis that seating arrangements influence the emergence of
leadership, Howells and Becker (1962) suggested that spatial
position in the group was a major factor. They arranged persons
around a table so that two persons would be on one side and three
on the other. Their hypothesis was that the two-person side would
develop more leaders than the three-person side. Fourteen persons
emerged as leaders from the two-seat positions but only six from the
three-person side.

Individuals who attempt to avoid leadership positions typically place themselves distant from those spots where a focus of attention might occur. This also lowers their potential for communication indeed, using a variety of measures to assess leadership—for example the number of interactions directed to and from a particular individual—one can determine that this seating factor is of critical importance. It is difficult to sit in the middle of a group and not receive some remarks. Heckel (1973) attempted to determine the relationship between leadership and voluntary seating at head positions during meal times. Subjects were fifty-five professional persons (forty-one participants, fourteen staff)—psychiatrists, psychologists, social workers, administrators, nurses, and technicians working in mental health centers, hospitals, and universities. All were attending a week-long workshop on experimental learning and community mental health held in a rural North Carolina setting which afforded maximum contact between participants and minimal intrusion by outsiders and outside activities.

Data were obtained by two methods. On the last full day of the workshop, participants and staff were asked to list those persons they felt were the true leaders in the community. Since the workshop was not staff-designed, and participants were required to design the laboratory experience, it was felt that the staff of fourteen persons would not be inordinately represented in leadership roles, a fact subsequently borne out by the data. Data on seating arrangements were obtained by observing dining-room behavior for the entire group during the full period of the workshop. Serving was family style, and all persons were fed simultaneously at all meals. The room in which food was served was large, containing ten tables. There were sixteen seats that could be conceived as either the head or the foot of the long tables (four tables were placed in such a way that one head-foot position could not be utilized). The arrangement afforded no clear definition of one area as foot or as head. The important factor in the end seat is that it affords more contact (visual, verbal) than any other seat.

Observations were made for sixteen meals. No person other than the researcher was aware that data were being collected. Participants questioned at the end of the workshop indicated no awareness that observations were being made. No comments beyond that level were noted. Reasons for choice of seating were not elicited.

Leadership ratings were obtained by requesting each person in the workshop to list up to 6 persons who performed major leadership roles during the week. The 55 participants and staff made 276 ratings.

There was high agreement on those performing leadership roles. Six persons received 157 nominations. The 3 highest ratings were given to participants, suggesting that the goal of a participant-centered experience was attained. Separation of ratings into staff and participants shows excellent agreement about who performed major leadership roles (r = .929). The correlation obtained between the group's rating of leadership during the workshop and seating was .20. Though this relationship is low, there were individuals who showed rather remarkable consistency both in avoiding the head-foot role or taking it. Five individuals, all of whom played major leadership roles, sat at the head or foot for at least half of their meals.

Considering the many problems which exist in attempting to take such measurements in a naturalistic setting, the results are encouraging. Had this been done in a laboratory setting where each individual who would choose a "head" seat had 100 percent opportunity to do so, it is felt that the outcome would have been clear-cut. In the naturalistic setting, those who for some reason were delayed in arriving at the dining room, may have found seats at the heads of tables already occupied. The findings do suggest a tendency for individuals in leadership roles to choose a focal seat in their spontaneous activities.

Most recently Heckel has studied the relationships between seating choice under varying conditions of group size, distance from others in the group and positions of maximal and minimal visual contact, and leadership, which is defined in terms of a series of personality and attitudinal variables: locus of control, Machiavellianism, future time perspective, perceptions of the past, life-style, and academic performance. In his series of studies he has found small positive relationships between leadership and related personality variables and seating choice: persons rated as high internals on locus of control and those highest on Machiavellianism tend to choose the "leader" seat when it is available more often than do persons scoring lower on these factors. From the study of these interactions he would hope to provide a multidimensional models for describing the parameters of "leader" and "follower" behaviors.[1]

Observations on the Physical Properties of Chairs

Several authors have expressed the feeling that specific psychological information can be derived from a variety of styles and shapes of chairs or couches within the group setting. They go on to infer certain personality characteristics from the choices made by group members. Even though these dynamic observations may be lost, it is felt that having chairs of uniform size, shape, color, and quality has proved most satisfactory. Chairs should be comfortable but not to the extent that it would detract from the attention of group members. Such uniformity of seats does not provide for a uniformity of behavior on the part of patients who sit in them. They angle, slant, tilt, and otherwise engage in a variety of postures in these "uniform" chairs so that nonverbally they communicate a great amount of potentially decodable data which the therapist or observer may wish to deal with. With uniformity of equipment, it is highly probable that variations which occur are personal variations rather than some feature of the chair or object on which the patient is sitting.

The authors had the experience of conducting group therapy in a variety of settings utilizing a wide range of seating objects such as couches, chairs, folding chairs, and at times even benches. Some of these rooms also contained many extraneous objects, such as tables

---

1. Concern with interpersonal space is of growing interest to social psychologists. Innovative studies concerned with responses to invasion of personal space, need for privacy, crowding, and other manifestations of physical interactions occurring between individuals are appearing in increasing numbers in the literature. The works of Leibman (1970), Byrne (1971), Patterson, Mullens, and Romano (1971), Sommer (1959, 1966), and Mehrabian and Diamond (1971) are representative. Careful study of their data is recommended for those who would wish to study further space factors in psychotherapy.

lamps, elaborate ash trays, planters, flowers, desks, and even in one case an aquarium. In every instance, objects which extend beyond the bare essentials for group psychotherapy—that is, sufficient chairs to seat all individuals, or ash trays for those who smoke, have at one time or another acted as a block or distraction which affected group behavior and interaction. In one case, in a group of acutely disturbed patients, the presence of a couch was an invitation for one to stretch out full length and feign sleep. While dynamically this was interesting, it did not facilitate group activity or interaction. Variations in equipment produce physical problems (and sometimes status problems—"Who gets the best chair?") for the group to deal with. Such situations do not lend themselves to creating the most effective group psychotherapeutic situation, and quite certainly these variations would affect any attempt to exercise at least minimal controls for experimental purposes over the group setting. Even the presence of pictures and other art objects, while generally pleasant and stimulating, may distract group members from their task orientation. It is felt that for the most effective conduct of group psychotherapy, seating should be arranged to minimize external stimuli, except those emitted by other group members and the therapist.

Often the therapist will be accorded what others perceive to be the most comfortable chair in the room. This may permit access to interesting dynamics and perceptions of some patients who would support preferential seating for therapists. However, it is felt that the most satisfactory system is for the therapist to be seated in a chair similar to those of other group members. Even when this is done, group members tend to reserve a certain chair or certain spot for the group therapist. Some manipulations of the chair in which the therapist sits have been carried out with very interesting results, which will be discussed at some length under the problem of transference and countertransference. Research should be conducted to ascertain the relative advantages and disadvantages of the therapist and group members taking different seats each session or retaining a "regular" seat, especially in view of the importance of territoriality in our culture and the frequency with which one's chair can reflect a territorial orientation.

Physical Properties of the Group Room

As has already been indicated the setting of the room should minimize external perceptual cues. Thus, too many windows may be a negative factor, at least in terms of maintaining a focus of attention. It has been noted that, in hour to hour-and-one-half group therapy sessions, patients will often spend a certain amount of time looking out the window. This is not limited to patients alone. Therapists can also be distracted by external stimuli. The most effective group therapy/group research setting appears to be one in which the room is an inner room with an outer chamber providing several openings for observation of the group process and opportunity to film the groups. One-way glass is effective for observation and has been used on two or three sides of a room without difficulty.

The inner room (or any group room) should be sound-shielded. Acoustical properties comfortable to the ears will not record on that same level. Extraneous noise sources, often over 100 feet distant, will be picked up by most sensitive audio equipment. The use of acoustical tile on walls and ceiling, carpet and thick rubber pad on the floor, and drapes where possible are effective for successful transcribing of audio portions of film or video. However, this will *not* approach studio quality in any sense. In order to achieve studio quality, a sound stage, which can be the inner room, will be required. Consultation with a sound engineer is highly desirable.[2]

One-way glass has certain limitations for effective filming. Illumination is decreased, in some cases as much as 80 percent. This is, of course, sufficient for proper viewing of the group room but it provides insufficient illumination for filming of activity taking place in the room. Thus, a dummy window partially silvered but allowing a camera lens access is almost essential when filming is to take place. The illumination demands for videotaping are considerably less than for films, and most research centers now use videotaping. However,

2. These cautions are based on experience. One of the authors was part of a program which set up a studio for film production and "lived through" the long and tedious process of constructing a sound studio. During this time, one hum remained in an otherwise "clean" studio. It was finally traced to an elevator over one hundred feet from the studio and was almost inaudible even at close range.

microanalysis of nonverbal behavior (gestures, movements, and facial expression) requires filming for adequate enlargement and close viewing.

The flexibility of video equipment, the ease of handling, and the lower demands on the skill of the operator make such equipment ideal for both training and research. Videotape equipment is cheaper than films. A basic package of video equipment should cost no more than $4,000, while a quality camera and necessary support equipment for filming requires at least a $10,000 investment.

In a recent article, Heckel (1975b) has proposed a unique use of video equipment in group psychotherapy. The camera is in the room with the group, as sometimes is necessary where external filming is not possible. Instead of the camera representing an intrusion—like any recording instrument, it becomes a group issue—it is incorporated into the group as cotherapist. Operated by each patient, the camera becomes an extension of the patient which, when played back for him and the group, reveals his face, his selective perceptions and his omissions in a way that permits an access to the patient not possible with other techniques. By rotating the camera operator's role among all patients each is revealed to the group.

Innovations such as those indicated represent only a beginning of the possible uses of the physical environment and recording apparatus in the study and practice of group therapy.

The Effects of External
Auditory Stimuli on Group Behavior

Heckel, Wiggins, and Salzberg engaged in a series of studies to determine the effects of external auditory stimuli on the behavior of patients in a group therapeutic setting. These auditory stimuli ranged from tonal signals through white noise to music.

In a study by Heckel, Wiggins, and Salzberg (1963), background music was played during group psychotherapy sessions in four different groups. Utilized were two musical selections: (1) "Midsummer Night's Dream: Nocturne" by Mendelssohn, and (2) "Thunder and Lightning Polka" by J. Strauss, Jr. The selections were played at an audible level which did not require group members to increase their volume of speech in order to communicate. The first selection has a slow tempo of approximately 60 beats per minute while the latter has a fast tempo and is played at approximately 172 beats per minute. Each group was subjected to 5 trials. A trial consisted of 6 minutes of the 60-beats-per-minute selection and 2 minutes, 47 seconds of the 172-beats-per-minute selection. In order to control for the "warming-up period" of group interaction nothing was played during the initial 9 minutes of each session. There was a 30-second interval of silence between trials. Subjects were given no information regarding the music. Rate of speech was recorded and scored by two independent raters who were pretrained in a word-counting technique. Coefficients of concordance for raters were high in pretrials and there was almost perfect agreement in the scoring of both raters. Obtained differences were averaged. Analysis of the results of 20 trials for the 4 groups revealed that the fast music elicited a significantly greater number of words per minute than the slow music (p. < .001). Although there was only an average (difference) of 22 percent in the rate of speech between the fast and slow music, results were consistent across trials. While the results of this study should not be taken as indicating that rate of speech in itself will greatly affect psychotherapy one way or the other, it certainly indicates how external auditory stimuli can influence and significantly alter verbal behavior in a group.[3]

In a second study, Heckel, Wiggins, and Salzberg (1962) attempted to produce a change in the operant levels of verbal behavior in group psychotherapy. The experimental variable was introduced during ongoing psychotherapy sessions without the patients' awareness of any planned change in the sessions. The theoretical basis from which this work was developed is dated from Thorndike and Rock's (1934) work on learning without awareness and elaborated upon by some of the verbal conditioning studies by Greenspoon (1955), Philbrick and Postman (1955), and Postman and Jarrett (1952).

In this study, Heckel et al. utilized white, male, psychiatric

---

3. An interesting sidelight occurred when the senior author presented a seminar on this research. As part of the presentation, the two numbers were played as background. At one point the audience dissolved in laughter as they noted that the author unknowingly was varying *his* speech rate to that of the music.

n-patients. The experiment was carried out in an air-conditioned, soundproofed, experimental room which was equipped with a one-way observational mirror and two microphones for monitoring and recording the sessions. Through a speaker hidden in an air-conditioning vent, an auditory stimulus was transmitted into the room. The auditory stimulus was produced by an audiometer and consisted of a continuous tone of 85 decibels (db) at 4,000 cycles per second (cps). The group had been functioning for several months on a twice-weekly basis with two therapists. In the initial stage of the experiment, for the first fifteen minutes of each of the first four meetings, the total number and duration of silences following a ten-second period of silence were recorded. This served as a baseline or operant level of silences. For the experimental treatment, during the first fifteen minutes of four sessions the auditory stimulus was presented after each ten-second period of silence and continued until some member of the group "broke" the silence by speaking. The last four sessions, when no auditory stimulus was presented, served as extinction trials and again the number and duration of silences were recorded. For each phase of the experiment the therapist refrained from initiating comments or statements during the first fifteen minutes of each group meeting. The subjects were given no information about the experiment nor the sound, other than to inform them in response to their questions that there was probably some malfunctioning of the recording apparatus. Though none of the subjects recognized the meaning of the auditory stimulus, they did learn to make the correct response. These findings seem to support Thorndike's hypothesis and our general contention in this article that the impact of external stimuli upon a group setting cannot be underestimated.

Wiggins and Salzberg (1966) have performed a more extensive development of this basic experiment and extended the manipulated variables to other dimensions of the group therapy setting. Wiggins and Salzberg attempted to condition members of psychotherapeutic groups, through auditory stimulation, to eliminate both silences and therapist-directed responses.

Ss were seventy recently admitted, male, neuropsychiatric Veterans Administration in-patients. Ss were observed for twenty-eight sessions in three continuing, open-ended psychotherapy groups which met for one-hour sessions two times a week and which previously had been in progress for several months. Group 1 had a total of twenty-two Ss, group 2 had twenty-three Ss, and the control group had a total of twenty-five Ss. Each group had a nucleus of six to ten members who were present during all twenty-eight sessions. The remaining members were typically present for only one or two sessions and contributed little to the total responsiveness of the group.

All groups were seen in an air-conditioned, soundproofed room, equipped with two microphones for listening and recording purposes, a one-way vision mirror for observation, and a speaker hidden in an air-conditioning vent for transmission of the auditory stimulus. A Maico audiometer was used to generate a continuous stimulus of 4,000 cps at 65 db. This stimulus was chosen through previous experimental investigations as meeting the criteria of a tone with a combination of frequency and intensity that rendered it uncomfortable enough for the listener to rate it as "unpleasant." All sessions were taped stereophonically.

In all of the twenty-eight group sessions the number and duration of silences and number of therapist-directed responses were scored "live." The tape recordings allowed for reliability checks by two independent raters. The experimental treatment was administered only during the first fifteen minutes of each group hour; during this time the therapist remained silent. During the remainder of each hour the therapist actively participated in the group. In each group when members inquired about the introduction of the tone, the therapist explained that it was probably due to some malfunction of the sound system. This was accepted by the groups and no further inquiry was made. As a result, group members were minimally aware of the experimental procedure.

Two groups received different experimental treatments and the third group served as a control. Table 3 presents the design for this experiment.

During the operant level, responses were scored but no reinforcement was administered to any of the groups. During the first treatment phase for group 1, a tone was sounded after seven seconds of silence and continued until some member of the group "broke" the silence by speaking. In the second treatment phase for group 1,

Table 3

Experimental Design

No. of sessions		6	8	8	6
Phase	N	Operant level	First treatment	Second treatment	Extinction
Group 1	22	No tone	Tone for silence	Tone for therapist-directed responses	No tone
Group 2	23	No tone	Tone for silence	Tone for silence & therapist-directed responses	No tone
Control Gp	25	No tone	No tone	No tone	No tone

Reprinted by permission of *Psychological reports*, p. 593. Copyright © 1966

the tone was introduced as soon as a patient made a therapist-directed response and continued until a response was made to someone other than the therapist (group interaction). During the extinction phase, no tone was introduced.

The procedure during the first treatment phase for group 2 was identical with the procedure for group 1. During the second treatment phase, however, both silences and therapist-directed responses were followed by the tone and continued until one group member interacted with another. No tone was introduced in the control group. Otherwise, this group was treated in the same manner as the two experimental groups.

The number of silences, total time silent, and the number of therapist-directed comments were recorded for the three groups during the four treatment phases. Analyses of variance yielded no significant differences among the operant levels of the three groups on any of the above measures.

An analysis of variance (Lindquist Type II) of number of silences yielded significant mean effects of groups ($F = 33.14$, df = $2/63$, $p < .001$), treatments ($F = 18.06$, df = $3/63$, $p < .01$), and of the interaction of treatment X groups ($F = 3.72$, df = $6/63$, $p < .01$). Separate analyses of variance for experimental groups yielded significant treatment differences in group 1 ($F = 10.57$, df = $3/63$, p

$< .01$) and group 2 (F = 14.08, df = 3/63, p $< .01$). There were no significant treatment differences in the control group. There was a steady decrease in the number of silences in group 2 with little recovery during the extinction phase. Group 1 dropped less markedly and less consistently, with a greater increase during the extinction phase, and the control group was very inconsistent and variable, showing little progressive change over the course of the experiment. The difference between group 1 and group 2 can be explained by the fact that silence was negatively reinforced during both treatment phases for group 2 but only during the first treatment phase for group 1.

An analysis of variance of total time silent yielded significant group differences (F = 17.49, df = 2/63, p $< .001$), no significant treatment effects, and a significant treatment X group interaction (F = 2.49, df = 6/63, p $< .05$). Analyses of variance in each of the three groups separately yielded no significant treatment differences, although treatment differences in group 2 approached statistical significance (F = 2.86, df = 3/63, p $< .10$). Inspection of the data indicates that the control group demonstrated the most variability following the operant phase and group 2 the least variability. Group 1 showed a marked increase in duration of silence during the second treatment phase when silence was no longer negatively reinforced but a tone was administered for therapist-directed responses. Inspection of the data further reveals that the groups responded as expected, with the control group spending the most time in silence and group 2 spending the least. In fact, following the operant phase of the experiment, there was no overlap of the three groups.

An analysis of variance of therapist-directed responses indicated no significant group differences, nor was the treatment X group interaction significant. Treatment differences were significant (F = 4.21, df = 2/63, p $< .01$). Analyses of variance in the three groups separately yielded no significant treatment differences. Inspection of the data shows no clear trend in the control group but a good deal of variability from session to session. Both experimental groups were variable in therapist-directed responses during the operant phase and the first treatment phase when only silence was negatively reinforced. Both groups then decreased in therapist-directed responses rapidly during the second treatment phase when the tone was presented with therapist-directed responses. There was a sharp rise in therapist-directed responses in both experimental groups when negative reinforcement was terminated during extinction.

In general, the results of the present study substantiated the findings of Heckel, Wiggins, and Salzberg (1962), Salzberg (1962), Peters and Jenkins (1954), and Drennen and Wiggins (1964), who all were able systematically to manipulate various classes of behavior or verbal responses in patient groups. This study expanded the number of sessions employed to twenty-eight; Heckel et al. (1962) used only twelve sessions. In Heckel's study the small number of sessions led to a good deal of variability. Increasing the number of sessions in the present investigation tended to smooth out the variability and resulted in much more clear-cut effects. During extinction, in Heckel's study, silences increased rapidly and approached initial operant levels.

The decrease in number and duration of silences was most dramatic in group 2, as it received twice as many sessions of negative reinforcement as group 1. Theoretically, one would expect this difference between the two experimental groups to be reflected in extinction by fewer and shorter periods of silence in group 2 than in group 1. The results did show group 2 to be considerably more resistant to extinction. The number and duration of silences continued to decrease in group 2, averaging less than 1 silence per session and less than 5 seconds of silence per session. There was a slight increase in frequency, with a slight decrease in duration of silences during extinction for group 1, which averaged more than 5 silences per session and almost 130 seconds of silence per session. During extinction, although silence did not reach operant levels in either group, it was virtually eliminated in group 2 but not in group 1. It is a tenable hypothesis that as silence drops out, other, more adaptive behaviors are instituted and tend to perpetuate themselves. If this is the case, then it may be possible to eliminate permanently silence or other undesirable behaviors in group psychotherapy, using for a sufficient period of time conditioning techniques similar to the one used here.

The attempt to condition against therapist-directed responses yielded quite interesting, if not the most striking, results. The control group was as inconsistent as it had been on the other measures but there was very little difference in therapist-directed responses across phases of the experiment. The experimental groups were more consistent and responded very similarly across phases of the experiment. There was some variability in therapist-directed responses with no tone and when silence was being negatively reinforced. Then a sharp drop in responding occurred in both groups when therapist-directed responses became negatively reinforced. During extinction both groups rose again to initial operant levels. If the same principles of group behavior are operating in this case as with silences, the initial rise in therapist-directed responses could be explained as a substitution for the now absent silences. The rise which, during extinction, followed the drop after negative reinforcement, could be attributed to an insufficient number of conditioning sessions. Both groups responded similarly with therapist-directed responses, as they received the same number of conditioning sessions. It is possible that, had we increased the number of sessions in which therapist-directed responses were negatively reinforced a greater decrease would have resulted during conditioning, and there would have been less recovery during extinction.

It is tempting at this point to speculate considerably beyond the present data to future research possibilities with similar conditioning techniques. Is it possible to select two comparable groups, have an experienced therapist agree with E on the behavior to be manipulated, and make it a contest to see if E is more successful in manipulating behavior in a group without a therapist than the group psychotherapist, using all of his vast experience and knowledge about behavior in group psychotherapy? Is it possible selectively and consecutively to reinforce or extinguish a number of behaviors in the group psychotherapeutic situation with simple conditioning techniques so that only one or two desirable behaviors would eventually remain?

The combined effect of these several studies is to indicate that a stimulus, whether ranked as pleasant (as in the case of the music) or unpleasant (as in the case of the tonal stimuli) can markedly affect group behavior. It can be instrumental in extinguishing silences and other categories of behavior as well as having potential for manipulating verbal rate. Even when the tone is presented as merely a signal at a low intensity, as was the case with the Wiggins and

Salzberg study, the effects produced are the same. The behavior of group members does shape according to the desired ends of the tone manipulation. Naturally, with such studies some high degree of variability is encountered. It is not possible, at this stage, to predict which subjects will respond by breaking silence or which subjects may not be affected at all. However, it is possible to say conclusively that there is enough effect produced in the whole group that a significant change can be measured and observed. The authors feel that variables such as length of conditioning period, numbers of extinction trials, and complexity of the behavior to be changed form an interaction which may produce variations among subjects, yet they believe that all subjects exhibiting necessary behavioral base-lines will reflect behavioral change.

Length of Session and Time
of Day as Factors in Group Therapy

Most of the observations on group psychotherapy have been made on an informal basis. These observations point to the fact that there is a relationship between meeting hours and verbal rate. Not unsurprisingly, this seems to follow existing curves on work rate for production workers in industry. That is, the group therapy sessions that have been held at the early hours—8:00 or 8:30 A.M.—tend to show a lower verbal rate than those meeting at a somewhat later period in the morning, as 10:00 or 11:00 A.M. Also, the first hour in the afternoon, 1:00 P.M., appears to produce a fairly consistent effect. While some groups have responded quite effectively and efficiently immediately after lunch, most have been slow, sluggish, and unresponsive. In an institutional setting, time of day is extremely important because typically patients receive medicine at specified periods, and the length of time since the last medication period will often have a marked effect on group activity.

In out-patient settings and private practice, the time figure is typically determined by patient needs. The working patient prefers therapy at times which do not conflict with his occupation, and minimally with his family life. Such requests are realistic and are only occasionally signs of resistance to the therapist or to treatment. The highly resistive patient typically finds no convenient time to meet and is usually fairly easily distinguished from the patient who requests a time convenient to his life-style. This forces the private practitioner to hold most of his groups between 11 A.M. and 2 P.M. during the day (lunch-hour therapy) and in the evenings between 4 and 10 P.M. Patients who are unable to pay or those who are in-patients are made more manipulable by their geographic or financial circumstances and are most often seen at the pleasure of the therapist. No research has been done on this important factor, largely because of the confounding social-class variables involved.

The individual therapist would appear to be the best judge of how long he can properly function in this setting. Utilizing groups of no larger than ten, a single therapist characteristically runs his sessions between one and one-and-one-half hours. It is our subjective opinion that beyond one hour and a half it is difficult to attend to remarks and make proper responses even when utilizing a cotherapist.[4] It would be possible to determine the effectiveness and appropriateness of therapist responses to other group members in a comparative study between longer and shorter sessions in an attempt to establish which is more effective. There may also be an optimum period of time in which particular group members can function effectively. But while individual variations do exist, it is possible to subject each of these conditions to experimental verification. There are a great many parameters that can be used to measure effectiveness. It would be possible to compare verbal rate of patients, longer sessions, the degree of task orientation, the number of patient responses, amount of interaction, or proportion of relevant responses during sessions of varying length.

4. The special problems and circumstances of marathon session and therapist are dealt with in chapter 7.

6

GROUP THERAPY WITH ALCOHOLICS

Special Characteristics of Alcoholics

Before discussing specific group therapy procedures for alcoholics it seems valuable to describe how the alcoholic differs from the typical clinical population. Although alcoholism is frequently described as a disease, following a medical model, most definitions center on a sociological-psychological orientation; this is the one that is most in keeping with our views.

Alcoholism is a serious problem in the United States and the world. There are an estimated 9 million alcoholics in the United States, but it is estimated that fewer than 10 percent seek treatment and an even smaller percentage get involved in psychotherapy. There are 70 million users of alcohol in the United States—a majority of the adult population. There are an estimated 200,000 new alcoholics each year, and alcoholics compose 15–20 percent of first admissions to mental hospitals. The life-span of the alcoholic is 12 years shorter than for the average individual, and alcohol accounts for half of all automobile fatalities.[1] Rate of suicide is considerably higher in the alcoholic, and alcohol ranks third as a cause of death in the United States.

An alcoholic may be defined as an individual whose drinking behavior has seriously interfered with his physical and mental health, his marriage, his home life, and his work situation. The problem is

1. This figure is minimal. Research conducted by the Alcohol Safety Action Project has revealed that no determination of blood alcohol levels was conducted in a high percentage of fatal accidents, even though this is supposed to be a routine procedure.

most prevalent during early and middle adulthood, whereas the drug addict typically is under twenty-five years of age. Alcoholism is much more frequent among males but it is increasing in incidence among females. The current male to female ratio among alcoholics is about four to one.[2]

Action of Alcohol

Alcohol acts as a depressant of cortical centers, thereby lessening inhibitory control of behavior. It results in motor incoordination and lessens discrimination of perception of cold and pain. Alcohol is a high-calorie drug which contains congeners that may have a toxic effect on the human body. The incidence of liver damage is very high in alcoholics, and a multitude of other physical problems exists. Vitamin deficiencies are common because the alcoholic frequently does not eat while he is drinking. The alcoholic, like the drug addict, tends to build up a tolerance to alcohol. He experiences physical withdrawal symptoms, often in the form of delirium tremens, following a period of heavy drinking.

A person is considered intoxicated when he has .1 percent of alcohol in his blood stream. At a level of .5 percent he will usually lose consciousness. Fortunately, the individual typically passes out before he imbibes enough alcohol to kill himself. However, if he drinks quickly enough, it is possible that an alcoholic may drink sufficient quantities for his blood stream to reach a level close to .6 percent, at which point he will die.

Personality and Behavioral Characteristics

Attempts to discover "the alcoholic personality" have been notably unsuccessful (Golightly and Reinehr, 1969). Observing alcoholics in treatment programs for several years has led the authors to conclude, nevertheless, there are a number of common behavioral characteristics. As one consequence of his drinking behavior the alcoholic has frequently been divorced and is not living with his family when he volunteers for treatment. There is great social

---

2. There is some evidence that it is much easier for females to conceal their alcoholism from public recognition through their life-style, work situation, and lower number of driving miles. A recent work by Stenmark, Sausser, and Heckel (1973) suggest the ratio may be lower than 4 to 1.

censure associated with excessive alcohol usage, and therefore a feeling of guilt is common to almost all admitted alcoholics. This guilt is frequently antitherapeutic, since continued drinking serves to reduce the experiencing of guilt; this creates a vicious circle. The alcoholic also experiences a considerable lowering of self-confidence and self-esteem (Nocks and Bradley, 1969). One focus of treatment has to be on a reduction of guilt and an increase in self-confidence and self-esteem. An alternative explanation for the severe guilt feelings may be that the alcoholic is internally rather than externally oriented, and as a result feels that he should be able to control his drinking; his inability leads to a very low opinion of himself. Rotter (1966) originally predicted that alcoholics would be externally controlled because of the poor control of their drinking behavior but subsequent research by Goss and Morosko (1970), Distefano, Pryor, and Garrison (1972) and many others have concluded that the alcoholic scores in an internally oriented direction on Rotter's I/E scale.

Another factor which possibly contributes to guilt feelings in the alcoholic is his strong religious orientation. This may be an outgrowth of the Alcoholics Anonymous movement in the United States, which has a definite religious flavor. It has been the authors' experience in treatment centers in the southeastern United States that a much higher proportion of alcoholics profess a belief in God than does the population at large. It is rather rare to find an alcoholic who is an atheist.

Another common characteristic of the admitted alcoholic—probably an offshoot of the AA orientation—is the belief that one drink is his downfall. This leads to the feeling that he can never be a social drinker and that when he takes the first drink he is doomed. Although past research has indicated that alcoholics have not been very successful in becoming moderate drinkers or resuming social drinking, there has been some recent evidence that at least for some alcoholics social drinking might be a legitimate outcome of therapy. Schaeffer (1972) and Mills, Sobell, and Halmuth (1971) demonstrated how social drinking can be taught. In their study, where they had a bar and lounge as part of the experimental environment, the alcoholic is given an electric shock to his fingers when he takes sips larger than one-seventh of the drink and whenever he continues drinking beyond the stage (five ounces) at which a social drinker would stop.

A study originally conceived to investigate the effects of alcoholic blackouts resulted in some fascinating possible implications. Ryback (1970) invited alcoholics to an institutional setting and allowed them to drink as much as they wanted over a period of several days. Blood alcohol level was frequently monitored and there were frequent question periods to ascertain whether amnesia for drinking periods (blackouts) was experienced. Those experiencing blackouts could be clearly differentiated from those who did not have amnesic episodes. This differentiation was made not in terms of the total quantity of alcohol consumed nor the blood alcohol level reached, but solely on the basis of the *rate* of increase of alcohol in the blood stream. Those who drank very quickly and experienced a rapid rise in blood alcohol level in a short period of time experienced blackouts. Those who drank more slowly and whose blood alcohol level rose at a slow rate experienced no blackouts. Implications of these findings, if they hold up after replication, are that blackouts are associated with spree or binge drinking, and that teaching social drinking to spree drinkers who experience blackouts might be an effective treatment.

The typical alcoholic usually drinks in isolation, contrary to popular belief (Nathan and O'Brien, 1971). Studies investigating the behavioral effects of alcohol indicate that, although feelings of well-being increase during initial phases of drinking for the alcoholic (Mello, 1968), soon after the mood state becomes depressed and the alcoholic actually experiences psychological pain under the influence of alcohol (Mendelson and Mello, 1966).

The alcoholic has been frequently characterized as a psychopathic individual who denies problems and is therefore very difficult to treat. There is some evidence (Gibbons and Armstrong, 1957) that self-reports of alcoholics are not highly reliable, but our clinical experience has indicated that the admitted alcoholic who voluntarily seeks treatment is neither more denying nor less motivated for change than any other clinical population. It is probably much more efficacious to treat the voluntary admission rather than the involuntary admission. The results of studies by Schwarz and Fjeld (1969) and Mechanic (1961) bear this out.

Rosenberg (1969) found that the alcoholic is more likely to have lost at least one parent before the age of fifteen, and that alcoholic males are more likely to have an alcoholic father.

The female alcoholic frequently has different problems from the male alcoholic. Winokur, Reich, Rimmer, and Pitts (1970) and Curlee (1970) found that females become alcoholic at a later age and display less psychopathic behavior, and their alcoholism is more frequently associated with a specific traumatic life situation than is true for males. The female alcoholic most frequently is a woman in her early to late forties who has focused on being a mother and housekeeper for many years. Drinking is typically not a problem during her early years of marriage. When the children grow and leave home, she suffers what is known as the "empty nest syndrome," which leaves her feeling useless and unattractive. This is the most dangerous point for the female alcoholic who moves from occasional social drinking to regular drinking with the husband and eventually to isolated drinking in the home.

Countless histories of female alcoholics reveal the following pattern: during the early part of the marriage there frequently is a good marital relationship. Most often, the woman does not work, even if she has the skills for employment. Underlying this is an apparent need for her husband to be the sole breadwinner. As children come along there is less need and desire for work as she focuses on providing a good home for the children and her husband. The typical husband of an alcoholic female works long hours and is away from home a good part of the time. As the children grow older and go to school, drinking in the evenings with her husband becomes a routine. As the children become more independent, the female alcoholic becomes more dependent on her husband and drinking increases in the evenings. Frequently, the wife will have a cocktail before her husband comes home so that she "will be in a good mood" for his arrival. The next step is for the female developing an alcoholic pattern to need a "pick me up" at lunch time, first with her female friends, and later by herself if she is not with her friends. Soon after this, she increases her drinking in the evenings and feels so bad physically in the morning that she begins drinking right after her husband leaves for work and continues drinking during the day. She pays less attention to her housework and becomes ashamed of her drinking. Next she withdraws from all activities and from her friends. By this time her husband becomes concerned over her drinking and becomes critical of her and tries to get her to stop. She becomes defensive and afraid she will lose her husband and begins to hide her drinking.

Drinking becomes the major way in which she can get her husband's attention. In the long run it becomes the only way to keep their marriage together. She reasons, often falsely, that her husband will not leave her if she is helpless and unable to cope with her drinking problem. At this point, she feels completely inadequate to get and hold a job and she has become completely dependent on her husband and on alcohol. It is crucial at this point either to get the husband involved in the treatment program or to have the female alcoholic move toward establishing some independence from the symbiotic relationship she has formed with him. Unless radical environmental manipulation is undertaken, the marriage will dissolve and she will be in a very poor position to help herself. We will discuss other specific syndromes associated with alcoholism after the section on guidelines for group therapy.

Stenmark, Sausser, and Heckel (1973) described the rural southern alcoholic as an individual of upper lower-class status, limited in income, lacking much formal education, unsuccessful in interpersonal relationships, with a history of strict parental management without much affection. "Hobbies, social activities and friends play less a role in his life than they do for his normal neighbors. Instead, alcohol has become a substitute for the missing emotional supports in this world."

Treatment of the Alcoholic

Until recent years the alcoholic was considered a derelict and was not admitted to regular treatment facilities unless his physical health warranted emergency medical care. Schwarz and Fjeld (1969) pointed out that the alcoholic is in the best condition for psychological treatment when his physical health has not yet deteriorated. Most often in the past the alcoholic was admitted while having DT's or impending DT's, was dried out for several days on a medical ward, and then released. Group therapy on the medical ward was typically unavailable and little was done in terms of follow-up. The alcoholic was treated as a physically sick individual and when the physical symptoms subsided he was released. In some private facilities, alcohol was often part of the withdrawal program and no effort was made to deal with the problems the alcoholic was experiencing that led to and sustained his drinking behavior. Many centers were established to dry out the alcoholic who still had the ability to pay high fees, and every effort was made to conceal the fact that the individual was psychologically disturbed, so that he could comfortably return to his previous drinking pattern in his home environment. This treatment inevitably led to a deterioration in the family and work situation until the individual could no longer manage to pay for drying out, and had to be admitted to a facility like a state hospital. When the alcoholic was admitted to a treatment facility with other psychiatric patients he was often punished for his drinking behavior, in some instances receiving electric shock therapy as punishment if he went on a weekend pass and got drunk.

It has only been in recent years that the attitude toward alcoholism has been modified. Along with increasing federal and state interest in the problem of drug addiction, separate treatment facilities for alcoholics have finally emerged. The Veterans Administration has developed a number of drug and alcohol treatment units in their hospital system where alcoholics and/or drug addicts are treated as a separate population with separate problems. Many treatment modes are available in these settings, but they may be differentiated mostly in terms of whether they are primarily based on a psychological model or a medical model. Basically, in the medical model, the alcoholic is treated as a sick person who cannot control his drinking behavior and is given drugs as a substitute for alcohol. It has been the authors' experience that tranquilizing drugs are incompatible with the most effective means of treatment for the alcoholic, except during withdrawal from alcohol. Drugs may simply substitute one way of escaping from conflict situations for another.

It is the authors' belief that medical treatment for emergency medical crises of the alcoholic should be separate from his psychological treatment. If the alcoholic is not in good enough physical condition to withstand a drug-free environment, he should be hospitalized, withdrawn from the alcohol, and then sent to a treatment facility that is based on a psychological model. Available evidence suggests that at least in the early stage residential treatment is more effective than nonresidential treatment for the alcoholic. It also appears that the alcoholic can gain more if he is treated in a group with other alcoholics. This homogeneity of symptom is not typically a necessary or advisable ingredient for group therapy, but because of the tremendous social censure consequent upon being an alcoholic, it seems important to have the alcoholic treated in a homogeneous group. It is also desirable that this residential treatment be time-limited, so that the treatment center does not become a haven and so the individual will recognize that he must, within a specified period of time, go back into the real world and try out his newly learned behaviors with an increase in self-confidence and self-esteem.

It is important to avoid the revolving door technique which has been the model in many VA and state hospitals throughout the country until recent years. The revolving door has been particularly notable in many county jails and workhouses, where the alcoholic becomes an indentured worker with little chance of breaking out of the pattern. This was particularly evident to Salzberg when conducting a study in a county jail in Tennessee. Many of the inmates had been jailed over one hundred times for public drunkenness and were usually picked up on the same day as released and sentenced to another term on the county work gang.

A desirable model would be one in which the alcoholic was refused readmission to a residential treatment center until a specified period after discharge. It is, of course, important to provide for follow-up treatment and for some help in job placement or training. The alcoholic has essentially given up on life by the time he admits himself to a residential treatment center. Some alternative behaviors are necessary for him to get a new lease on life. Sessions (1964) suggested that, in order to recover, the alcoholic must go back and evaluate his personal resources, which he had previously under-estimated. Elimination of the drinking behavior is only one aspect in the treatment of the alcoholic. Frequently it is extremely helpful to have the alcoholic's family included in the treatment program, both in the residential treatment center and after discharge in follow-up therapy.

Surprisingly, in a drug-free, alcohol-free residential treatment program the urge to drink is not frequently a serious problem for the alcoholic and very few infractions of the rules regarding abstinence occur. Haberman (1966) found ability to achieve some period of sobriety just prior to admission was correlated with improvement in abstinence following group therapy. Problems arise when the alcoholic is faced with going from a protective, supportive drug-free and alcohol-free environment back to the original stress-producing situations. The more that can be done in the treatment program to change the stress situations outside the treatment center, the more likely it is that the changes in the alcoholic as a result of treatment will be effective in forestalling a return to an alcoholic way of life. The alcoholic's family has almost always become a major source of conflict and therefore should be a major focus for change both during and after psychological treatment. Some studies have indicated that in some instances the alcoholic's spouse has difficulty accepting nondrinking behavior (MacDonald, 1956; Gliedman et al., 1956; Igersheimer, 1959).

In addition to group therapy for the patient, it is desirable to provide family group therapy both for the children involved, who have suffered considerable psychological damage as a result of the disruption of family life, and for the alcoholic, who needs to receive some understanding and help from all the members of his family in embarking on a different life-style after treatment. The alcoholic with a family and a job to return to is much more likely to be able to function effectively than the alcoholic who has lost all remnants of his family and who is unemployed and unemployable.

Guidelines for Group
Therapy with Alcoholics

The alcoholic, compared to other individuals with psychological problems, is a highly verbal individual who is, typically, not lost for words in an individual interview situation or in group therapy. While consulting at a residential treatment center for alcoholics over a period of seven years, Salzberg has found only rare instances where, in interviewing, the alcoholic has been reticent to talk about himself or how alcohol has disrupted his life. This, of course, is true primarily for the alcoholic who voluntarily admits himself for psychological treatment, and may not be characteristic of the alcoholic population in general.

There appears to be a large group of individuals whose lives have been seriously disrupted, primarily by drinking, who neither seek treatment nor acknowledge their dependence on alcohol. In any case, the alcoholic who comes to treatment has a high degree of motivation to change. His initial focus is on his drinking as the source of all his misery. As a result, early sessions in group therapy are overwhelmingly centered on drinking as the sole problem, and long "drunk-a-logs" characterize these early sessions (a drunk-a-log is a monologue or dialogue on alcohol as the cause of all problems). This is comparable to the "drug-a-logs" of the drug addict. Many researchers have found that alcohol plays a primary role in the beginning discussions in group therapy, but that the group progresses toward more traditional psychotherapy after a while (Strayer, 1961; Burton, 1962; Scott, 1963; Pixley and Stiefel, 1963). Part of the reason for a major emphasis on drinking may be that alcohol is the main element common to all individuals in the group, and therefore the focus of early concern. In effective treatment with alcoholics, individuals who initially engage in drunk-a-logs soon change their response patterns and, in the course of several weeks of intensive therapy, drinking plays a progressively smaller role. The therapist should expect this early focus on drinking behavior and he should not attempt to extinguish it prematurely. He should be attuned to the idea, however, that if it does not undergo a sharp decline after the first four sessions the group is not progressing well. The length of time that these drunk-a-logs continue is a function of the skill and experience of the therapist, and the experience and motivation of individuals in the group.

Group therapy appears to be the treatment of choice for the alcoholic. It is less expensive and more efficacious than individual therapy, at least in a residential treatment center. Treatment should be intensive in these centers since alcoholics are there for a limited time. Groups should meet every day, preferably for an hour and a half to two hours. The rest of the day may be spent in activities such as industrial and recreational therapy. The most important factor is to keep the groups of individuals working together on an intensive basis throughout their treatment program.

With the short time frame and the need to reach deep therapeutic levels quickly, it is desirable for groups to begin and remain together throughout their stay at a residential treatment center (closed therapy groups) as opposed to having new members join ongoing groups of more experienced residents (open therapy groups). The authors have studied open and closed groups (Salzberg, Brokaw, and Strahley, 1964) and more progress is made in the closed psychotherapy group at the residential treatment center. In the closed group, each individual is essentially at the same stage of therapy as everyone else in the group. Group members need to support one another and progress with one another at the same pace. In an open group, when new members who are added engage in drunk-a-logs, they are often prematurely censured by other group members who have been at the center for some time. This often leads to scapegoating by cliques that have formed in the group, and has a tendency to result in individual therapy during group sessions as the therapist attempts to ward off potentially negative interactions. In the closed group, with mutual support from each member, group cohesiveness is more likely to be established.

Group therapy also appears to be the treatment of choice for nonresidential follow-up treatment. In some instances this may be supplemented by individual, marital or family therapy. Frequently, both forms of therapy may go on simultaneously after residential treatment. Homogeneity of groups is less important in nonresidential than in residential treatment settings, particularly if the nonresident group is a follow-up of residential treatment. By the time of discharge from a center, most have shifted focus from the drunk-a-log to relevant causal problems.

In comparing alcoholic and nonalcoholic treatment groups, certain aspects of treatment for the alcoholic group appear to need special consideration. A focus on the present is more appropriate for the alcoholic group, since a great amount of time could be spent in going over past tragedies, with no possibility of undoing the devastation already caused by the drinking behavior. Smart (1968) found that alcoholics differed from social drinkers in that they showed shorter time extensions and demonstrated an astonishing inability to order events on a time continuum either consistently or logically. This factor suggests that one therapeutic goal should be to help the alcoholic reestablish meaningful personal relationships in his current life and environment and to focus on short-term goals. He has probably reached a point, by the time he admits himself to a residential treatment center, where he has isolated himself from all meaningful relationships, with alcohol as his only source of support. His loss of self-esteem and self-confidence is usually clearly evident. Recognizing this, the therapist can work to help him develop acceptance, understanding, and support from people important to him. With these supports he can reach a level where he can deal with and resolve his problems by the end of therapy.

The content of the group sessions inevitably moves from drunk-a-logs to interpersonal crises, which are pivotal environmental events that lead to drinking behavior. These crises need to be faced squarely and dealt with emotionally and rationally so that the alcoholic will be able to choose behaviors other than drinking when he is faced with new crises. It is more realistic to focus on short-term goals and decision-making than on long-term plans, since the alcoholic in a time-limited residential treatment program needs to face the outside world immediately after treatment. He must have available some effective alternative behaviors to cope with leaving the protection of his group at the center. A focus on long-term goals often leads to immediate discouragement when the alcoholic leaves the residential treatment center if he has not made any immediate short-range plans. As a result, he may be forced back to his previous drinking pattern. Employment and a place to live are basic to survival and must be provided for upon release.

The therapist is a powerful agent for behavioral change in the group. He should foster group cohesiveness throughout the treatment program so that members of the group can be mutually supportive in and out of group therapy sessions. He should avoid being the sole source of support for individual group members. Although guilt and repentance are common in group therapy with alcoholics, particularly during initial phases, they are antitherapeutic, particularly when elicited and focused on early in the history of the group. Both guilt and repentance can keep the alcoholic from facing real decisions that he needs to make, serving as a screen for real problems. They can result in his avoiding close interpersonal relationships. Both can serve as a reason for the alcoholic to continue drinking when he leaves the center, since he views himself as unworthy of rehabilitation because of his past transgressions.

As in all other groups, intellectualization and denial can serve as defenses against change for the alcoholic. Kepner (1964) notes that increasing self-awareness, by eliminating the defensive behavior of denial, will enable the alcoholic to see more clearly the aversive consequences of his drinking. The therapist needs to be aware of these characteristics as they emerge in the group and should help the group to focus on emotions rather than on ideas or intellectual solutions.

Guidelines for Therapists' Behavior

The group therapist needs to have special training for the treatment of alcoholics, although training in group therapy with other clinical populations is of considerable help. It is of primary importance that the therapist who would work with groups of alcoholics has "worked through" his own attitudes and reactions toward drinking. He must also work through some of the social attitudes that are common in both the general public and in people who treat psychiatric groups. The authors have found that the graduate student frequently has attitudes and biases about alcoholics that are common to the general population and do not disappear as a result of sophistication about clinical psychology or about treatment of other clinical populations. To be effective with alcoholics, the therapist must serve as a model for appropriate behaviors without presenting himself as so different from the group that he is not credible or acceptable. Whatever his background, his effectiveness will be related to his ability to identify with the problems the alcoholic faces, and to give each member of the group an opportunity to see alternative methods of dealing with interpersonal crises. Scott (1961), Moore (1961), Glud (1962), and Benedict (1960) believe a firm, directive approach is most successful in treating alcoholics. This is true only to a certain extent.

The therapist must learn how to lead and to shape behaviors

without being the autocrat or controller. The very directive therapist does not train group members to support one another. He also fosters a great deal of transference and dependency on himself. This prevents the alcoholic from functioning on his own and being able to make independent decisions when he leaves the residential treatment center. On the other hand, a therapist who does not lead but who is psychologically absent from the group fails to use his experience and skill to guide the group when members are moving in antitherapeutic directions.

A therapist can be a potent reinforcer of genuine feelings expressed in the group. He can also be very constructive in shaping group cohesiveness and reducing the incidence of intellectualization and denial, often a major defense of the alcoholic. The therapist can and should serve as a model for confrontation, when confrontation is appropriate, and especially when the group is intellectualizing and is fostering the denial of problems.

The therapist needs to support group members when appropriate, but should not monopolize this role. Eventually, his role as supporter for individual members will be minimal as he shapes group members to take on this function when it is realistic and appropriate. It is necessary for the therapist to be able to distinguish between "real support" and the pseudo-supportive behavior among group members early in therapy which leads to denial and intellectualization.

It is particularly important for the therapist to consider the different environments from which alcoholics come in setting expectations for how far an individual should progress or for what gains are realistic in group therapy. There should be significantly different expectations for lower class individuals than for upper middle class individuals, in terms of behavior in the group, levels of aspiration, and the ability to deal effectively with life's problems.

It is also important to differentiate between the goals and expectations of the male and female alcoholic. There does seem to be some real advantage, however, in treating both sexes in a group instead of treating one sex alone. Unfortunately, in many VA-hospital, private, and state-supported alcoholic units, the male alcoholic is treated separately. This deprives him of female support and understanding—a critical source of feedback in the restructuring of behavior.

The Cotherapist

As is true in other groups, a cotherapist can be a valuable asset in group therapy with alcoholics. The cotherapist can often pick up on subtle cues given out by members of the group who are not actively participating at the moment, and between-session discussions of the therapist and cotherapist can speed up the progress of the group. Most comments later made in describing the role of the cotherapist apply when working with alcoholics.

Specific Problems in Treating Alcoholics

In the younger male alcoholic, drinking is sometimes associated with "machismo," and other exaggerations of the male role. Therefore, it is important to treat the rebellion, the competition, and the need for recognition in the young alcoholic while simultaneously dealing with his drinking problem.

Drinking, unlike other symptoms, has immediate positive reinforcement, and its negative effects are usually delayed over an extended time period. One is, therefore, working against the effects of that immediate reinforcement in trying to deal with the drinking problem. There is a vicious cycle operating in which negative social and psychological effects increase feelings of inadequacy and worthlessness in the alcoholic. These he attempts to assuage with alcohol, which further decreases his self-concept, and increases his need to continue drinking.

At times, the alcoholic has strong motivation to stop drinking. However, he is not necessarily motivated to change attitudes and behaviors that are not, in his thinking, linked to drinking. This is frequently difficult to deal with in therapy, because once he finds that he is able to discontinue his drinking, he often loses motivation to change other behaviors and attitudes that may be linked intimately to his drinking without his awareness of the connection. Thus the conditions that lead to a return to drinking may be unchanged.

Another concept that has been seriously considered, but not systematically tested, involves a tailoring of treatment to specific individual characteristics, rather than the use of only one treatment modality. On the basis of the authors' experience, two major groups can be differentiated in the alcoholic population. One is the neurotic or depressive alcoholic who drinks to relieve anxiety. This person uses alcohol primarily as a means of escaping conflict situations. In effect, alcohol operates as a tranquilizer. A clinical example of this type of individual was seen in a residential treatment center by Salzberg several years ago. He was an office worker for a large firm who was in jeopardy of losing his job as a result of absenteeism associated with the bad hangovers that followed heavy drinking in the evenings. He was married and had two teenage children, who were both in school and doing well. His wife worked, took care of the children, and made most of the household decisions. The patient had isolated himself from the family and had no outside interests, though at one time in his life he had been interested in golf and in going out with his wife and children. When admitted for treatment he was almost exclusively preoccupied with his work at the office; the only way he felt he could relieve this preoccupation was to go to his room and drink. He felt very guilty about his drinking, and increasingly apprehensive that his employer would find out about it, for his job efficiency had been steadily diminishing. He led a very drab existence, increasingly seeking alcohol as an escape from the terrible and increasing feelings of inadequacy he experienced. This type of individual seems to benefit most from group psychotherapy, since the focus is on developing responses and skills for resolving difficult conflict situations, as well as on building self-esteem and self-confidence which, in the depressed alcoholic, lowers his need to drink for relief.

The other class is that of the psychopathic alcoholic, who does not experience a great deal of anxiety but who drinks as a means of releasing his inhibitions and acting out. This individual seeks exciting situations, and alcohol enables him to act on his impulses. An example of this type is a very attractive woman in her mid-twenties who was admitted to the same residential treatment center. She came from a home where the male members (stepfather and uncles) had made numerous attempts to seduce her sexually in her early teens. At the age of fifteen she left home and went to New Orleans where she worked as a waitress and lived off men who became sexually interested in her. She moved from place to place and eventually met and married a young man who lived in a rural environment in the northeastern United States. He was a solid, hard-working individual who worshipped her and tried to satisfy her every whim. They had a child, but our patient soon became bored with such a routine, humdrum existence and left her husband and child to begin traveling again. She met a long-distance truck driver with whom she lived and traveled for two years. This man was an alcoholic and would subject her to very severe physical beatings during alcoholic episodes. He broke several of her bones and caused bruises and lacerations of her face and body on numerous occasions. In spite of this, our patient expressed a strong emotional attachment toward him, in contrast to the apathy she felt toward her husband, who treated her so kindly and was willing to give her anything she wanted. This girl had been to several treatment centers for her alcoholism but had achieved no sobriety following each admission. She got along very well while in a center and experienced no anxiety during these admissions. She was very seductive in her behavior toward both staff and other residents and was treated as the "belle of the ball" by most of them. Drinking gave her license to act on her whims outside of the treatment center and group therapy seemed to have little long-range effect on her behavior.

Rubin and Lawlis (1970) suggested that readiness for therapy is associated with three types of alcoholics and different treatment modalities. They found that the individual most ready for therapy is the inhibited neurotic, with whom the treatment of choice is group therapy. Somewhat less ready is the aggressive neurotic, who also benefits some from group therapy. Least ready is the sociopath, who benefits more from a "hard-nosed" or highly controlled treatment program than he does from group therapy.

Eysenck and Beech (Bergin and Garfield, 1971) believe that sociopathy is the primary difficulty with the alcoholic, and that group therapy would not be effective with this type of individual, for whom they prescribe behavior therapy, particularly aversive therapy with electric shock. They cite research to indicate that it is effective for the alcoholic and more effective than group therapy. Nevertheless, there has been no systematic attempt to apply different treatment modalities to different types of individuals to demonstrate the relative effectiveness of one mode of treatment over another. Comparative approaches are an exciting area of research that, we hope, will be more extensively investigated in the future.

Outcome of Therapy with Alcoholics: Recent Research Findings

As with all other groups, follow-up research is a painstaking and frustrating procedure. It is particularly difficult with alcoholics because they tend to be a transient population whose lives are so disrupted that frequently they are difficult to locate after treatment. In an unpublished survey on the effects of time-limited residential treatment involving intensive group therapy with alcoholics, Salzberg found that although only 13 percent reported abstinence during the 8 to 14 months since they had left the center, 77 percent reported that they drank less than before treatment. Only 10 percent reported they drank as much or more. Eighty-five percent felt more certain of their ability to control their drinking behavior after treatment and 73 percent reported that their families felt they were doing better since treatment. Ninety-nine percent of those surveyed felt that they had been helped by treatment at the center and 81 percent had recommended the program to other alcoholics. The questionnaire was returned by 53 percent of the total sample of 216 former residents. A surprisingly large number were deceased or not locatable. There was a 4-to-1 male to female ratio and a 9-to-1 white to black ratio in the sample.

Generally, studies of the effectiveness of psychotherapy with alcoholics have found that the individual who has a good premorbid adjustment prior to treatment and who is better educated, more intelligent, and comes from a higher socioeconomic level is more likely to benefit from treatment than the one who is less well endowed or less fortunate (Gillis and Keet, 1969). This is very similar to therapy-outcome studies with other clinical populations.

Abstinence is the typical criterion used for outcome with alcoholics. Several recent studies have questioned whether this is a valid or even the sole criterion (Ludwig, 1972; Sobell, Sobell, and Christelman, 1972; Bigelow et al., 1972; Bigelow and Liebson, 1972). Using abstinence from alcohol for a period of over six months as a criterion, the results have been disappointing for both verbal psychotherapy and the behavior therapies. Neither result in greater than 50 percent success rates, with abstinence rates frequently much lower.

Schaeffer, Sobell, and Sobell (1972) gave videotape feedback of their behavior while intoxicated to groups of alcoholics to give them some idea of how they looked and acted while they were drinking. This feedback resulted in a great deal of anxiety in individuals who viewed their alcoholic behavior. When compared to a group who had not had videotape feedback, more of this group resumed drinking after release from the facility. Unfortunately, the videotape feedback was not combined with group psychotherapy in this study. It is very possible that such a combination might be a catalyst for change in group therapy. It is not enough to raise an alcoholic's anxiety level. His past learning has established a pattern of alcohol usage to reduce anxiety.

Gottheil et al. (1972, 2 studies) found that fixed-interval drinking results in a moderate drinking schedule. By allowing alcoholics access to alcohol at fixed intervals, he was able to control the amount of drinking engaged in. Cohen, Liebson and Faillace (1971a, 1971b) found that a patient could consistently decrease his drinking behavior for weeks at a time when an enriched environment and social contact was made contingent on such behavior. Schaeffer, Sobell, and Mills (1971) were able to show that controlled drinking can be maintained by monetary reinforcers. Chafetz (1970) has indicated that a substitution of some type for the alcohol is essential for successful treatment.

Meeks and Kelly (1970) dealt with family groups in treating alcoholics. They found better communication and increased mutual support after therapy. Smith (1969) found that when a wife of an alcoholic is in treatment, the alcoholic has a more favorable abstinence record. Reinehr (1969) and Ludwig (1968) found that therapists rate patients more favorably if they like them but that these ratings do not agree with patients' self-ratings or with outcome of therapy. This implies the need for study of other factors associated with a good outcome of treatment.

Ends and Page (1957) compared a learning orientation with a psychoanalytic and a client-centered orientation in group therapy. They used as a measure a pre- and post-therapy Q sort. They found that for the learning theory group there was a healthier post-therapy ideal self, but the post-therapy self-image had become worse. This latter change was due to heightened self-criticism. Therefore the overall effect was a deleterious one. The analytic group decreased self, ideal-self discrepancy primarily by changing the self-concept. In the client-centered group there was a healthier self-concept and a decreased ideal self-concept near the end of the therapy. This was seen as the most beneficial change. The control group showed a less healthy ideal self over the same time period. In a one- to one-and-a-half-year follow-up it was found that analytic and client-centered therapy had led to fewer alcoholic episodes than the control group experienced. However, only the client-centered therapy group had less recidivism than the control group.

It would appear that the abstinence rates for alcoholics following all present forms of treatment are disappointing. When one examines other criteria, such as control of drinking behavior and better interpersonal and family relationships following treatment, the results are much more encouraging. Behavior therapists focus on eliminating the symptom of drinking, often using aversive methods. The results of these studies and others that have used Antibuse or other aversive methods vary in reported effectiveness. None are highly effective, though these methods do show some promise. There are almost no published studies comparing the effectiveness of different treatment methods for different types of alcoholics. A most promising area for future research in treatment of alcoholics would be to assess the differential effects of specific treatment approaches to specific types of individuals. Certainly group therapy is an important method of treatment for the alcoholic; but the uncovering of supporting data showing which alcoholics it would benefit most could greatly increase its efficacy.

7

SPECIAL GROUP TECHNIQUES:
THE MARATHON

Few psychotherapeutic events in recent times have had the impact in the United States of the marathon or encounter group. It has been portrayed in films and on television; articles have been written about it in virtually every popular magazine. It has been used by neighborhood churches, business organizations, social organizations, and even in some instances the local public school. The theoretical orientation and techniques have taken many forms and have included T groups, Transactional Analysis, Gestalt therapy, personal growth laboratories, human potential experiences, sensory awareness, and even those bearing a more religious label. Many enter hoping to shorten their course of psychotherapeutic treatment to several intensive weekends. Others see the marathon as a continuing process of self-growth and exploration. Whatever the reasons for any one person's participation, the results, other than subjective impressions of the therapist, or testimonials by patients, have been quite limited. The only extended study, one that raises many questions about the effectiveness of marathon techniques as well as about persons leading such activities is the book by Lieberman, Yalom, and Miles (1973). They describe the encounter movement as follows:

It employs the newest, the oldest; its strategies sometimes stress safety, sometimes danger; it reveres anger and love, words and deeds, old western drama, old eastern meditation. Encounter groups are the interpersonal equivalent of sky diving. They are high risk, high-adrenalin endeavors, partially controlled, semi-regulated surprises. All participants share some idea of what will unfold, but there is sufficient ignorance of the details to lend qualities of mystery and easy adventure into the unknowns of self and others.

The authors go on to indicate that in many instances these groups fall outside the major therapeutic disciplines in our culture. They feel that part of their popularity is a reaction against the standard, highly institutionalized help-giving that is part of our society. Their study of seventeen groups provided one of the first yardsticks for measuring marathon groups. Their conclusions suggest that people seeking radical change in their life-styles, themselves, and their reactions with others are apt to be disappointed. What does occur is an intense, brief, interpersonal experience which can have some lasting effect. It may be positive, negative, or it could precipitate an emotional crisis. Lieberman et al. see the marathon as a dangerous device if the goal of the approach is to produce a new individual. They view it as a psychological form of radical surgery. From their results, they feel that success in marathon groups can only be achieved when both therapist and participants view the technique as less than magic, as no panacea. The value of marathons lies in their use as socially sanctioned opportunities for persons to engage in self-exploration and to develop greater ability to communicate. With scientific study, techniques may be refined to make the marathon a constructive, highly developed therapeutic tool.

This chapter will attempt to describe some of the techniques, the theories, and the operation of the marathon encounter from our point of view and from that of some proponents of the method. We will also review the research evidence related to the efficacy of the marathon as an instrument for producing behavioral change.

In spite of the many divergent approaches utilized in the marathon encounter group, there are a series of commonalities which are discussed at some length in the main body of this chapter. Size tends to be highly similar, with, typically, eight to sixteen participants; the modal number is about twelve which, as we have seen, allows for considerable interaction, especially when the encounter group is considered in terms of its time—eight or more hours per day. Other commonalities—such as a focus on the here and now, the support of self-disclosure, and the scrupulous avoidance of labeling participants "patients"—lead to a degree of comfort not possible in the traditional group, wherein individuals come because they are "sick" and are clearly labeled "patient" by virtue of the billing system, and the concurrence among various medical insurance programs that this constitutes treatment.

In encounter marathons, the goals may be change in specific behaviors, but more often they are aimed at changes in personal values, the release of inhibitions, an increase in self-acceptance, and perhaps above all the release of oneself to be able to enjoy life more fully.

Techniques

We have deferred discussion of some of the more innovative techniques of group psychotherapy to this section because they are identified with the marathon encounter, rather than with the more traditional models of group psychotherapy. However, it is possible in most instances to fit them into the framework described in our chapter on therapist behaviors. We will discuss the marathon in this section in terms of our five classes of therapist behaviors. While this suggests a high degree of concurrence between our approach and that of the marathon, there are also important and vital differences between the two. Chief among these is the difference in the therapist/leader roles. For example, the leader spends considerable time early in most marathon encounter groups in gaining membership in the group as a peer or coequal with other group members. As this particular behavior is achieved, the traditional protective and leadership roles played by the therapist become the property of the group, and leadership is a fluid role which moves between the participants and the participant/leader. It is doubtful that the leadership is ever totally given to the group, in that its best-informed and most-experienced member, the leader, continues to be highly influential and to play a protective and balancing role. However, he does engage in a level of self-disclosure not unlike that of other participants. In this respect he most sharply breaks with more traditional forms of group psychotherapy. It is interesting to note that in recent times, the marathon encounter model has had profound impact on traditional forms of group psychotherapy, in that many of the techniques, particularly the exercises and warm-up behaviors used in the marathon encounter, have been adapted and modified to fit the traditional psychotherapy group.

Instruction

As in group psychotherapy, the ground rules are laid out in an instructional model, perhaps even more so in marathon encounter groups than in traditional group therapies. The exercises or experiences are described in detail, often through the use of printed handouts or other materials, to the participants. Excellent representative examples of the exercises utilized in the marathon encounter groups are available in several publications, for example, the four-volume series by Pfeiffer and Jones (1969, 1970, 1971, 1973), where many of the exercises used by the National Training Laboratory Organization and similar groups are presented. In a volume derived from Gestalt principles (Stevens, 1971), the exercises used to open the participant to the "Gestalt experiences" are presented in sufficient detail to be used as a guide. There are many other published volumes which offer similar materials.

The group leader uses exercises of varying types to structure the learning experience for participants. There are a number of exercises designed for initial stages of interaction, while others illustrate specific interpersonal blocks, communication problems, and other events as they unfold in the group process. The rationale for use of each exercise is described in the typical manual. For example, there are exercises to aid self-disclosure, the development of trust, seeking closure on a topic, giving feedback, and other processes common to the group.

Once an exercise has been selected, other therapist behaviors are employed in carrying out the task. The leader, in many instances, may model the exercise or interaction. This is particularly vital when a high degree of self-disclosure is desired. In such instances, the leader may use a process such as the "lifeline exercise" in which an individual traces his key life experiences from the past to the present, and finally predicts his future. To be effective, it is deemed essential that the leader reveal meaningful, affective experiences rather than provide a demographic history of his life to that time. In such instances, modeling plays a major role. Once other participants become involved, then the additional factors of reinforcement, aversive control, data gathering, and various combinations of these principles are utilized.

The therapist may also utilize techniques such as relaxation, which is common to behavioral group psychotherapy and individual behavior therapy. He may instruct the individuals in the appropriate ways to relax in the group, a procedure similar to some of the Gestalt exercises, which have this as a secondary goal.

Another type of instructional technique is given to individuals under the heading of assertion or assertiveness training. This technique involves a number of skills beyond the instructional process—reinforcing by observers of an individual's efforts to be assertive, as well as confronting and forcing him to become directly expressive in dealing with people. Once ground rules have been established, then the modeling process or other techniques may be used to prepare the individual to engage in the assertive behaviors. Other techniques, such as systematic desensitization and role playing or behavioral rehearsal, also require an instructional process as part of the preliminaries for group behavior, though a training process is rarely used in encounter groups.

Modeling

We have already discussed the value of modeling for the acquisition of behavior in groups. This same principle obtains in the marathon encounter group, where the therapist's modeling of openness and other behaviors is highly desirable. Most of the exercises used in the marathon encounter groups should be modeled. Typically they are modeled first by the leader and coleader, then by the participants. It appears from observation that this is one of the most effective means of involving individuals in the marathon process.

Reinforcement

Reinforcement is a cornerstone of group psychotherapy and it is no less so in the marathon encounter group. It is used initially by the therapist or group leader, modeled by other participants in dealing with members of the group, and used extensively when new roles and new behaviors are undertaken. In most marathon experiences, reinforcement is not utilized systematically.

Aversive Control

Aversive control, as seen in our earlier discussion, plays an important role, in combination with reinforcement, in shaping desired behaviors and in decreasing those less desirable. There is a tendency in some marathon encounter groups to utilize punishment, as when certain group members are confronted and challenged by the leader and other group members regarding their undesirable responses or behaviors. Punishment is most effective when it is coupled with the reinforcement of alternative desired responses.

There are forms of aversive control that may diminish undesirable behaviors through techniques such as "breaking in," "giving feedback," and "secret sharing," which can be understood from a behavior modification orientation. In fact, some aspects resemble the procedures recommended by behavior therapists, but there are considerable differences. On the other hand, some specifically labeled behavior therapy procedures, such as systematic desensitization and implosion, have been adopted by encounter group leaders, even though the theoretical foundation and the manner in which they are applied are grossly different.

Unfortunately, most of the nonbehavioral marathon encounter techniques are not presented systematically or consistently. The description of the categories of the therapist's responses can only very loosely be applied to what occurs in the marathon encounter group. Too often the leader is inclined to operate on some intuitive level, wherein he utilizes techniques and behaviors "he feels" are appropriate at a given moment, rather than responds to explicit patient or participant behaviors. Further, while some techniques and principles may be fitted into a learning model, many cannot and appear to be applied randomly, sometimes in conflict with previously utilized techniques. Some marathon encounter groups seem to be an endless chain of exercises, without explicit goals and with little systematic attempt to move into more relevant material and to develop a strong group interaction.

In spite of the many problems and shortcomings inherent in any description of marathon encounter groups, it is possible to examine some of the commonalities and the results that are a part of the marathon experience. In the following pages we will look at these results and the evaluations which have been made of marathon encounters.

The Time Factor

The distinguishing feature of the marathon encounter is that the group members meet continuously over a period of several days, usually a weekend. The first reported continuous contact weekend, the original "marathon," was coconducted by Frederick Stoller and George Bach with private patients of Bach's in the winter of 1963. Their particular model of the marathon lasts from twenty-four to thirty hours, sometimes without a break for sleep (Stoller, 1967). Bach (1966) feels that this longer time period makes it easier to strip people of the roles and images they maintain in order to hide honest expressions of feeling. As time goes on, with increasing exhaustion and fatigue, the group exhibits a decreasing tolerance for defensiveness and a refusal to expend energy on playing roles. As Bach puts it, "Tired people tend to be truthful" (Bach, 1966, p. 998). Although Bach presents his argument that the longer period for interaction leads to a breakdown in defensiveness in a very convincing manner, he offers no evidence in support of this contention. The uniqueness of the marathon rests upon its extended period for interaction but, in the absence of controlled and systematic observation, Bach's account of the effects of this extended interaction remains very much within the realm of theory.

Stoller (1968) feels that there are a number of advantages inherent in the marathon's prolonged time span. First, the extended period of interaction leads to a steady, continuous rise to unprecedented heights of group tension, which, Stoller believes, is an index of the degree of involvement of the group members. He likens the marathon to a pressure cooker in that, like a pressure cooker, the marathon can also compress the amount of time required to do its work. Consequently, the progress of the group is accelerated and levels of tension and involvement are reached that are only rarely matched in the conventional therapeutic setting. Second, the marathon, by virtue of the greater amount of time spent in continuous contact, produces a feeling of having lived with other individuals.

Instead of merely talking about their life situations in short segments of time, group members can be seen actually to live through their struggles and difficulties. Third, the marathon's unusual arrangement of time and place sets the occasion aside as something special and out of the ordinary. A change-inducing setting is created. Expectations for such out-of-the-ordinary occurrences are different and the investment of effort directed toward change is greater. Gibb and Gibb (1969) share Stoller's opinion that increased benefits can be derived from extended periods of interaction. They maintain that the marathon is the most powerful and economical time format for the breakdown of fear-inspired roles and the development of trust-inspired personal contact. "The continuous uninterrupted personal contact of the marathon is important. Groups meeting for only two hours at a session are significantly less powerful than continuous groups" (p. 48).

Like Bach, Stoller and the Gibbs offer nothing more than their own observations in support of their analyses of the advantages of the marathon's extended period for interaction. Stoller presents no evidence in support of what he sees as a steady rise in group tension and involvement. His assumption that the marathon's continuous contact leads to greater intimacy among group members seems logical enough, although it too awaits experimental confirmation. Even if we accept as fact that a climate of greater intimacy is produced, what evidence is there that this intimacy in and of itself can create lasting behavioral change? Finally, Stoller's contention that the extraordinary setting produces a different set of expectancies among the participants also seems likely, though it too remains unverified. A more likely interpretation would seem to be that the novelty of the situation provides little more than a catalyst for producing behavioral change.

The notion that a single interpersonal experience, no matter how prolonged or intense, can alter established patterns of behavior is subject to question. Hersko and Winder (1958) found that length of time in treatment was significantly related to patients' attitudes toward themselves and others. Likewise, Lorr (1962), after reviewing a number of studies related to frequency and duration of psychotherapy and its effectiveness, concluded that change would appear to require the passage of time. The span of time covered by treatment seemed to be a more influential factor in outcome than the sheer number of treatments. Bates (1968) found that a group counseling format of weekly class periods was superior to a marathon-type format, involving an equal amount of time, for producing classroom behavioral changes in high-school students.

Of central importance to the marathon is not only that the group meets continuously over an extended period of time, but that the amount of time is limited. Stoller (1968) feels that these limits create a sense of urgency and heighten the motivation of all parties concerned to face themselves and change those parts of their behavior which they find unsatisfactory. However, here again Stoller fails to provide any evidence that there is a relationship between time-limited interaction and heightened motivation for change. A study by Loar, Young, Roth, Rhudick, and Goldstein (Phillips and Wiener, 1966) does address itself to the efficacy of time-limited treatment. The researchers, working with patients' pre- and post-treatment self-reports, found that time-limited individual therapy was superior to an equal amount of time-unlimited therapy in terms of improvement in somatic distress, tension, depression, bewilderment, and fatigue. On the other hand, there were no significant differences in therapists' ratings between the time-limited and time-unlimited treatment groups. The authors felt, however, that in their ratings the therapists may have been biased against the time-limited therapy.

In addition to the increased motivation for change that he sees, Stoller (1968) also feels that the time-limited feature of the marathon reduces the degree of patient dependency on the therapist. He believes that group members, knowing that the group experience is of fixed, limited duration, tend to create expectancies of independence from the group leader; long-term dependency situations are thereby avoided.

Although marathons were originally run on a twenty-four- or thirty-hour continuous basis, Mintz (1967), Casriel and Deitch (1968), Ellis (1969), and others have concluded that it is usually advisable to divide the marathon into two parts, separated by an interlude for sleep. Berne (1966) states that without an intermission for sleep there is little chance to assimilate the events and experiences of the day and to put into effect and solidify any changes that have occurred. Where there is a regularly scheduled interval for sleep, the participants do not go home for the night, but sleep at the actual site of the marathon or somewhere close by. It is thought that this avoids interrupting the continuity of the group with home problems.

Selection and Setting

Marathon groups contain anywhere from eight to sixteen people. At present, there is no generally accepted criterion for screening potential participants, and most practitioners admit nearly all applicants (Stoller, 1968). Settings for marathon groups vary with the demands of the situation. Weekend retreats and the therapist's office are the most commonly used settings, but the primary considerations appear to be comfort, convenience, and most of all privacy. Most experts feel that the setting, compared to the attitudes of the group leader and the participants, is a secondary consideration. Although perhaps not of primary importance, the choice of setting should not be left up to the whim or personal preference of the group leader and some research would be in order.

The Group Leader

One of the most unusual and at the same time most controversial aspects of marathon group therapy has to do with the role of the group leader. As practiced by Bach, Stoller, and most other marathon group leaders, the function of the leader is to guide by modeling. The group leader's major responsibility is to create an atmosphere where experiences which provide opportunities for change can occur. In carrying out this responsibility he functions simply as another group member. The leader must build up his impression of the participants exactly as do the other members of the group and, like all other group members, he must share with the group the impact made by each participant. Relegating technical considerations and clinical training to the background, he must learn to direct his attention to and react to his own inner responses to people, for once he sets the group experience in motion he cannot remain detached and clinically aloof, but must be an active participant (Stoller, 1967). Like Stoller, Toll (1968) is of the opinion that the group leader can function most effectively by accepting full, equal membership in the group. She feels that many psychotherapists fail in group therapy because they are preoccupied with the problem of control and that the moment the therapist attempts to control the group deliberately, its whole purpose and spirit are lost. The group becomes a functioning unit only when the therapist lets himself become a complete partner and member of the group. Likewise, Kovan (1968) considers the need to be an authority and the need for detachment to be the two primary destructive influences evident in therapists' using the group process.

There is a need for further investigation into the effectiveness of leadership by modeling. Scheidlinger (1968) points out that there are major differences among group therapists on the issue of whether and in what manner the group leader should genuinely reflect himself as an individual. Truax and Carkhuff (1965) have found that therapist transparence, i.e., the degree to which the therapist acts as a real person "devoid of the usual professional-confessional screen," is significantly related to the patient's level of self-disclosure. They present evidence that, in turn, the patient's level of transparence or self-disclosure is a relevant condition of constructive personality change.

Bach (1967) has detailed the facilitative services of professional group leaders, including: screening of potential participants, proper timing and focusing of feedback so as to present behavioral alternatives, channeling of interaction, helping people to share their feelings rather than hide them through defenses, revealing self-defeating interaction patterns, reinforcing behavioral changes, maintaining optimum levels of group tensions and a selective focus on the here and now, and providing safe channels for the full exploration and non-destructive expression of conflicts and aggression. In addition to the apparent nonexistence of any screening procedures, one cannot help but wonder how the group leader can time feedback, channel interaction, gauge group tension, etc., and still function as a full and equal member in the group. Isn't this having your cake and eating it too? It would seem as if at least two group leaders would be needed, one to serve as a model for reacting to one's feelings and another to direct the interaction of the group.

Procedure and Process

At the beginning of each group, the leader explicitly states what is going to occur, outlining the hours of the meeting, the goals of the group, the general content of the interaction, and his role. This is considered necessary in order to create an atmosphere of honesty and directness from the very onset of the group experience (Stoller, 1968). The basic procedures employed in the marathon have been outlined by Bach (1966). First of all, no subgrouping is permitted. Everyone stays together until the prearranged time for the group to take a break or end. Shifting of positions within the room is encouraged in order to prevent the tendency of any group to develop into cliques or mutually protective relationships. Second, except for the early phases of the marathon, concentration is upon what is present and actually going on within the group. The emphasis is on the here and now, rather than on historical or extra-group data. Third, honesty and spontaneity are emphasized, while being "right" is downgraded. All group members are expected to participate actively and to call attention to their true feelings. Fourth, group members must be given feedback, that is, information as to the effects they have on other group members. Emotional reactions rather than cognitive understanding must be a consistent group goal. Fifth, no physical threats or assaults are permitted. Sixth, nonverbal techniques are often utilized, permitting group members to explore new ground and enabling them to risk what they ordinarily avoid. Seventh, changes and improvements in participation should be attended to and reinforced by the group. Finally, information exchanged during the marathon is confidential.

It is thought that the here-and-now orientation of the marathon, focusing on the what and how of the problem and not its origin, is one of the factors that accounts for the great emotional impact that the marathon has been alleged to have. Even if we accept the idea that focus on the present generates greater emotionality within the group—although this is unproven—what evidence is there that this emotionality is any more than cathartic? A cathartic experience may be pleasurable and even healthy, but does not by itself justify claims for lasting behavioral change.

Perhaps an even greater force directed toward creating an emotional impact is the marathon's emphasis on honesty and the expression of feelings. To Rogers (1969), the sharing of subjective truths is one of the most change-producing aspects of a group experience. Similarly, Stoller (1968) believes that the honest expression of feelings leads to positive change:

To show oneself to others in a face-to-face encounter is to be vulnerable and exposed. To be open reveals our weaknesses, inadequacies, inconsistencies, guilts and inner wishes. It is the enormous energy which goes into remaining hidden which constitutes much of the difficulties and limitations with which we struggle. Without our disguises, we have potential for greater use of our resources of intellect and organization, a greater depth of feeling as well as a greater strength and resilience for recovering from disappointment and injury. An important key to personal change lies in permitting oneself to drop some masks, staying with the consequences of this exposure, and learning that the masks are not so necessary. The accelerated group (marathon) gives time and opportunity for this to happen. [p. 224]

The marathon group is geared toward stripping away the masks behind which people hide their feelings. The reactions of the participants are designed to penetrate defenses such as denial, rationalization, and particularly intellectualization. In Stoller's words, the group seeks to "provide experiences, not intellectual exercises—and experiences have the power to reshape us" (Stoller, 1967, p. 33).

Stoller's belief in the power of experience is certainly compatible with behavioral as opposed to more insight-oriented approaches. However, the marathon, because it is not followed up at a later time by other like experiences, represents a *single,* though massed, experience and, as was pointed out earlier, the therapeutic value of massed treatment is still subject to doubt. When considering the marathon's ability to break down defense mechanisms, one must take into account the fact that while defenses may not be very adaptive within the group, they may be very much so outside of the group, where openness is not always encouraged or positively reinforced. Where defenses are broken down by the group, it is quite possible that they will be built up again if the individual's outside environment does not provide models for or support for more open expression of feelings.

The giving of feedback to one another by the members of the group is supposed to be another of the marathon's prime mechanisms for inducing behavioral change. By means of feedback the individual is thought to be able to gain insights into how he appears to others; this often results in behavioral breakthroughs, where the individual begins to show different facets of himself. When people abandon their defenses and begin to face up to their feelings different feedback is received. "When people begin to talk to one another with an unmistakable quality of honesty and directness, the regard and appreciation they receive is highly reinforcing" (Stoller, 1968, p. 229).

The effectiveness of feedback in promoting behavioral change would seem to depend on the satisfaction of two important conditions. First, the atmosphere within the group should be such that group members do not feel threatened at the prospect of having to give feedback to other group members. Meeting this condition would seem to rest largely on the ability of the group leader to establish a climate of security. Second, in pointing out maladaptive behavior patterns and suggesting alternatives, the technique is no better than the observation and interpersonal skills of the participants. Obviously not all group members are equal in these skills, and there is a real danger that a few individuals may come to dominate the group. Such a situation is usually counterproductive, and the group leader must be on guard to prevent its occurrence.

Within the group, the kind of feedback that is given is quite varied. There are times when the term "feedback" is too mild to describe the emotional intensity of the interactions that take place, when perhaps it might be more accurate to state that one individual confronts another. Such confrontations may be positive but often they are quite negative and involve the expression of hostile feelings (Rogers, 1969). Differential feedback from various group members occurs a good deal of the time. However, typically there comes a time when a group consensus is reached and the resulting group pressure becomes a powerful force for change. The individual's regard for the group and his concern for their feelings about him is often a significant influence toward self-exploration and examination of alternatives to usual behavior patterns (Stoller, 1969) Studies on conformity leave little doubt that group pressure can exert a powerful force on the individual. If anything, assurances would seem to be needed that group members will not be coerced into a phony acceptance of the group consensus.

Thus far we have described some of the basic procedures—such as the emphasis on honesty and openness, the focusing of attention on the immediate present, and the use of feedback and group pressure—which the marathon employs in attempting to change behavior, and we have given a general description of the kind of behavioral change for which the marathon experience strives. However, it may be worthwhile to note the more specific changes which proponents claim it produces. Stoller (1968) takes the position that a marathon can only be judged as successful if it produces significantly different conduct. He believes that self-understanding, in the sense that it enables a person to talk more about himself, to explain himself, is irrelevant. With real change there is an increase in self-confidence, manifested in an ability to act decisively and spontaneously without undue regard for the opinion of others. There are those who undergo a marked and startling change, while others are better able to meet crises and arrive at more purposeful and less self-defeating solutions. Still others emerge from the marathon with an enhanced self-regard and a new appreciation for their own strengths and resources. At the risk of being redundant, we can only point out that once again Stoller offers only his own subjective, and hardly impartial, observations to attest to these kinds of changes.

In order to reinforce and evaluate some of the changes which have taken place during the marathon, some group leaders hold follow-up sessions. Stoller (1968) reports that he conducts follow-up sessions approximately six weeks after the original group situation. Casriel and Deitch (1968) have instituted a more elaborate follow-up procedure. After the conclusion of the marathon, they hold subsequent "static groups," composed of the same people who have taken part in the marathon. These groups meet regularly, and Casriel and Deitch feel that the advantage of this arrangement lies in the intimate awareness members have of one another's problems and behavior patterns. After meeting regularly for a period of eight to twelve weeks, the static group then meets for a second marathon.

Follow-up procedures may be quite important to marathon-group participants in helping them to overcome problems they may be

facing in sustaining whatever gains they made during the marathon
This is a question which certainly merits experimental investigation
If follow-up sessions do prove to make significant contributions
toward maintaining behavioral changes stemming from the marathon experience, it will in no way serve to refute the therapeutic value of the marathon but will lend credence to the view
that spaced treatment is necessary for lasting modifications in
behavior.

Stages

Individuals who have studied the marathon extensively have come
to the conclusion that its course is fairly predictable. According to
Stoller (1967), in the first phase, participants try to present themselves to the group as they would like to appear. However, invariably
they encounter unexpected reactions from the group, which they
find difficult to accept. The second stage is characterized by a
conflict between the desire to withdraw from this uncomfortable
situation and the demand of the marathon to become more involved.
During this phase the group members learn not only a good deal
about each other but also how to react more openly and honestly
with each other. The interactions during this period are intense and
make this the most "explosive" phase of the marathon. "Tears and
threats are not uncommon" (Stoller, 1967, p. 32). As the marathon
progresses, there is an increasing sense of intimacy among the group
members and "positive feelings emerge in a spontaneous and deeply
felt fashion" (Stoller, 1967, p. 32). Behavioral alternatives emerge as
the group members realize that they can show more of themselves to
the world than they thought safe in the past.

Casriel and Deitch (1968) find that in the initial phase of a
marathon each person takes an active part in presenting his own
problems and that the basic problems of most participants revolve
around an inability to accept love and to express anger. As the
marathon continues, the group members become more intensely
involved, progressing from interest to concern and finally to emotional involvement. During the concluding stage, some of the members have emotional breakthroughs and are able to overcome their
neurotic fears and defenses. As the defensive barriers are broken

down, a feeling develops of being both "free to love and be lovable."

A further description of the phases of a marathon is offered by Mintz (1967); she sees the initial phase, when the participants tell about their lives and problems, as marked by anxiety and defensiveness. In the next two stages there is a mixture of open hostility and open dependency. However, most individuals tend to release hostility first, and exhibitions of intense anger may break through. Following the expression and partial working through of hostile feelings, a new atmosphere begins to permeate the group. This, according to Mintz, is the most intense phase of the marathon. It is marked by a feeling of appreciation for one another, warmth, and closeness among group members, and by a desire to draw out and aid other group members to relax their defenses and experience their feelings more fully.

There is a common theme which can be seen in the three preceding descriptions of the stages of a marathon. In the opening phase, Stoller, Casriel and Deitch, and Mintz all see the participants as being in the grip of a fear and inability to express their feelings. Within the facilitative confines of the group, experiences are provided which make it possible for the participants to reveal more of themselves. By the close of the marathon many of the group members have overcome their former defensiveness and appear to be freer to express their feelings and more able to come into closer contact with others in the group.

Innovations

Although the marathon is a relatively new technique, several innovations have already been tried. Bindrim (1968) has conducted nude marathons and in one group of twenty participants, seventeen felt that the factor of nudity increased their ability to open up to each other emotionally and to achieve a greater degree of authenticity and transparency. Among the benefits cited by the participants were a feeling of revitalization, greater acceptance of self, increased self-confidence, a clearer perception of the roles they were playing in their daily lives, and a diminished fear of rejection. Bindrim felt that the group integrated and seemed to become therapeutically functional more rapidly than clothed marathon groups. He concluded that nudity facilitates group interaction and that

"Nudity in a group which encourages skin contact seems to be therapeutic in itself" (p. 187).

The total lack of experimental controls places Bindrim's optimistic conclusions within the realm of purely subjective observation, and even as such his conclusions appear rather tenuous. Control subjects are lacking, there are no pretreatment measures, no follow-up assessment is reported, and, since Bindrim does not say under what circumstances they were obtained, the possibility exists that the subjects' positive appraisals may contain an element of bias, in that they were directed toward the leader of the group. Furthermore, since many of the participants acknowledged that they had ambivalent feelings toward the nude marathon beforehand, their positive evaluations could easily be interpreted as attempts to reduce cognitive dissonance regarding the experience.

Ellis (1969) employs a marathon technique which he calls the "rational encounter." In the rational encounter, unlike most other forms of the marathon, cognitive and intellectual processes are strongly encouraged. The rational encounter does not merely induce feelings for their own sake. Instead, it follows up feeling with cognitive understanding and restructuring, and with behavioral activity. The techniques of the rational encounter are more directive than in most other kinds of encounter marathons and are consciously planned to provide both emotional experiences and help in personal problem solving. Finally, the participants are given homework assignments in order to implement and sustain in their daily lives what they have learned about themselves during the rational encounter. With its emphasis on planning, structure, leader direction, and cognitive insight, the rational encounter seems so different from the usual type of marathon that the key process variables are probably not the same. Only in its extended duration does the rational encounter appear to be modeled after the marathon as originated by Stoller and Bach.

Criticisms

Like most new developments in psychotherapy, the marathon has its share of critics. Spotnitz (1968) maintains that there is a need for better screening procedures. He believes that it is unjustifiable to expose people to an experience that may be desirable for some and undesirable for others without having established any objective criteria for participation.

A number of authorities object to the massed treatment which marathon groups offer. A. Burton (1969) believes that spaced learning is necessary for growth experiences and that the marathon represents a "hysterical form of encounter." Parloff (1968) also thinks that therapeutic improvement cannot be derived from massed treatment. According to Shapiro (1969), some of the most important effects of marathon groups seem to fade over time unless periodically and, preferably, regularly reinforced. As a psychoanalyst, Anthony (1968) wonders whether, in the absence of any working through, the impact created by marathon groups can endure. He suggests that there may be a correlation between the time it takes to develop a disturbance and the time it takes to repair it.

Many critics take issue with the great emphasis which the marathon group places upon intensity of experience and the expression of feelings. Spotnitz (1968) feels that the emphasis disregards the fact that some defenses are necessary for the protection of the ego. Spotnitz contends that the process of developing new behavior patterns requires an examination of the original causes of the disturbance and cannot be accomplished simply through exposure to a new experience. Anthony (1968) assesses the goal of the marathon as excitement and stimulation per se, as if this were a therapeutic end in itself. He maintains that there is an overemphasis on emotional interchange and a depreciation of insight, which make for a certain "mindlessness" about the approach. Furthermore, Anthony charges that the therapeutic setting of the marathon is too far divorced from the real world to be of any lasting value:

The participants may well become fixed to the overwhelming experience, as they might to a traumatic one, and crave its repetition compulsively. Life as it is, in its ordinariness and its conventions, and life as it could be under these special conditions is too sharply and suddenly contrasted and could well lead to lasting dissatisfaction with the type of life actually being lived. [Anthony, 1968, p. 251]

Parloff (1968) asserts that the assumption made by Stoller (1968) that all effective therapists are those who are open, personally involved with their patients, and self-revealing may be an unwarranted oversimplification. He contends that the literature suggests that with some types of patients reserved and impersonal types of behavior seem to be most successful in treatment. Parloff also questions the notion that honesty on the part of the therapist is necessarily therapeutic. He argues that the therapist, by becoming just another member of the group, may be restricting his effective role to the point where he slights or minimizes contributions based on his specialized skills.

Of all the criticisms directed against the marathon, the one most frequently heard, in this chapter and elsewhere, is that there is insufficient evidence to warrant the claims of lasting behavioral change. Parloff (1968) accepts the marathon experience as being strongly emotional but sees no evidence for its therapeutic value. Likewise, Spotnitz (1968) feels that until the efficacy of the marathon technique is ultimately proved or disproved on the basis of adequate evidence, it should be presented to the participants and to the profession at large as an unproven, experimental method. Bach (1968) acknowledges the need for further research into the effects of the marathon experience and believes that there is a need for longitudinal follow-up studies to examine its long-term consequences. The other leading proponent of the marathon, Stoller (1968), also recognizes that there is a need for more research into the efficacy of the marathon.

Research

A look at the existing research evidence related to the efficacy of the marathon as a psychotherapeutic tool finds the great majority of participants describing marathons, both immediately afterwards and a year later, as a worthwhile and moving experience. However, as Mintz (1967) has pointed out, for the most part there is only purely subjective observation as to the value of the marathon. Stoller (1968) reports that approximately 20 percent of the participants do not derive the kind of gain from the marathon that is sought and that about 1 or 2 percent seem worse after the experience. Stoller does not indicate where his figures come from. He cites no research efforts, so presumably they represent his own estimate. According to

Casriel and Deitch (1968), "roughly 14 out of every 15 participants have a beneficial emotional breakthrough during the course of the marathon" (p. 163). Where these figures come from is also uncertain. Nor do Casriel and Deitch indicate the ingredients of this "beneficial emotional breakthrough."

The individual who has done by far the most research into marathon groups is George Bach. He (1967b) claims that 90 percent of the participants in his marathons have evaluated the marathon as one of the most significant experiences of their lives. Bach (1968) reported a follow-up study of twenty-four subjects taken from two marathon groups in which creativity, joy, and stress were used as the parameters of change. The overwhelming majority of 92 percent reported a significant difference, with 13 percent reporting negative changes (less joy, more stress, and less creativity), and 79 percent reporting positive growth changes. Unfortunately, Bach does not specify how joy, stress, and creativity were measured.

From a sample of 612 self-reporting participants, Bach (1968) found that 12 percent reported feeling worse about themselves and their lives after the marathon experience. However, by the time of follow-ups (three to six weeks later) only four of the 612 subjects, or less than 1 percent, were unwilling to risk a repetition of the marathon experience. Bach maintained that these were the only true failures, the individuals who had been and remained hurt. However, is unwillingness to attend another marathon a valid index of failure? Are we to assume that if a participant will repeat the experience then it could not have had an adverse effect on him? On the contrary, people often want to repeat experiences which are anything but therapeutic.

Bach's research into consequences suffers from methodological inadequacies which obscure his overall positive results. There is an absence of control subjects or pretreatment measures. Bach does not supply full information about how his data were collected and one cannot be sure whether the participants' posttreatment evaluations were gathered by someone who was not personally involved in conducting the marathon. Perhaps the most serious shortcoming is that Bach's results rest solely on the basis of self-reports. Considering that the participants had invested time and money and had risked what, for some, was probably unprecedented candor in expressing their feelings, their positive evaluations of the marathon experience hardly seem surprising. However, these positive evaluations tell us little about the participants' actual functioning following the marathon.

Bach (1967a) also compared expert-rich and expert-poor marathon groups by having the groups exposed to two different intensities of expert visitation. The expert-rich groups contained a nonprofessional and one senior expert who was present at least half the time, and also received two-hour consulting visits from each of the other two senior experts. The expert-poor groups were exposed to only one senior expert and then only for two very brief visits. By their own evaluations, the expert-rich group members felt they experienced significantly greater stressfulness and more constructive aggression (risking anger) than the expert-poor group. The expert-rich group were more probing and were generally rougher on each other while, at the same time, they were warmer and more accepting and trusting of one another. On the basis of this data, Bach came to the conclusion "that people in an expert-led group have the best chance to really touch one another with their fangs, and thereby gain trust and full acceptance in the group at the (same) time" (p. 45). In view of the emotional intensity which the marathon is said to generate, the advisability of having an experienced and capable group leader is easily accepted.

Bach (1967b) categorized the responses of subjects who had served as participants in nine different marathon groups in five dimensions of maximal therapeutic helpfulness: empathetic identification, acceptance-warmth, self-understanding, problem solving, and aggression-confrontation. The dimension of self-understanding or insight mediation was the category most often checked as helpful in marathon groups. The responses also supported the hypothesis that aggression-confrontation between participants contributes as significantly as does warmth-acceptance to the therapeutic value of group interaction. Bach (1967c) found further support for the notion that aggressive confrontation is a needed ingredient for effective group therapy when he asked his subjects to specify the kinds of interactional contact that they felt interfered with, rather than facilitated, the emergence of social intimacy. Five parameters of disjunctive or least-helpful contact were identified: strangeness (unlike me), noncaring indifference (alienation), narcissism (autistic preoccupation), disjunctive communication (irrelevancy-derailing), and aggression-phobia (conflict evasion). Noncaring indifference and aggression-phobia were found to be the two most disjunctive forms of contact.

Although Bach is to be commended for carrying out most of the process research on marathon groups that has been undertaken, there is, as with his outcome research, a need for dependent measures other than the participant's own appraisals of the experience. The group members' subjective recollections of the important process variables can hardly serve as a substitute for controlled and systematic manipulation or even observation of the variables under study, followed by measurement through the use of behavioral or psychometric criteria.

Weigel (1968) compared two groups of nine clients who received eighteen consecutive hours of marathon-group psychotherapy, which focused both on members' problems and here-and-now encounters among members, with a third group of nine clients who participated in eighteen consecutive hours of marathon-group discussion, which focused on topical, nonself-oriented interaction. There were changes in the direction of positive mental health in both of the marathon psychotherapy groups and also in the marathon discussion group. However, no differences between the groups were noted in the amount of change occurring. It would have been interesting to see whether the positive changes in both types of groups were long-lasting, but no follow-up was included. Nevertheless, Weigel's study represented a step forward in marathon-group research, in that a treatment control condition was included and psychological tests were utilized to assess the quantity and quality of change. In a similar study, Lewis (1968) compared two groups of married couples who participated in group psychotherapy for nine continuous hours with a third group of married couples who participated in an educational-discussion type experience for nine continuous hours. On the basis of a follow-up questionnaire administered two weeks later it was found that, although a majority of subjects in both types of group meetings thought they had benefited from the experience, there was no clear difference between the two different kinds of nine-hour sessions.

Mintz (1969) questioned ninety-three marathon-group participants immediately following their experience and eighty others three or more months afterward, asking how much they felt they had profited. While spontaneous comments were generally exuberant, after three months the subjects were less enthusiastic but still felt that they had achieved a measure of permanent gain. Only fourteen of the respondents felt that nothing worthwhile had resulted. This research appears to contain the same methodological deficiencies as Bach's outcome research, but Mintz does attempt to assess the longevity of the group members' favorable reactions. Needless to say, more objective long-term follow-up measures are needed.

Recent studies have made greater use of parameters other than self-reports in attempting to determine the effects of marathon groups. Young and Jacobson (1970) administered the Edwards and the Marlowe-Crowne Social Desirability scale and the twelve scales of the Personal Orientation Inventory to college students four days before and four days after participation in a fifteen-hour marathon group. They found that the marathon-group subjects showed significantly lower defensiveness on the post-tests than a group of control subjects. The marathon-group participants also exhibited changes in the direction of more socially positive functioning on thirteen of the fourteen scales used. The performance of the control subjects renders the results of this study somewhat equivocal, particularly when we consider that a no-treatment control was employed, leaving any possible placebo effect among the marathon-group subjects uncontrolled.

Myerhoff, Jacobs, and Stoller (1970) used the Jacobs Adjective Check List as a measure of emotionality in comparing two groups of psychiatric patients; one group received a form of marathon-group treatment and the other a more traditional type of group psychotherapy. Although the authors reported "a generally higher rate of occurrence and variability in the expression of negative feelings" (p. 35) in the marathon group, there were no significant differences between the overall amount of emotionality in the two groups. However, the marathon-group subjects manifested a greater degree of group cohesion, as measured by the number of subjects who wanted to continue treatment and by their attendance record for six subsequent group sessions. The authors concluded, "The major impact of this study is the demonstration that hard data may be gathered on clinical material. This hard data corresponds quite clearly to the clinical impressions of the therapist and the observers of the groups" (p. 36). Regardless of whether the findings approximate the clinical impressions of the therapist and the observers of the groups, one gets the feeling that this study was not primarily intended to demonstrate the feasibility of obtaining hard data on clinical material. The suspicion is that this conclusion represents an attempt to divert attention from, or to gloss over, results that were less favorable than had been expected.

The work of Kilmann and his associates (Kilmann, 1974a, b, c; Kilmann and Howell, 1974; Kilmann and Auerbach, 1974; Kilmann, Albert and Sotile, 1975; Kilmann, Follingstad, Price, Rowland, and Robinson, 1975; Follingstad, Kilmann, and Robinson, 1975) represents the most comprehensive and best controlled studies of marathon-produced change in therapy patients and volunteer participants in small groups operating from a therapy model. In his work, comparisons have been made between various group models: directive and nondirective (structured vs. unstructured), scores on measures of personality (locus of control, POI State Trait Anxiety Inventory, Adjective Check List), and attitude measures (attitudes toward women). The results suggest the value of the marathon in producing measurable change on the instruments utilized (personality measures, attitudes), though they are not specific to either a structured or an unstructured model. Data suggested the internal individual, as measured by the Rotter, benefited more and was a better therapeutic risk than the external individual, using the marathon model as determined from several populations.

In another study, Dies and Hess (1970) found that "postnarcotic" marathon-group subjects did not display more interest in the present than control subjects who received an equal amount of short-term group therapy. The discussions in the marathon groups were rated by two judges as being more personal and self-disclosing in nature than in the short-term groups, thus supporting the experimenters' hypothesis that there would be a greater degree of overall intimacy in the marathon groups. Finally, on seven-point semantic differential scales the subjects in the marathon groups also showed more favorable responses to their group experience than the control subjects. This latter finding may be explained on the basis of a study by Query (1964) in which high self-disclosure was positively related to group attraction. Since in Dies and Hess's investigation the marathon-group interactions were rated as being more self-disclosing than those in the control group, this increased openness may have contributed at least in part toward the marathon-group participants' more positive evaluations of their group experience.

Directions for Future Research

Research on the marathon group presently stands as a wide open area. There are a myriad of unanswered questions, both theoretical and practical, regarding the functioning of marathon groups. To begin with, some of the basic underlying assumptions have either not yet been experimentally demonstrated or are in need of further substantiation. For instance, there is little available evidence to support the claim that the extended time for interaction leads to greater involvement, truthfulness, or intimacy among group members. The relative merits of time-limited versus time-unlimited group therapy would also seem to warrant further research. Closely related to this question is that of the efficacy of massed treatment. If, as much of the available research seems to suggest, the effects of massed treatment are not especially enduring, then there would seem to be a strong case for greater utilization of follow-up sessions. Inherent in the marathon technique is the idea that heightened emotionality within the group facilitates behavioral change. The degree to which this may be true is uncertain. Marathon proponents also seem to equate increased openness and lowered defensiveness with personal growth. Many people would no doubt be in accord with this notion as a value judgment. However, the effects of increased openness on an individual's ongoing life activities have not been extensively studied in any systematic way.

There appears to be a well-thought-out rationale for each of the basic procedures that are employed in the marathon but, for the most part, it is only that—rationale. The effects of focusing the group interaction on the present have received little attention. Experts have debated the pros and cons of the group leader overtly involving himself emotionally in the group proceedings, but relevant research is lacking. Although feedback is cited as an important influence on the therapeutic value of groups (Lieberman, Lakin, and

Whitaker, 1968), few attempts have been made to vary feedback along either qualitative or quantitative dimensions. The degree to which feedback can promote self-exploration and reinforce altera- tion in maladaptive patterns of interaction remains unknown. The effect of critical feedback, an important feature of all encounter groups, has apparently been the subject of only one investigation (Brown, 1969). A number of studies suggest that the marathon's emphasis on the sharing of feelings is justified (Truax and Carkhuff, 1965). However, the relative therapeutic contributions of insight and affect, though hotly contested, have not received very much sys- tematic examination.

In spite of essential agreement about the progression of inter- action, there is no process research to confirm these impressions. Several scales exist which could be used for the purpose of quanti- fying interaction in marathon groups (Bales, 1950; Gorlow, Hoch, and Teleschow, 1952; Ohlsen and Proff, 1961). The methodology and design employed in a study of encounter-group process reported by Rogers (1969) could also easily be applied to the study of interactions in marathon groups. Bach's conclusions regarding the beneficial consequences of aggressive confrontation in marathon groups would seem to provide at least one impetus for further process research.

Pattison (1965) has cited three methods for evaluating the results of group therapy. First, is behavioral criteria, which include the overall clinical impression of the therapist, comparative behavioral rating scales, and measurements of the subject's behavior in the group using scales of verbal participation or interaction. Second, is psychometric criteria, which include the common clinical psychological tests. Third, is the use of construct criteria, involving the measurement of the individual's change in self-perception. Outcome research in mara- thon-group therapy has made very little use of the first two evalua- tive criteria. Most of the small amount of outcome research accom- plished has focused on the third evaluative criterion, the participants' own reactions to the experience. However, improve- ment in self-perception may be irrelevant to the person's actual ability to cope with the problems he faces in everyday life. In addition, there is reason to believe that group members may have a considerable stake in perceiving positive personal change. Studies utilizing self-reports have not contained adequate controls to insure that improvements in self-perception have been a direct outgrowth of the marathon, and not an artifact of the need to feel better about oneself after the experience is over.

An inescapable conclusion is that there is a need for more marathon outcome research based on psychometric and behavioral criteria. Weigel's (1968) use of standard psychological tests to assess outcome in marathon groups should serve as a model for other investigators. In a comparison of several different measures of self-disclosure, the results of Hurley and Hurley (1969) are certainly relevant to the measurement of openness, a key concept involved in the kind of change that the marathon tries to inspire. A number of techniques have been used to measure changes following group therapy; these could be applied to marathon outcome studies. The use of Q-sorts, especially of self and ideal, have been very popular in outcome research in group psychotherapy (Pattison, Brissenden, and Wohl, 1967; Truax, 1968; Truax, Schuldt, and Wargo, 1968). Another frequently used instrument for evaluating changes in personality resulting from group therapy is the Interpersonal Check List (Leary and Coffey, 1955; Laforge and Suczek, 1955). It provides descriptions of self and of how the individual is perceived by others and could easily be adapted to marathon outcome research. Judges' clinical impressions based on behavioral rating scales would also seem appropriate in assessing outcome. When these are used the design should include: control treatment groups; before- and after-treatment measures; ignorance on the part of the raters of the treatment conditions being employed, or of whether they are rating pretreatment or posttreatment behavioral segments; and the establishment of reliability among raters.

Several other points relevant to future research deserve mentioning. First, researchers must specify the kinds of behavioral outcomes they expect, so that not all changes can be cited as supportive of the technique. Second, there is a need to compare the effects of marathon therapy with those of other group therapies to determine what methods best meet given behavioral objectives. As Slavson (1965) has pointed out, "To impose upon patients indiscriminately a treatment of preference of the therapist's rather than a treatment of choice to suit the needs of the patient cannot but yield negative results" (p. 3). Third, individualized measures of therapy outcome would seem to be called for since different group members present different problems and measurement along a single criterion for all participants may be unnecessarily crude. Of course, the criterion measure for each subject must be specified before measurement of change takes place.

The effect of individual differences on marathon process and outcome has not been explored. It seems unlikely that the goals of the marathon are equally relevant to all people or that the experience has a similar impact on all participants. Rather, it appears more likely that the marathon's procedures may have varying effects upon different populations. We cannot, for example, assume that all kinds of people react to feedback in the same way. Nor can we assume that the experience as a whole benefits all people. Critics have assailed the lack of selection procedures for marathon groups, but until outcome research focuses on individual differences no fully adequate selection procedure will be forthcoming. In the meantime, practitioners might do well to make use of selection procedures which have proved useful in other types of group therapy (Neighbor et al., 1958; Salzberg and Bidus, 1966).

Although methodological controls and objective measures are largely lacking, observers of marathon groups almost unanimously agree that changes in behavior are manifested within the course of the group interaction. Results of the seventeen groups studied by Lieberman, Yalom, and Miles (1973), suggest that change does occur, but also that it may not last and that it is sometimes in a negative direction. However, an individual's behavior within the group may reflect social adaptation rather than therapeutic improvement. Alternatively, the behaviors manifested within the group may generalize to an individual's life outside of the group without first coming under the control of appropriate discriminative stimuli. For example, in ordinary life openness and intimacy may not always be the expected or accepted mode of interaction and their indiscriminate appearance may bring undesired consequences. In spite of these potential pitfalls, the question of transferring change to the participants' lives outside the group has barely been noticed. The same is true for the durability of the alleged changes where no long-term follow-up studies (six months or longer) have been accomplished.

Additional studies are needed before anything can be said about the permanence of the purported changes in behavior.

In spite of the many present deficits in knowledge of impact, long-range effects, and most-desired therapist characteristics, the marathon, by virtue of the fact that it is a massed form of treatment, offers several advantages to the potential researcher. Because there is no ongoing treatment, repeated outcome measures can be obtained at different follow-up periods without any concern about influencing treatment. In addition, problems caused by attrition among group members are avoided.

Conclusion

On the whole, the available evidence does not sustain Bach's statement that "The Marathon Group encounter has been found after the first three years of practice and research to be the most direct, the most efficient, and the most economical antidote to alienation, meaninglessness, fragmentation, and other hazards of mental health in our time" (Bach, 1967d, p. 995). Like Back (1972) and Lieberman, Yalom, and Miles (1973), one may legitimately criticize encounter groups in general for the near absence of objective measurement of the enduring benefit from an experience which lasts for such a relatively short period of time. This is not meant to serve as a total indictment of the marathon. At the very minimum, this type of group has the stimulating and enriching impact of any intense emotional experience shared with other people. If nothing else, this type of experience offers at least a temporary respite from the alienation between people that seems so commonplace in contemporary society. Whether the marathon helps people to continue in life more able to maintain close, open relationships is an unanswered question. Even though objective measurements of long-lasting behavioral change may be difficult to obtain, it is incumbent upon those who practice marathon-group therapy and those who espouse its benefits to prove their case. However, it should be pointed out that the marathon as an unproven technique is not unique to the psychotherapy field at large, where there is much need for further outcome research. In the meantime, those who practice marathon-group therapy will have to rely on its immediate emotional impact and the gratification of its consumers as justification for its continuance. Unless such measurements are undertaken, critics such as Back (1972) will continue to have ample justification for their attack on the marathon encounter movement.

8

TRAINING IN GROUP PSYCHOTHERAPY

Training in group psychotherapy does not involve the application of the same techniques, in the same fashion, as does individual psychotherapy. Indeed, generalizing from the study by Heckel, Froelich, and Salzberg (1962), it is possible to conclude that the application of individual psychotherapeutic principles to group psychotherapy may inhibit rather than foster interaction and the formation of meaningful relationships within a group. This is not to suggest that training in individual psychotherapy is undesirable or unnecessary. What *is* essential is that persons who conduct group therapy must have obtained first-hand observations of personality dynamics, and achieved self-knowledge and ability in self-evaluation. The use of the group setting for development of clinical theory is also an essential prerequisite for training in group psychotherapy. In addition, there is a need for training in the types of techniques that are peculiar to the group experience, that is, techniques which foster group interaction, shape group behavior, and guide persons to function on the level of social interaction deemed appropriate by the group therapist.[1] Such techniques are not found in individual psychotherapy because they are only present when three or more persons are involved in the group. Dyadic relationships offer only one alternative—that is, when the responder becomes the listener or the listener becomes the responder. In larger groupings, the possible permutations and combinations become enlarged and much more

1. The ability to move persons to deeper levels of interaction—from superficial environmental or irrelevant responding to the personal responses which more nearly parallel individual therapy and finally to the group- or other-centered response set—is crucial.

complex with the addition of each group member. These techniques are understood and thoroughly researched by social psychologists working in small-group research. The most relevant work is done under such labels as power, social distance, status, conflict management, interaction process analysis, and leadership, to mention some of the most directly applicable. In order satisfactorily to pursue clinical research in group psychotherapy or to be an effective and sensitive group psychotherapist, one needs a fundamental and formalized knowledge of group process.

Transference and countertransference, common phenomena in the individual therapeutic setting, show themselves in many obvious forms in that setting. These are easily identified by the therapist and can effectively be dealt with as part of treatment through analyzing the transference responses, as some therapists do, or simply by working with or around them as nondirective psychotherapists do. In the group setting, however, we have felt that the manifestations of transference and countertransference are best indicated by therapist-directed responses not reinforced by a group psychotherapist. We have also felt that transference is not easily divided into positive and negative transference because most transference responses grow out of ambivalence and a projection of these mixed feelings onto others. In training, the group therapist must be aware that there seldom will be the direct and obvious transference responses seen in individual psychotherapy. Instead, it may be no more obvious than an increase or decrease in responsivity or in the number of responses directed toward him. He must also be able to recognize when certain attitudes are being transferred to other members of the group. Several simplistic techniques may be applied in achieving this. The therapist may mentally keep a tally of the group members who are emitting responses and to whom these responses are directed. He might also keep a paper and pencil tally of responding, though this could interfere with his attending to group activity or cause some concern in group members. Retrospective analysis from video or audio tapes is useful. The bug-in-the-ear which is discussed in greater detail in this chapter can be used with data fed to the therapist by an observer.

Special training also seems to be necessary in establishing an understanding of the various roles that the student therapist must play within the group setting, in addition to the special techniques previously mentioned. This knowledge of a mass of techniques and behaviors that is required of a group psychotherapist has caused some group trainers to throw up their hands and feel that maintaining awareness of all the dynamics and interactions within the group therapy situation is impossible. As a result they turn their backs on the group approach and limit their work to individual psychotherapy. One way to overcome this tendency to avoid group procedures is to develop ease in self-disclosure in the novice therapist through experience in T-groups, sensitivity groups, or personal growth groups. Experience with the dynamics of self-disclosure need not come through having been a "patient" in a group therapy setting. These various groups offer much to the training of the group psychotherapist because they appear to operate along the same continuum as therapy groups[2] yet provide opportunities for the normal, adjusted individual to attain a degree of sensitivity to other people and deeper insights into his functioning within group settings, and to study the group process. One must not overestimate the learning opportunity and the efficacy of T-groups, encounter groups, and growth groups, however. We previously indicated that Lieberman, Yalom, and Miles (1973) presented research on seventeen groups utilizing a variety of approaches, most of which were relatively ineffective in producing measurable and lasting behavioral change. This negative evidence does not destroy the usefulness of such procedures but it should put the purveyors of these approaches on notice to isolate, through research, those procedures that do produce change.

Formal Training in Group Psychotherapy

Early group psychotherapists report no formalized training in the techniques of group psychotherapy. Nearly all persons practicing group therapy techniques who were trained within the last ten years report that they have received some formal training in group techniques, either in their university setting, in their psychiatric resi-

2. The concept of a continuum of groups, from those composed of patients to the advanced personal growth model, was well stated some years ago by Martin and Hill (1953).

dency program, in an apprenticeship training with an experienced group psychotherapist, or through T-group experiences. An even higher number of these same individuals report that they had received formal training in the techniques of individual psychotherapy or counseling. In many instances their progression into group psychotherapy came as follows: training and experience in individual psychotherapy, small-group experience with play therapy in groups, group therapy with special interest groups (such as mothers of disturbed children, mothers of handicapped children, etc.), and, finally, group psychotherapy, often as a preferred treatment technique for heterogeneous groups of individuals.

Today, probably a slight majority of all persons doing group psychotherapy would report no formalized program in group psychotherapy beyond assisting as a cotherapist or an observer with someone skilled in group therapy techniques, and attendance at brief workshops which are now available in all regions of the country.

It is apparent from exploring the many books about group psychotherapy and from the numbers of persons who are currently engaged in conducting group psychotherapy that professionals diverge greatly in determining what is considered valid training in group psychotherapy. Some would hold that the prerequisites are a personal analysis, personal experience in a group psychoanalytic setting, and formal coursework in an analytic institute; all of this, followed by an apprenticeship as a cotherapist in a group, finally produces a polished analytic group psychotherapist. While these might be appropriate goals within the analytic system, current approaches to group psychotherapy would not appear to require such a lengthy experience to develop the insights and skills for effectively conducting group psychotherapy. One should not discount a formal framework for training. It is possible to acquire formal group skills and training in many psychotherapeutic orientations ranging from lengthy neoanalytic programs to shorter, highly intensive training conducted in workshop settings. Some of the orientations are Gestalt, existential, directive, client-centered, rational-emotive, systematic desensitization, operant conditioning, transactional, and primal.

The other, and perhaps the more negative, pole of professional views about group psychotherapy is provided by those who would hold that only training in individual psychotherapy is necessary for the practice of group psychotherapy. They see little beyond the types of responses needed for individual psychotherapy as necessary for conducting group psychotherapy. Analysis of groups conducted with an individually oriented approach reveals sharp differences in response patterns from group-oriented approaches (Heckel, Froelich, and Salzberg, 1962). That is, the groups are, in essence, a series of individual psychotherapies in a group setting where interaction only occasionally occurs and the therapist is preeminent or dominant in all functioning within the group. In effect, in order to maintain the same types of controls over the behavior of each member of the group, the group-individual psychotherapist becomes the focal point of all group activity. In the terms defined by Martin and Hill (1957), such groups rarely get beyond a parental or leader-centered level of social interaction. Mullan and Rosenbaum (1963) suggest that those therapists that do use leader-centered methods may do so for non-therapeutic or even pathological reasons. That may somewhat overstate the situation. However, there are therapists who are unwilling to give patients either control of or responsibility for behaviors emerging in the group setting. Instead they feel that they should maintain control, permitting patients to work on problems which they deem appropriate, whereas our position holds that the patients' taking of responsibility and experiencing a variety of roles in the group is necessary in the treatment process, and, in turn, serves as a measure of his improvement.

A further issue in the training of group psychotherapists accounts for some of the divergence among professionals—the definition of what constitutes actual group psychotherapy. Some persons would classify all educative, reorientation, and remotivation groups as group psychotherapy. Yet by their very definition these groups do not constitute true group psychotherapy, for they are not geared to dealing with the individual and his problems in relating to others, but rather, they use techniques slanted to a given end—that is, causing persons to respond in a specific fashion or to engage in a special social or work activity. Often these specific and short-term goals can be readily and easily accomplished, primarily because many personal needs and dynamics are considered secondary to those goals. Many of these techniques have maintained the illusion of being group psychotherapy simply because, historically, the earliest attempts at influencing behavioral change through groups utilized a teacher-pupil educative process.[3] We would attempt to limit the term "therapeutic group" to those whose goals are to aid individuals to improve functioning in the group, and to foster the development of insight into their actions and reactions to other persons and, ultimately, into their personal and interactional responses in their home environments. We would exclude groups that are geared to other goals such as recreation, relaxation, or special social skills, even though all may ultimately have therapeutic implications and offer benefit to the individual.

Training Approaches by Other Theorists

Problems in training group psychotherapists have been long in existence. Sadock and Kaplan (1971) indicate that as early as 1947 Slavson described a program on qualifications and training of group psychotherapists. Even though standards advanced in his description were minimal, many universities and residency training programs do not meet them over a quarter of a century later.

Mullan and Rosenbaum (1963) suggest the following intensive training program for the group psychotherapist: 1. Didactic—includes basic lectures, reading and clinical seminars, and elective courses. 2. Clinical workshops—required and elective. 3. Personal group psychotherapusis (treatment)—required. 4. Supervised group psychotherapy—required. They then elaborate extensively upon each of these factors. It should be noted, however, that Mullan and Rosenbaum utilize psychoanalytic group psychotherapy, which may in some ways represent an extreme on the continuum. They also include an extended series of advanced seminars, lectures, and other didactic approaches.

Sadock and Kaplan (1971) describe a series of psychiatric training centers and their programs, among them Stanford University, Columbus State Hospital, University of Cincinnati, Mt. Sinai School of Medicine, the Post-Graduate Center for Mental Health, in New

3. Joseph Hersey Pratt, a Boston physician, as early as 1907 utilized an instructional group approach with patients having similar diseases (i.e., tuberculosis), though his model appears to have been a teacher-pupil model.

York City, and the New York Medical College. These psychiatric residency programs have a number of commonalities in their training in group psychotherapy. Stanford University is described as requiring a T-group experience for all students at the start of their residency; four to six months of group observation through a one-way mirror; seminars dealing with the basic principles and practice of group psychotherapy; and finally, a two-year supervisory group experience as cotherapist. The program at Columbus State Hospital was described as: lectures in general psychopathology, individual psychotherapy initially, followed by lectures on group psychotherapy; participation as an observer during the second year of residency training, as cotherapist, and finally as an independent group therapist in the third year of residency; participation in a personal group psychotherapy experience. The University of Cincinnati listed lectures in group psychotherapy during the first year; the second year it involved participants in groups as an observer, and in the third year as group leader with supervision. Mt. Sinai School of Medicine required a thorough background in psychopathology and individual psychotherapy, followed by lectures and demonstrations of group therapy, and finally, leading a therapy group under close supervision. Also required was personal participation in a psychotherapy group. At the Post-Graduate Center for Mental Health training extended over a two-year period, and included both individual and group supervision of long-term intensive psychotherapy groups and a personal group psychotherapy experience for the trainee. Extensive use of videotape plays an important role in their program. Kaplan and Sadock's description of The New York Medical College was quite thorough, owing to their affiliation with that institution. In their program, the first year included extensive lectures in group psychotherapy; the second year consisted of working with out-patients in group psychotherapy as cotherapist; the third year involved an extended, advanced group psychotherapy seminar and the independent leading of a psychotherapeutic group with supervision.

Each program represents training provided in a psychiatric residency. It has been indicated that only approximately 40 percent of psychiatric residency training settings have well-developed programs of training. Few programs have more elements than those described, others may have much less. One state hospital residency setting familiar to the authors provides no formalized training in group psychotherapy. Another has extended practical training through close supervision, by videotape, and as a cotherapist, but only on an elective basis. This would be the more typical situation for psychiatric residents. They may, but are not required to, have training in group psychotherapy.

In schools offering advanced training in clinical psychology, group psychotherapy typically is not a required course offering. Instead, it is an elective program often covering no more than a single semester's work. Typically, there is the requirement of prior course work in individual therapy, psychopathology, and group dynamics. In one such course offered by Heckel the requirement is a sensitivity group experience or training in individual psychotherapy prior to being accepted in the group psychotherapy course. Ideally, students would have both experiences prior to enrollment. Schools of social work frequently offer elective work on group psychotherapy but it is rarely required. There has been in recent years an increase in group training in counseling programs. Many of the counseling programs now offer students extended training in group counseling techniques, some of which are aimed at group vocational guidance, others at counseling for personal adjustment.

In addition to the above training programs, many universities and training settings periodically offer workshops in special techniques in group psychotherapy and group dynamics. These may last only a few days or may extend over a period of a week, a month, or even longer. The content of such programs is most often experiential, though some didactic material is made available. Most often an intensive group experience is the basis for learning.

To summarize, most persons come out of a professional training program—as a psychiatric resident, social worker, clinical psychology graduate student—which is a hodgepodge, offering varying levels of experience. There is no nationally recognized standard for certifying proficiency in this area. To date, no organization offers clear-cut criteria for minimal standards as a group psychotherapist. However, the American Group Psychotherapy Association does require minimal levels of training and experience for admission to its organization. While standards for training in group psychotherapy may be somewhat unclear and variable, the related areas of sensitivity and encounter groups are in even more serious difficulty because no minimal base of training and no background in any behavioral science has been established. In great numbers the American public is reaching out to these various kinds of groups and their leaders, often viewing them as the new model of group psychotherapy.

Unfortunately, there are few textbooks which present a logical and scientifically substantiated position with regard to many of the questions which are raised about group procedures or training techniques. Nonetheless, the few important clinical observations which have been made in a number of books on group psychotherapy are considered worth investigating.

There is little question about the value of a formalized lecture, seminar, and reading program as part of the necessary training for group psychotherapy. Unfortunately, most of the books on group psychotherapy do not provide research evidence for the techniques they present. With the exception of the three volumes published by the American Psychological Association on Research in Psychotherapy, and the work by Bergin and Garfield (1971), both of which are heavily weighted toward research on individual psychotherapy, little scientifically valid research is available for the reader. Much of the published literature in journals is anecdotal or observational—indeed, that is one reason this book was written.

For the individual who has completed formal training and wishes to expand his group skills, the American Group Psychotherapy Association's regular workshops held throughout the country offer an excellent opportunity to learn more of current techniques, as do similar workshops held at universities, major training centers, and other professional meetings. Such experiences are of great help to the group psychotherapist who works in the applied setting without the stimulation of academically oriented colleagues or in a teaching framework. These workshops can do much to lessen the "cultural lag" which inevitably occurs between newly developed and researched ideas in the practical and applied settings and the professional isolated in the field. The trained professional also must renew and refine his techniques. Training is an unending process, and workshop participation, even for the most experienced, can provide new insights or refurbish one's skills by blending them with new ideas.

We would emphasize the importance and the value of a human growth experience, as exemplified by the National Training Laboratories conducted at Bethel, Maine. While they are not group therapy in a strict sense, they do provide the group therapist with increased insight into his impact on other individuals and on a group's activities. Today, group laboratories are found virtually everywhere in the United States (though not always led by fully trained professionals).

There is some question of the necessity of a personal therapeutic group experience as a precondition for functioning as a group psychotherapist. We would not entirely agree with those who hold that this is an absolute requirement. However, we would agree on the necessity of some meaningful form of group involvement.

Because the group therapist presumably operates on a higher level of adjustment in his personal behavior, the sensitivity group experience may be sufficient to permit personal understanding and insights into his functioning in groups and the impact of others on him. We feel that it is through a deep involvement in a group that the group therapist is able to experience the many interactions and transferences that exist in therapy. Entering and participating in a group also permits the experiencing of the anxieties, problems, and group decisions which are never a part of the individual therapeutic experience. Without some extended group experience, the beginning group therapist may never become aware of the many group actions and reactions which an effective group therapist must comprehend.

We would agree on the importance but not necessarily on a fixed level or certain length of time for this experience for each trainee. Personal needs and individual situations would set these guidelines.

What arguments are there to support the group training experience as opposed to some other approach? Certainly the evidence published in research by Heckel, Froelich, and Salzberg and additional data of the authors on this subject indicate the fallacy of attempting group psychotherapy utilizing techniques derived from an individual psychotherapeutic approach. One might infer that any form of interpersonal group experience with a trained professional cannot help but enhance the individual's understanding of his role in the group setting.

It is our belief that individuals being trained in group psychotherapeutic techniques must be under the careful scrutiny of their trainers, to provide an individual prescription of the kinds of group

experiences each person might need and the length of time necessary
for close supervision. A forty-five-hour intensive group experience,
plus a strong background in the study of personality dynamics and
pathological behaviors, would seem to be a minimal learning base for
group therapy.

A further question can be raised whether this group experience
should be of an experiential/didactic nature with peers (colleagues,
classmates, residents, etc.). Some professionals feel that such an
undertaking may have very limited value. While we do not choose to
argue the limitations of such an approach, studies on attitude formation suggest that behavioral change is indeed possible, even when
such group procedures are applied to a group with a high degree of
peer relationship. Heckel, Kraus, and Beck (1964) measured shifts in
attitudes toward patients and authority figures utilizing an attitudinal scale developed by Brown and McCormick (1957). The authors
found that this technique was useful in shaping the attitudes and the
behavior of nursing aides who functioned with patients in a series of
informal group settings and in other key relationships.

Heckel (1964), in a later paper, describes the theoretical observations of the practical function of the nurse as a cotherapist in group
psychotherapy. Training began with a nurse serving as a participant
observer and later as a cotherapist. However, there is no statistical
evidence, only subjective judgments, to support the efficacy of this
particular approach in broadening dynamic understanding or increasing the efficiency of nurses.

These studies imply that while a deep, searching, personal experience may not take place in groups of peers who share other common
experiences as students, residents, etc., a personal understanding of
the principles of interaction and behavioral change may be gained.
This understanding is achieved primarily by a focus not on early
history, as would be the case in the more psychoanalytically oriented groups, but on understanding what is taking place in the here
and now.[4]

4. The most recent experience by one of the authors (1973–74) in the use
of therapeutic group as a training medium for student therapists met with
mixed results. Some were open and active, though the group ethic which
evolved was one of limited involvement and self-revelation. Detrimental to the
process was the desire of many in the group to maintain a greater social

Supervised Group Therapy

There is little doubt that ideal training would include lectures, seminars, cotherapy training, and personal supervision over a period of one year on a weekly basis. Intensive supervision is an absolute necessity during the early stages of training. The supervisory system utilized by the authors may serve as an example of one approach. The initial exposure of interns, students, and professionals consists of a review of principles of short-term, intensive group therapy followed by a series of sessions of observation of group therapy through a one-way mirror. Each session is extensively processed for the observers. In this manner trainees are able to observe the group therapist and his actions with the group with points of reference. During the post-group seminars, portions of the group session might be replayed from the tape recordings, with further comments on various techniques used and their purpose in the development of therapy.

Following a series of observation seminars, those who would work in group therapy are permitted to join the group initially as participant-observers[5] and later as cotherapists. The length of time involved in this form of apprenticeship is variable, depending upon the skills and desires of the trainee. Generally, only a few weeks are necessary before trainees can participate as cotherapists. Shorter time frames are achieved by setting up an intensive program of group psychotherapy and the frequency (three times per week) of meetings for all groups. In addition to the direct group therapeutic experience some chance at active participation in a more structured group setting—that of a group screening technique for patients—was prescribed for all trainees. This process has been described by Salzberg and Heckel (1963), Salzberg and Bidus (1966). The prospective trainee might serve as a cotherapist for periods ranging up to nine months or even longer. Those showing special skills and aptitude

---

distance with their peers than group therapy would permit, the limitations of a two-hour, once-per-week model, and the desire to maintain a positive image with the faculty member conducting the group.

5. The role of the participant observer is a unique one. In our approach, it might involve collecting research data and making specific observations of therapist or patient behavior, while responding only when brought into ongoing discussions by patients in the group.

might, after six months intensive training, be given group leadership
During the cotherapist experience, there is much discussion of the
different roles performed by the two therapists, patient reactions to
them, and the conflicting opinions which might arise as a result of
the actions of one or the other therapist. Such actions were never
discussed in front of the patient group nor were conflicting opinions
voiced which might contradict the statements of one or the other
group therapist.

After sufficient experience and insight had been gained by the
trainee as a cotherapist, he was permitted to function as therapist
with a group. Again, this is not done without intensive supervision.
The senior therapist supervising the student therapist's work ob
serves his actions within the group room through a one-way mirror
By requiring tapes (video or audio) on sessions it is possible to
discuss in the tape seminar the role which the therapist was playing
and the actions which he undertook while dealing with his own
group. The total program as conducted by the authors, like other
training programs, covers a period of six to twelve months. Even
with the indicated intensity over this period of time, both authors
feel that training limitations still exist in it.

Two additional techniques require special comment. They are the
bug-in-the-ear technique, and the use of closed circuit television.

Bug-in-the-ear

The use of a compact transitorized receiver in the ear of the
beginning group therapist, operating independently, offers the super
visor the opportunity to intervene in difficult situations, to "bail
out" the trainee, or to place in his hand important strategies with
which he may be only partially familiar. This technique insures
maximum therapeutic benefit for the patients being seen, and per
mits some external control over therapist's behavior by the super
visor. Its limitations are obvious. It provides the beginning group
therapist with a crutch on which he may become overly dependent
Patients may become overly curious about its use and purpose and
feel less confidence in their group leader. It also makes the student
therapist quite anxious and, in some instances, leads to a serious
reduction in his effectiveness during sessions when it is in use.

Currently, there are no studies that measure the effectiveness of this technique. Anecdotal evidence suggests that it can be useful in critical situations during a therapy session. This instrument is of inestimable value for group psychotherapy research wherein specific inputs, time signals, and other required controls may be presented in a way minimally obtrusive in the group.

Closed-circuit TV offers the obvious benefits of the immediate monitoring of therapist behavior and may be utilized in conjunction with a bug-in-the-ear or other signaling devices.

Special Training Techniques,
Devices and Strategies

An important part of postgraduate seminars and advanced training for students are the special techniques and procedures for group processes, such as the use of the TV camera as cotherapist (Heckel, 1975b) or special group manipulations as utilized by Heckel, Wiggins, and Salzberg (1962). Training in the use of such special techniques involves thorough processing of the strategies, implications, goals, and possible outcomes of such efforts.

Training in research is an essential element in the adequate development of the group psychotherapist. The present state of group psychotherapy allows of few absolutes. Thus it is essential that those in training develop a sense of inquiry about what they do, its effectiveness, and its relevance to the group process. It is often necessary for them to experiment with the mechanics of the group— time, frequency, setting, as well as the verbal structure of interaction. Research is learned best from good models. This is not to suggest that research should be preeminent. Rather, research should be taught as the method by which techniques are refined and the effectiveness of psychotherapy raised.

Special Problems in
Group Psychotherapeutic Training

Certain factors regarding group psychotherapy require special handling in the training of group psychotherapists, and in selecting those who would wish to practice group psychotherapy. The group, with its larger numbers of patients and the relatively public display of the therapist's wares, inevitably is more anxiety-producing and more personally threatening. No longer is the therapist able to present his skills in the relative security of a one-to-one relationship; he must perform therapeutically in the presence of, in some cases a cotherapist, and in most instances seven to ten patients, some of whom may have had more experience in group psychotherapy than he. Because of these potential threats, some therapists develop extensive defenses, most often through exerting greater control over the group's actions and behaviors as a protection against real or imagined functional deficits as a group therapist.

Even utilizing the many techniques available to the supervisor, bug-in-the-ear, closed-circuit television, or video and audio recordings of sessions, changing the behavior of the therapist in a group is much more difficult than in an individual therapy session. In the group, there are seven to ten individuals responding, challenging, questioning, seeking answers and providing a host of verbal and nonverbal cues to the therapist. In the press of this therapeutic situation the therapist cannot easily shift his behavior, or engage in the thoughtful pauses available in individual therapy which may allow a more effective response, or the development of a strategic plan for directing behavior.

The problems of training are increased in the therapeutic training model utilized by the authors because it is one in which a constant research component is maintained, in the interest of refining techniques, proving procedures, and making the best use of therapists and patients. It may be that the trainee in group psychotherapy may function effectively as a research instrument and a therapeutic tool yet feel that these roles conflict with his need to be concerned and involved with his group of patients. Yet the discipline afforded by working within this model is felt to maximize the therapeutic skills of trainees.

Use and Training of
Other Professional Persons
in the Group Psychotherapeutic Setting

Statements made by Heckel (1964) on the function of the nurse as a cotherapist may in general be applied to all supporting personnel who might function in a group psychotherapeutic setting. "It is felt that within any professional group there are persons who can more effectively achieve the goals of good group psychotherapy than some members of any given discipline." Mintz (1963), Lundin and Aronov (1952), Hulse et al. (1956), Demarest and Teicher (1954), and others have provided illuminating discussions on the particular values of the cotherapist in the group setting. Though in general they are referring to others of similar professional training and not particularly to supporting personnel, their ideas might equally be applied in support of the thesis advanced by Heckel, who says,

Psychiatrists and psychologists working toward providing a total therapeutic community have recognized the need for changing the image of the nurse from that of a service person for maintaining order and dispensing medication to recognition of the nurse as a fully qualified professional person. By including those nurses in group therapy who have sufficient training, maturity and background the image of the nurse becomes more closely identified with patient treatment rather than patient control. From this unique vantage point the nurses are then able to provide adequate feedback to other staff nurses on the treatment and functioning of the patient in the interpersonal world of group psychotherapy. The nurse also injects into the group therapeutic setting the ward reality. This fact tends to link treatment with patient functioning on the ward.

Such a statement can equally apply to other persons who are involved in the care and treatment of patients. Though their image may be different from that of the physician, nurse, psychologist, or social worker, they can impart an aspect of reality into the group therapy situation. It is felt that a most valuable part of group psychotherapy is its use as a "work sample" of interactions in life. At times treatment and group discussion may become somewhat abstract. At that point there is a need to come to grips with the reality of adjustment both to the group and to the immediate environment in which the patient presently operates. Of special value are persons who when serving as cotherapists or participants-observers offer longer-term contact with the patient. The psychologists, psychiatrists, and social workers who function as therapists for a series of patients are seldom identified as part of a ward environment when dealing with hospitalized individuals in group psychotherapy. Characteristically, they make rounds or come on the ward to see specific patients. Often they do not even enter wards but have patients sent to their offices or to meeting rooms which are located outside the ward environment. It might be argued that such a technique would limit the depth of therapeutic penetration by the group therapist. However, this would appear to apply only if the patients in the group psychotherapeutic setting were unable to solve the problems of their immediate reality—the ward. Once these problems have been solved their efforts might be shaped and guided by the group therapist and cotherapist to ever-increasing personal and interactional insights.

Group Parameters to be
Considered in the Training Setting

There are a number of considerations regarding the structure of patients groups to be used for beginning group therapists during their training period. Such factors as group size, length of time to be spent on each session, the frequency with which groups should meet, and the level the therapist should seek to attain would seem to be legitimate questions to consider. Observations of trainees would indicate that they operate on the old adage of "safety in numbers." They show preference for larger groups in the group psycho-therapeutic setting. There seems to be an overwhelming preference for at least ten group members rather than the six or seven group members which group dynamicists have shown to be best for communication (Bales, 1950). Frequently group therapy trainees may wish to cancel therapy groups when as few as four members are present.[6] The obvious reasoning behind this is that the therapist in the smaller group is more on the spot, more is apt to be demanded of him by members, more silences may occur, and the depth attained in discussion of personal problems may go beyond the level most comfortable for the therapist. In a larger group where interaction is encouraged and participation required of everyone, con-

6. Therapists in training have been observed by the authors doing effective therapy and maintaining effective group functioning with only three members.

siderable time is used in the amenities which are a part of nearly all group settings (more time is spent on environmental responding). Thus, warm-up and preparing to close the session take much longer in the larger group than is the case with a small, intensive group relationship.

Because of the usual running time of most tape recordings the sixty-minute or fifty-minute session has become extremely popular. Nearly all cassette or tape recorders utilized today can satisfactorily record this length of session without any attention. Recent developments in tape-recording equipment have allowed for continuous recording for up to four hours, though to date it is not known that anyone except those using marathon sessions takes full advantage of such a length of time for group sessions. Group therapists reporting on session lengths, primarily those for outpatients, have indicated the most popular time length was ninety minutes, as preferred by 60 percent of practicing group therapists. This would seem to be the more desirable time limit when larger groups of persons are seen and when they are seen for only one or two sessions per week.

Some of our insights into the framework of training and experience for group psychotherapists have been derived from research into the usual procedures and some variations. Many, however, have been arrived at informally and may represent the most comfortable level of functioning in the relationships which exist between the group therapists' trainer and his trainees.

Bibliography

Anthony, E. J. 1968. Discussion. *International Journal of Group Psychotherapy* 18:249–55.

Bach, G. R. 1966. The marathon group: Intensive practice of intimate interaction. *Psychological Reports* 18:995–1002.

_____. 1967a. Group and leader-phobias in marathon groups. *Voices* 3:41–46.

_____. 1967b. Marathon group dynamics. I: Some functions of the professional group facilitator. *Psychological Reports* 20:995–99.

_____. 1967c. Marathon group dynamics. II: Dimensions of helpfulness: Therapeutic aggression. *Psychological Reports* 20:1147–58.

_____. 1967d. Marathon group dynamics. III: Disjunctive contacts. *Psychological Reports* 20:1163–72.

_____. 1968. Discussion. *International Journal of Group Psychotherapy* 18:244–49.

Back, K. W. 1972. *Beyond words.* New York: Russell Sage Foundation.

Bales, R. F. 1950. *Interaction process analysis: A method for the study of small groups.* Cambridge, Mass.: Addison-Wesley Press.

Bandura, A. 1969. *Principles of behavior modification.* New York: Holt, Rinehart and Winston.

_____, Lepsher, D., and Miller, P. 1960. Psychotherapists' approach-avoidance reactions to patients' expression of hostility. *Journal of Consulting Psychology* 24:1–8.

Bass, B. M., and Klubeck, S. 1952. Effects of seating arrangements in leaderless group discussions. *Journal of Abnormal and Social Psychology* 47:724–27.

Bates, M. 1968. A test of group counseling. *Personnel and Guidance Journal* 46:749–53.

Benedict, P. K. 1937. Psychotherapy in alcoholism. *Progress in Psychotherapy* 5:148–55.

Benne, K. D., and Sheats, P. H. 1948. Functional roles of group members. *Journal of Social Issues* 4:41–49.

Bergin, A. E., and Garfield, S. L., eds. 1971. *Handbook of psychotherapy and behavior change.* New York: John Wiley & Sons.

Berne, E. 1966. *Principles of group treatment.* New York: Oxford University Press.

Bigelow, G., Cohen, M., Liebson, I., and Faillace, L. A. 1972. Abstinence or moderation? Choice by alcoholics. *Behavior Research and Therapy* 10:209–15.

Bigelow, G., and Liebson, I. 1972. Cost factors controlling alcoholics' drinking. *Psychological Record* 22:305–10.

Bindrim, P. 1968. A report on a nude marathon: The effect of physical nudity upon the practice of interaction in the marathon group. *Psychotherapy: Theory, Research and Practice* 5:180–88.

Bion, W. R. 1961. *Experience in groups.* New York: Basic Books.

Brammer, L. M., and Shostrom, E. L. 1960. *Therapeutic psychology.* Englewood Cliffs, N.J.: Prentice-Hall, Inc.

Brown, J. B. 1969. Some factors in response to criticism in group therapy. *Dissertation Abstracts International* 30:376.

Brown, R. L., and McCormick, E. J. 1957. *Employee supervisor statement study.* Greenville, S.C.: Copyrighted by the authors.

Burton, A. 1969. Encounter, existence, and psychotherapy. In *Encounter: The theory and practice of encounter groups,* ed. A. Burton. San Francisco: Jossey-Bass.

Burton, G. 1962. Group counseling with alcoholic husbands and their non-alcoholic wives. *Marriage and Family Living* 24:56–61.

Byrne, D. 1971. *The attraction paradigm.* New York: Academic Press.

Carkhuff, R. R. 1969. *Helping and human relations.* New York: Holt, Rinehart and Winston.

Cartwright, D., and Zander, A. 1968. *Group dynamics.* 3rd. ed. New York: Harper and Row.

Casriel, D. H., and Deitch, D. 1968. The marathon: Time extended group therapy. In *Current Psychiatric Therapies,* ed. J. H. Masserman. New York: Grune and Stratton.

Chafetz, M. E. 1970. The alcoholic symptom and its therapeutic relevance. *Quarterly Journal of Studies on Alcohol* 31:444.

Cohen, M., Liebson, I. A., and Faillace, L. A. 1971a. Modification of drinking in chronic alcoholics. In *Recent advances in studies of alcoholism,* ed. N. Mello and J. Mendelson. Washington, D.C.: U.S. Government Printing Office.

_____. 1971b. The role of reinforcement contingencies in chronic alcoholism: An experimental analysis of one case. *Behavior Research and Therapy* 9:375–79.

Collins, B. E., and Guetzkow, H. 1964. *A social psychology of group processes for decision making.* New York: John Wiley and Sons.

Conger, J. C. 1971. The modification of interview behavior by client use of social reinforcement. *Behavior Therapy* 2:52–61.

Curlee, Joan A. 1970. A comparison of male and female patients at an alcoholism treatment center. *Journal of Psychology* 74:239.

Cutler, R. L. 1958. Countertransference effects in psychotherapy. *Journal of Consulting Psychology* 22:349–56.

Demarest, E., and Teicher, A. 1954. Transferences in group therapy: Its use by co-therapists of opposite sexes. *Psychiatry* 17:187–202.

Dies, R., and Hess, K. 1970. Time perspective, intimacy, and semantic differential changes in marathon and conventional group psychotherapy. *Proceedings of the Annual Convention of the APA* 5:531–32.

Dinoff, M., Rickard, C., Salzberg, H. C., and Siprelle, C. 1960. An experimental analogue of three psychotherapeutic approaches. *Journal of Clinical Psychology* 16:70–73.

Distefano, M. K., Pryor, M. W., and Garrison, J. L. 1972. Internal-external control among alcoholics. *Journal of Clinical Psychology* 28:36–37.

Drennen, W. T. 1963. Transfer of the effects of verbal conditioning. *Journal of Abnormal and Social Psychology* 66:619–22.

_____, and Wiggins, S. L. 1964. Manipulation of verbal behavior of chronic hospitalized schizophrenics in a group therapy situation. *International Journal of Group Psychotherapy* 14:189–93.

Ellis, A. 1969. A weekend of rational encounter. In *Encounter: The theory and practice of encounter groups,* ed. A. Burton. San Francisco: Jossey-Bass.

Ends, E. J., and Page, C. W. 1957. A study of three types of group psychotherapy with hospitalized male inebriates. *Quarterly Journal of Studies on Alcohol* 18:263–77.

Eysenck, H. J., and Beech, R. 1971. Counter-conditioning and related methods. In Bergin and Garfield (1971), pp. 543–611.

Follingstad, D. R., Kilmann, P. R., and Robinson, E. A. 1975. Effects of marathon group therapy for male subjects on attitudes toward women and levels of self-actualization. Paper presented at the Southeastern Psychological Association, March 1975, at Atlanta, Ga. Xeroxed.

Ford, D., and Urban, H. 1963. *Systems of psychotherapy.* New York: John Wiley and Sons.

Franks, C. 1969. *Behavior therapy: Appraisal and status.* New York: McGraw-Hill.

French, J. R. P., Jr. 1956. A formal theory of social power. *Psychological Review* 63:181–94.

Frey, J., Heckel, R. V., Salzberg, H. C., and Wackwitz, J. In press. Demographic variables as predictors of outcome in psychotherapy with children. *Journal of Clinical Psychology.*

Gibb, J. R., and Gibb, L. M. 1969. Role freedom in a TORI group. In *Encounter: The theory and practice of encounter groups,* ed. A. Burton. San Francisco: Jossey-Bass.

Gibbons, R. J., and Armstrong, J. D. 1957. Effects of clinical treatment on behavior of alcoholic patients. *Quarterly Journal of Studies on Alcohol* 18:429–50.

Gillis, L. S., and Keet, M. 1969. Prognostic factors and treatment results in hospitalized alcoholics. *Quarterly Journal of Studies on Alcohol* 30:426–37.

Glanzer, M., and Glaser, R. 1959. Techniques for the study of group structure and behavior. 1: Analysis of structure. *Psychological Bulletin* 56:317–32.

――――. 1961. Techniques for the study of group structure and behavior: Empirical studies of the effects of structure in small groups. *Psychological Bulletin* 58:1–27.

Gliedman, L. H., Rosenthal, D., Frank, J. D., and Nash, Helen T. 1956. Group therapy of alcoholics with concurrent group meetings of their wives. *Quarterly Journal of Studies on Alcohol* 17:655–70.

Glud, E. 1962. Psychoanalytic techniques with alcoholics. *British Journal of Addiction* 58:29–37.

Goldstein, A. P. 1973. *Structured learning therapy: Toward a psychotherapy for the poor.* New York: Academic Press.

Golightly, C., and Reinehr, R. C. 1969. 16 PF profiles of hospitalized alcoholic patients: Replication and extension. *Psychological Reports* 24:543–45.

Gorlow, L., Hoch, R., and Teleschow, E. 1952. *The nature of nondirective group psychotherapy.* New York: Columbia University Press.

Goss, A., and Morosko, T. 1970. Relation between a dimension of internal-external control and the MMPI with an alcoholic population. *Journal of Consulting and Clinical Psychology* 34:189.

Gottheil, E., Corbett, L. O., Grasberger, J. C., and Cornelison, F. S. 1972. Fixed interval drinking decisions. I: A research and treatment model. *Quarterly Journal of Studies on Alcohol* 33:311–25.

Gottheil, E., Murphy, B. F., Skoloda, T. E., and Corbett, L. O. 1972. Fixed interval drinking decisions. II: Drinking and discomfort in 25 alcoholics. *Quarterly Journal of Studies on Alcohol* 33:325–40.

Gottschalk, L. A., and Auerbach, A. H. 1966. *Methods of research in psychotherapy.* New York: Appleton-Century-Crofts.

Greenspoon, J. 1955. The reinforcing effect of two spoken sounds on the frequency of two responses. *American Journal of Psychology* 68:409–16.

Gross, R. S. 1969. The effects of structuring and therapist absence or presence on behavior in a group therapy setting. Ph.D. dissertation, University of South Carolina, 1969.

Grotjahn, M. 1971. The qualities of the group therapist. In *Comprehensive group psychotherapy,* ed. H. I. Kaplan and B. J. Sadock, pp. 757–73. Baltimore, Md.: The Williams and Wilkins Co.

Gutride, M. E., Goldstein, A. P., and Hunter, G. F. 1973. The use of modeling and role playing to increase social interaction among asocial psychiatric patients. *Journal of Consulting and Clinical Psychology* 40:408–15.

Haberman, P. W. 1966. Factors related to increased sobriety in group psychotherapy with alcoholics. *Journal of Clinical Psychology* 22:229–35.

Hare, A. P. 1962. *Handbook of small group research.* New York: Free Press.

Heckel, R. V. 1964. The nurse as co-therapist in group psychotherapy. *Perspectives in Psychiatric Care* 2:18–22.

_____. 1965. Characteristics of early dropouts from group psychotherapy. *Mental Hygiene* 49:574–76.

_____. 1966a. Effects of northern and southern therapists on racially mixed psychotherapy groups. *Mental Hygiene* 50:304–7.

_____. 1966b. Verbal rates in group psychotherapy using two different therapist procedures. Columbia, S.C.: University of South Carolina. Xeroxed.

_____. 1971. Precausal thinking as a criterion of therapy choice. *Psychiatric Forum* Summer: 22–26.

_____. 1972a. *Leadership: A brief introduction.* Columbia, S.C.: Social Problems Research Institute.

_____. 1972b. Predicting role flexibility in group therapy by means of a screening scale. *Journal of Clinical Psychology* 28:570–73.

_____. 1973. Leadership and voluntary seating choice. *Psychological Reports* 32:141–42.

_____. 1975a. Blocks to treatment: A white therapist treating blacks in the South. *International Journal of Group Psychotherapy,* in press.

_____. 1975b. Camera vs co-therapist in group psychotherapy. *Psychiatric Forum,* in press.

_____, Froelich, R. E., and Salzberg, H. C. 1962. Interaction and redirection in group therapy. *Psychological Reports* 10:14.

Heckel, R. V., Holmes, G. R., and Salzberg, H. C. 1967. Emergence of distinct verbal phases in group therapy. *Psychological Reports* 21:630–32.

Heckel, R. V., Kraus, R., and Beck, E. W. 1963. Measurement of attitude change in nursing aides. *Psychological Reports* 13:639–42.

Heckel, R. V., and Levenberg, S. 1975. A comparison of process data from family therapy and group therapy. *Journal of Community Psychology.*

Heckel, R. V., Wiggins, S. L., and Salzberg, H. C. 1962. Conditioning against silences in group therapy. *Journal of Clinical Psychology* 18:216–17.

_____. 1963. Joining, encouraging, and intervention as means of extinguishing a delusional system. *Journal of Clinical Psychology* 19:344–46.

Heller, K., Myers, R. A., and Klein, L. V. 1963. Interview behavior as a function of standardized client roles. *Journal of Consulting Psychology* 27:117–22.

Hersko, M., and Winder, A. E. 1958. Changes in patients' attitudes toward self and others during group psychotherapy. *Group Psychotherapy* 11:309–13.

Hollingshead, A. S., and Redlich, F. C. 1958. *Social class and mental illness.* New York: John Wiley and Sons.

Howells, I. T., and Becker, S. W. 1962. Seating arrangements and leadership emergence. *Journal of Abnormal and Social Psychology* 64:148–50.

Hulse, W. C., Lulow, W. V., Rindsberg, B. K., and Epstein, N. B. 1956. Transference reactions in a group of female patients to male and female co-leaders. *International Journal of Group Psychotherapy* 6:430–35.

Hurley, J. R., and Hurley, S. J. 1969. Toward authenticity in measuring self-disclosure. *Journal of Counseling Psychology* 16: 271–74.

Igersheimer, W. L. 1959. Group psychotherapy for non-alcoholic wives of alcoholics. *Quarterly Journal of Studies on Alcohol* 20:77–85.

Kelley, G. A. 1955. *The psychology of personal constructs. Vol. I, A theory of personality.* New York: Norton.

Kelley, H., and Thibaut, J. 1969. Group problem solving. In *The handbook of social psychology.* 2nd ed. Vol. 4. *Group psychology and phenomena of interaction,* pp. 1–101, ed. G. Lindzey and E. Aronson. Reading, Mass.: Addison-Wesley.

Kepner, E. 1964. Application of learning theory to the etiology and treatment of alcoholism. *Quarterly Journal of Studies on Alcohol* 25:279–91.

Kilmann, P. R. 1974a. Locus of control and preference for type of group counseling. *Journal of Clinical Psychology* 30:226–27.

____. 1974b. Anxiety reactions to marathon group therapy. *Journal of Clinical Psychology* 30:266–67.

____. 1974c. Direct and nondirect marathon group therapy and internal-external control. *Journal of Counseling Psychology* 21: 380–84.

____, Albert, B. M., and Sotile, W. M. 1975. The relationship between locus of control, structure of therapy, and outcome. *Journal of Consulting and Clinical Psychology,* in press.

Kilmann, P. R., and Auerbach, S. M. 1974. Effects of marathon group therapy on trait and state anxiety. *Journal of Consulting and Clinical Psychology* 42:607–12.

Kilmann, P. R., Follingstad, D. R., Price, M. G., Rowland, K. F., and Robinson, E. A. 1974. Effects of a marathon group on self-actualization and attitudes toward women. Columbia, S.C.: University of South Carolina. Xeroxed.

Kilmann, P. R., and Howell, R. J. 1974. The relationship between locus of control, structure of therapy and therapeutic outcome. *Journal of Consulting and Clinical Psychology* 42:912.

Kohlberg, L. 1963. Moral development and identification. In *Child psychology: The sixty-second yearbook of the national society for the study of education. Part I,* ed. H. W. Stevenson, pp. 277–332. Chicago: The National Society for the Study of Education.

Kovan, R. A. 1968. Resistance of the marathon facilitator to becoming an intimate member of the group. *Psychosomatics* 9:286–88.

Krasner, L. 1958. Studies of the conditioning of verbal behavior. *Psychological Bulletin* 55:148–70.

————. 1963. Reinforcement, verbal behavior and psychotherapy. *American Journal of Orthopsychiatry* 33:601–13.

————, and Ullmann, L. P. 1973. *Behavior influence and personality.* New York: Holt Rinehart and Winston.

Krumboltz, J. D. 1966. *Revolution in counseling.* New York: Houghton Mifflin Company.

Laforge, R., and Suczek, R. F. 1955. The interpersonal dimension of personality. III: An interpersonal check list. *Journal of Personality* 24:94–112.

Land, E. C. 1962. Comparison of patient improvement resulting from two therapeutic techniques. Augusta, Ga.: V. A. Hospital. Xeroxed.

Leary, T., and Coffey, H. S. 1955. Interpersonal diagnosis: Some problems of methodology and validation. *Journal of Abnormal and Social Psychology* 50:110–24.

Lewis, R. W. 1968. The effect of long group therapy sessions on participant perceptions of self and others. *Dissertation Abstracts* 28:3879.

Lieberman, M. A., Lakin, M., and Whitaker, D. S. 1968. The group as a unique context for therapy. *Psychotherapy: Theory, Research and Practice* 5:29–36.

Lieberman, M. A., Yalom, I. D., and Miles, M. B. 1973. *Encounter groups: First facts.* New York: Basic Books.

Liebman, M. 1970. The effects of sex and race norms on personal space. *Environment and Behavior* 2:208–46.

Lorr, M. 1962. Relation of treatment frequency and duration to psychotherapeutic outcome. In *Research in psychotherapy, II*, ed. H. H. Strupp and L. Luborsky. Washington, D.C.: American Psychological Association.

Luchins, A. S. 1964. *Group therapy, a guide*. New York: Random House.

Ludwig, A. M. 1968. Studies in alcoholism and LSD (1): Influence of therapist attitudes on treatment outcome. *American Journal of Orthopsychiatry* 38:733–37.

____. 1972. On and off the wagon: Reasons for drinking and abstaining by alcoholics. *Quarterly Journal of Studies on Alcohol* 33:91–97.

Lundin, W. H., and Aronov, B. M. 1952. Use of co-therapists in group psychotherapy. *Journal of Consulting Psychology* 16:76–80.

MacDonald, Donald E. 1956. Mental disorders in wives of alcoholics. *Quarterly Journal of Studies on Alcohol* 17:125–32.

Mahoney, M. J., and Thoreson, C. E. 1974. *Self-control: Power to the person*. Monterey, Cal.: Brooks/Cole.

Mahrer, A. R. 1967. *The goals of psychotherapy*. New York: Appleton-Century-Crofts.

Martin, E. A., Jr., and Hill, W. F. 1957. Toward a theory of group development: Six phases of therapy group development. *International Journal of Group Psychotherapy* 7:20–30.

McGrath, J. E., and Altman, I. 1966. *Small group research: A synthesis and critique of the field*. New York: Holt, Rinehart and Winston.

Mechanic, David. 1961. Relevance of group atmosphere and attitudes for the rehabilitation of alcoholics: A pilot study. *Quarterly Journal of Studies on Alcohol* 22:634–45.

Meeks, D. E., and Kelly, C. 1970. Family therapy with the families of recovering alcoholics. *Quarterly Journal of Studies on Alcohol* 31:399.

Mehrabian, A., and Diamond, S. G. 1971. Effects of furniture arrangement, props and personality on social interaction. *Journal of Personality and Social Psychology* 20:18–30.

Mello, N. K. 1968. Some aspects of the behavioral pharacology of alcoholism. In *Psychopharacology, a review of progress, 1957–1967,* ed. D. Efron. Washington, D.C.: U.S. Government Printing Office.

Mendelson, J. H., and Mello, N. K. 1966. Experimental analysis of drinking behavior of chronic alcoholics. *Annals of the New York Academy of Science* 133:828–45.

Miller, N. E., and Dollard, J. 1941. *Social learning and imitation.* New Haven: Yale University Press.

Mills, K. C., Sobell, M. B., and Halmuth, H. H. 1971. Training social drinking as an alternative to abstinence for alcoholics. *Behavior Therapy* 2:18.

Mintz, E. E. 1963. Special value of co-therapists in group psychotherapy. *International Journal of Group Psychotherapy* 13:127–32.

———. 1967. Time extended marathon groups. *Psychotherapy: Theroy, Research, and Practice* 4:65–70.

———. 1969. Marathon groups: A preliminary evaluation. *Journal of Contemporary Psychotherapy* 1:91–94. Abstract.

Mischel, W. 1968. *Personality and assessment.* New York: John Wiley and Sons.

Moore, Robert A. 1961. Reaction formation as a counter-transference phenomenon in the treatment of alcoholism. *Quarterly Journal of Studies on Alcohol* 22:481–86.

Moos, R. H., and Clemes, S. K. 1967. Multivariate study of the patient-therapist system. *Journal of Consulting Psychology* 31:119–30.

Mowrer, O. H. 1964. *The new group therapy.* Princeton, N.J.: Van Nostrand.

Mullan, H., and Rosenbaum, M. 1962. *Group psychotherapy.* New York: Free Press of Glencoe.

Myerhoff, H. I., Jacobs, A., and Stoller, F. 1970. Conditionality in marathon and traditional psychotherapy groups. *Psychotherapy: Theory, Research and Practice* 7:33–36.

Nathan, P. E., and O'Brien, J. S. 1971. An experimental analysis of the behavior of alcoholics and non-alcoholics during prolonged experimental drinking: A necessary precursor of behavior therapy? *Behavior Therapy* 2:455.

Neighbor, J. E., Beach, M., Brown, D. T., Kevin, D., and Visher, J. S. 1958. An approach to the selection of patients for group psychotherapy. *Mental Hygiene* 42:243–54.

Nocks, J. J., and Bradley, D. L. 1969. Self esteem in an alcoholic population. *Diseases of the Nervous System* 30:611–17.

Ohlsen, M., and Proff, F. 1961. A method for the quantification of psychotherapeutic interaction in counseling groups. *Journal of Counseling Psychology* 8:54–61.

Palisi, A. T., and Ruzicka, M. F. 1974. Practicum students' verbal responses to different clients. *Journal of Counseling Psychology* 21:87–91.

Parloff, M. B. 1968. Discussion. *International Journal of Group Psychotherapy* 18:239–44.

Patterson, M. L., Mullens, S., and Romano, J. 1971. Compensatory reactions to spatial intrusion. *Sociometry* 34:114–26.

Pattison, M. E. 1965. Evaluation studies of group psychotherapy. *International Journal of Group Psychotherapy* 15:382–93.

____, Brissenden, A., and Wohl, T. 1967. Assessing specific effects of inpatient group psychotherapy. *International Journal of Group Psychotherapy* 17:283–97.

Peters, H. N., and Jenkins, R. L. 1954. Improvement of chronic schizophrenic patients with guided problem solving motivated by hunger. *Psychiatric Quarterly Supplement* 28:84–101.

Pfeiffer, J. W., and Jones, J. E. 1969–71, 1973. *A handbook of structured experiences for human relations training,* vols. 1–4. Iowa City: University Association.

Philbrick, E. B., and Postman, L. 1955. A further analysis of learning without awareness. *American Journal of Psychology* 68:417–24.

Phillips, E. L., and Wiener, D. N. 1966. *Short-term psychotherapy and structural behavior change.* New York: McGraw-Hill.

Pixley, John M., and Stiefel, John R. 1963. Group therapy designed to meet the needs of the alcoholic's wife. *Quarterly Journal of Studies on Alcohol* 24:304–14.

Postman, L., and Jarrett, R. F. 1952. An experimental analysis of learning without awareness. *American Journal of Psychology* 65:244–55.

Query, W. T. 1964. Self-disclosure as a variable in group psychotherapy. *International Journal of Group Psychotherapy* 14: 107–15.

Reinehr, R. C. 1969. Therapist and patient perceptions of hospitalized alcoholics. *Journal of Clinical Psychology* 25:443–45.

Roby, T. B., and Lanzetta, J. T. 1958. Considerations in the analysis of group tasks. *Psychological Bulletin* 55:88–101.

Rogers, C. R. 1951. *Client centered therapy.* Boston: Houghton-Mifflin.

_____. 1969. The group comes of age. *Psychology Today* 3:27–31, 58–61.

Rosenberg, C. M. 1969. Young alcoholics. *British Journal of Psychiatry* 115:181–88.

Rotter, J. B. 1966. Generalized expectancies for internal versus external control of reinforcement. *Psychological Monographs* 80(1).

Rubin, S. E., and Lawlis, G. F. 1970. A mode for differential treatment for alcoholics. *Rehabilitation Research and Practice Review* 1:53.

Russell, P. D., and Snyder, W. V. 1963. Counselor anxiety in relation to amount of clinical experience and quality of affect demonstrated by clients. *Journal of Consulting Psychology* 27:358–63.

Ryback, R. S. 1970. Alcohol amnesia: Observations in seven drinking alcoholic inpatients. *Quarterly Journal of Studies on Alcohol* 31:616.

Sadock, B. J., and Kaplan, H. I. 1971. Training and standards in group psychotherapy. In *Comprehensive group psychotherapy,* ed. H. I. Kaplan and B. J. Sadock, pp. 774–98. Baltimore: The Williams and Wilkins Co.

Sager, C. J. 1968. The group psychotherapist: Bulwark against alienation. *International Journal of Group Psychotherapy* 18:419–31.

Salzberg, H. C. 1962. Effects of silence and redirection on verbal responses in group therapy. *Psychological Reports* 11:455–61.

_____. 1967. Verbal behavior in group psychotherapy with and without a therapist. *Journal of Counseling Psychology* 14:24–27.

_____. 1969. Group psychotherapy screening scale: A validation study. *International Journal of Group Psychotherapy* 19:226–28.

_____, and Bidus, D. R. 1966. Development of a group psychotherapy screening scale: An attempt to select suitable candidates and predict successful outcome. *Journal of Clinical Psychology* 12:478–81.

Salzberg, H. C., Brokaw, J. R., and Strahley, D. 1964. Effects of group stability on spontaneity and problem-relevant verbal behavior in group psychotherapy. *Psychological Reports* 14:687–94.

Salzberg, H. C., and Heckel, R. V. 1963. Psychological screening utilizing the group approach. *International Journal of Group Psychotherapy* 13:214–15.

Schaeffer, H. H. 1972. Twelve month follow up of behaviorally trained ex-alcoholic social drinkers. *Behavior Therapy* 3:286–90.

_____, Sobell, M. B., and Mills, K. C. 1971. Baseline drinking behaviors in alcoholics and social drinkers, kinds of drinks and sip magnitude. *Behavior Research and Therapy* 9:23.

Schaeffer, H. H., Sobell, M. B., and Sobell, L. C. 1972. Twelve month follow up of hospitalized alcoholics given self-confrontation experiences by videotape. *Behavior Therapy* 3:283–85.

Scheidlinger, S. 1968. Group psychotherapy in the sixties. *American Journal of Psychotherapy* 22:170–84.

Schwarz, L., and Fjeld, S. P. 1969. The alcoholic patient in the psychiatric hospital emergency room. *Quarterly Journal of Studies on Alcohol* 30:104–11.

Scott, E. M. 1961. The technique of psychotherapy with alcoholics. *Quarterly Journal of Studies on Alcohol* 22:69–80.

———. 1963. A suggested treatment for the hostile alcoholic. *International Journal of Group Psychotherapy* 13:93–104.

Sessions, P. 1964. The alcoholic and his world. *Southeastern School of Alcoholism Fourth Proceedings,* pp. 79–96.

Shapiro, S. B. 1969. Tradition innovation. In *Encounter: The theory and practice of encounter groups,* ed. A. Burton. San Francisco: Jossey-Bass.

Shaw, M. E. 1971. *Group dynamics.* New York: McGraw-Hill.

Slavson, S. R. 1955. Criteria for selection and rejection of patients for various types of group psychotherapy. *International Journal of Group Psychotherapy* 5:3–30.

Smart, R. G. 1968. Future time perspective in alcoholics and social drinkers. *Journal of Abnormal Psychology* 73:81–83.

Smith, C. G. 1969. Alcoholics: Their treatment and their wives. *British Journal of Psychiatry* 115:1039–42.

Snyder, W. U. 1961. *The psychotherapy relationship.* New York: Macmillan.

Sobell, L. C., Sobell, M. B., and Christelman, W. C. 1972. The myth of "one drink." *Behavior Research and Therapy* 10:119–25.

Soloman, L. N., and Bergon, B., eds. 1972. *New perspectives on encounter groups.* San Francisco: Jossey-Bass.

Sommer, R. 1959. Studies in personal space. *Sociometry* 22:247–60.

———. 1966. The ecology of privacy. *Library Quarterly* 36:234–48.

Spotnitz, H. 1968. Discussion. *International Journal of Group Psychotherapy* 18:236–39.

Steinzor, B. 1950. The spatial factor in face to face discussion groups. *Journal of Abnormal and Social Psychology* 45:552–55.

Stenmark, D., Sausser, E., and Heckel, R. V. 1973. *The Rural Southern Alcoholic.* Social Problems Research Institute Monograph 5, Columbia, S.C.: University of South Carolina.

Stevens, J. O. 1971. *Awareness: Exploring, experimenting, experiencing.* Moab, Utah: Real People Press.

Stoller, F. H. 1967. The long weekend. *Psychology Today* 1:28–33.

———. 1968. Accelerated interaction: A time limited approach based on the brief, intensive group. *International Journal of Group Psychotherapy* 18:220–35.

———. 1969. A stage for trust. In *Encounter: The theory and practice of encounter groups,* ed. A. Burton. San Francisco: Jossey-Bass.

Strayer, R. 1961. Social integration of alcoholics through prolonged group therapy. *Quarterly Journal of Studies on Alcohol* 22:471–80.

Szasz, T. S. 1961. *The myth of mental illness.* New York: Hoeber-Harper.

Tamerin, J. S., and Mendelson, J. H. 1969. The psychodynamics of chronic inebriation observations of alcoholics during the process of drinking in an experimental group setting. *American Journal of Psychiatry* 125:886–99.

Thoresen, C. E., and Mahoney, M. J. 1974. *Behavioral self-control.* New York: Holt, Rinehart and Winston.

Thorndike, E. L., and Rock, R. T., Jr. 1934. Learning without awareness of what is being learned or intent to learn it. *Journal of Experimental Psychology* 17:1–19.

Toll, N. 1968. Non-conformist group therapies. *Voices* 4:44–45.

Truax, C. B. 1968. Therapist interpersonal reinforcement of client self-exploration and therapeutic outcome in group psychotherapy. *Journal of Counseling Psychology* 15:225–31.

Truax, C. B., and Carkhuff, R. R. 1965. Client and therapist transparency in the psychotherapeutic encounter. *Journal of Counseling Psychology* 12:3–9.

———. 1967. *Toward effective counseling and psychotherapy.* Chicago: Aldine Publishing Company.

Truax, C. B., and Mitchell, K. E. 1971. Research on certain therapist interpersonal skills in relation to process and outcome. In Bergin and Garfield (1971), pp. 299–344.

Truax, C. B., Schuldt, W. J., and Wargo, D. G. 1968. Self-ideal concept congruence and improvement in group psychotherapy. *Journal of Consulting and Clinical Psychology* 32:47–53.

Ullmann, L. P., and Krasner, L. 1969. *A psychological approach to abnormal behavior.* Englewood Cliffs, N.J.: Prentice Hall.

Walker, H., and Lev, J. 1953. *Statistical inference.* New York: Holt.

Weigel, R. G. 1968. Outcomes of marathon group therapy and marathon group topical discussion. *Dissertation Abstracts* 29.

Whitaker, D. S., and Lieberman, M. A. 1964. *Psychotherapy through the group process.* New York: Atherton Press.

Wiggins, S. L., and Salzberg, H. C. 1966. Conditioning against silences and therapist-directed comments in group psychotherapy using auditory stimulation. *Psychological Reports* 18:591–99.

Williams, R. L., and Long, J. D. 1975. *Toward a self-managed life style.* Boston: Houghton Mifflin.

Winder, C. L., Ahmad, F. Z., Bandura, A., and Rau, L. C. 1962. Dependency of patients, psychotherapists' responses, and aspects of psychotherapy. *Journal of Consulting Psychology* 26:129–34.

Winokur, G., Reich, T., Rimmer, J., and Pitts, F. N. 1970. Alcoholism. III: Diagnosis and familiar psychiatric illness in 259 alcoholic probands. *Archives of General Psychiatry* 23:104.

Yalom, I. D. 1970. *The theory and practice of group psychotherapy.* Basic Books, Inc.

Young, E. R., and Jacobson, L. I. 1970. Effects of time extended marathon group experiences on personality characteristics. *Journal of Counseling Psychology* 17:247–51.

Author Index

Subject Index